CAMBRIDGE LIBRARY COLLECTION

Books of enduring scholarly value

Literary studies

This series provides a high-quality selection of early printings of literary works, textual editions, anthologies and literary criticism which are of lasting scholarly interest. Ranging from Old English to Shakespeare to early twentieth-century work from around the world, these books offer a valuable resource for scholars in reception history, textual editing, and literary studies.

Shakesperiana

James Orchard Halliwell-Phillipps (1820-1889) was an enthusiastic collector of books on Shakespeare (including nearly all the pre-1660 editions) and a respected and prolific scholar of Elizabethan literature. His extensive collection is now housed at Edinburgh University Library. This volume contains a selection of his early writings and includes: 'A catalogue of the early editions of Shakespeare's plays and of the commentaries and other publications illustrative of his works' (1841); 'An account of the only known manuscript of Shakespeare's plays, comprising some important variations and corrections in the Merry Wives of Windsor' (1843); 'An introduction to Shakespeare's Midsummer Night's Dream' (1841); 'On the character of Sir John Falstaff, as originally exhibited by Shakespeare in the two parts of King Henry IV' (1841); 'Curiosities of Modern Shakespearian Criticism' (1853); 'Observations on some of the manuscript emendations of the text of Shakespeare and are they copyright?' (1853).

Cambridge University Press has long been a pioneer in the reissuing of out-of-print titles from its own backlist, producing digital reprints of books that are still sought after by scholars and students but could not be reprinted economically using traditional technology. The Cambridge Library Collection extends this activity to a wider range of books which are still of importance to researchers and professionals, either for the source material they contain, or as landmarks in the history of their academic discipline.

Drawing from the world-renowned collections in the Cambridge University Library, and guided by the advice of experts in each subject area, Cambridge University Press is using state-of-the-art scanning machines in its own Printing House to capture the content of each book selected for inclusion. The files are processed to give a consistently clear, crisp image, and the books finished to the high quality standard for which the Press is recognised around the world. The latest print-on-demand technology ensures that the books will remain available indefinitely, and that orders for single or multiple copies can quickly be supplied.

The Cambridge Library Collection will bring back to life books of enduring scholarly value across a wide range of disciplines in the humanities and social sciences and in science and technology.

Shakesperiana

*A Catalogue of the Early Editions of Shake-
speare's Plays, and of the Commentaries and
Other Publications Illustrative of his Works*

JAMES ORCHARD HALLIWELL-PHILLIPPS

CAMBRIDGE
UNIVERSITY PRESS

CAMBRIDGE UNIVERSITY PRESS

Cambridge New York Melbourne Madrid Cape Town Singapore São Paolo Delhi

Published in the United States of America by Cambridge University Press, New York

www.cambridge.org
Information on this title: www.cambridge.org/9781108000024

© in this compilation Cambridge University Press 2009

This edition first published 1841
This digitally printed version 2009

ISBN 978-1-108-00002-4

Shakesperiana.

A CATALOGUE

OF THE EARLY EDITIONS OF

Shakespeare's Plays,

AND OF THE

COMMENTARIES AND OTHER PUBLICATIONS

ILLUSTRATIVE OF HIS WORKS.

BY

JAMES ORCHARD HALLIWELL, Esq., F. R. S., F. S. A.,

&c. &c. &c.

LONDON:

JOHN RUSSELL SMITH,

4, OLD COMPTON STREET, SOHO SQUARE.

M DCCC XLI.

PREFACE.

THIS little publication has been undertaken chiefly with a view of supplying the critic and student with the means of ascertaining at once what sources are available on any particular points of inquiry in Shakesperian criticism, and affording the latter a manual of bibliographical information which is indispensable to the attainment of any correct knowledge in that department of literature.

Something of the same kind was undertaken by Mr. Wilson, and published in 1827; but, besides being very concise in the list of the early editions of the plays, it offers us no correct accounts of the different impressions. Moreover, the scarcity of this last mentioned work, and the rapid progress which this class of literature has made since its publication, are sufficient reasons for the present undertaking.

The list of Shakesperiana in Lowndes' Bibliographer's Manual, has been found of great use, as also the Prolegomena of Boswell's Malone, the Catalogue of Malone's library, and the second part of Bibliotheca Heberiana. All the copies of the early quartos in the library of the British Museum, have been carefully examined; but it is to be regretted that our national library should still want many of the most valuable. As an example of the great deficiency of the Museum library in Shakesperiana, it does not appear that a single copy of any edition of so common and popular a work as Dodd's " Beauties of Shakespeare," is to be found in the whole collection.

It may be as well to state that Capell's collection of early English literature, so frequently referred to in the following pages, is preserved in the library of Trinity College, Cambridge.

J. O. H.

June 21*st*, 1841.

Shakesperiana.

SINGLE PLAYS.

I. TEMPEST.

1. The Tempest, or the Inchanted Island, a Comedy alter'd by Davenant and Dryden, 4to. Lond. 1670, 1674, 1676, 1690.
2. —— An Opera, by D. Garrick, 8vo. Lond. 1756.
3. —— Altered by Sheridan, 8vo. Lond. 1777.
4. —— By J. P. Kemble, 8vo. Lond. 1789, 1806.
5. —— Italian, 8vo. Pis. 1815.

II. THE TWO GENTLEMEN OF VERONA.

1. The Two Gentlemen of Verona: a comedy: with alterations and additions. By Benjamin Victor, 8vo. Lond. 1763.
2. —— Altered by J. P. Kemble, 8vo. Lond. 1808.

III. MERRY WIVES OF WINDSOR.

1. A most pleasaunt and excellent conceited comedie of Syr John Falstaffe, and the merrie wives of Windsor. Entermixed with sundrie variable and pleasing humors of Syr Hugh, the Welch Knyght, Justice Shallow, and his wise cousin M. Slender. With the swaggering vaine of auncient Pistoll, and Corporal

B

Nym, 4to. London, *Printed by T. C. for Arthur Johnson*, 1602.
The first edition, extremely rare. Bibl. Heber. Pt. 2, No. 5443,
£40. Copies in Capell's Collection and the Bodleian Library.

2. —— 4to. London, *Printed for Arthur Johnson*, 1619.
Reprinted by Steevens in 1766. Bibl. Heber. Pt. 2, No. 5444,
£7. Copies in Capell's Collection, Bodleian Library, and the
British Museum.

3. —— Newly corrected, 4to. London, *Printed by T. H. for R. Meighen*, 1630.
Copies in Capell's Collection, Bodleian Library, and the British
Museum.

4. —— Altered by Denis, under the title of " The Comical Gallant," 4to. Lond. 1702.

5. —— Altered by J. P. Kemble, 8vo. Lond. 1797. Second edition, 1804.

IV. TWELFTH NIGHT.

1. Love Betray'd; or, The Agreeable Disappointment. Altered from *Twelfth Night* by C. Burnaby, 4to. Lond. 1703.

V. MEASURE FOR MEASURE.

1. Measure for Measure; or, Beauty the best Advocate. Altered from Shakespeare by Charles Gildon, 4to. Lond. 1700.

2. —— Revised by J. P. Kemble, 8vo. Lond. 1803.

VI. MUCH ADO ABOUT NOTHING.

1. Much adoe about Nothing. As it hath been sundrie times publikely acted by the right honourable, the Lord Chamberlaine his servants, 4to. London, *Printed by V. S. for Andrew Wise and William Aspley*, 1600.
Reprinted by Steevens in 1766. Bibl. Heber. Pt. 2, No. 5445,
£18. Copies in Capell's Collection, Bodleian Library, and the
British Museum.

2. —— Altered by James Miller, under the title of " The Universal Passion," 8vo. Lond. 1737.

3. —— Altered by J. P. Kemble, 8vo. Lond. 1799.

VII. A MIDSUMMER NIGHT'S DREAM.

1. A Midsommer nights dreame. As it hath beene sundry times publickely acted by the Right honourable the Lord Chamberlaine his servants, 4to. London, *Imprinted for Thomas Fisher,* 1600.
   Bibl. Heber. Pt. 2, No. 5442, £36. Copies in Capell's Collection and the British Museum.

2. —— 4to. London, *Printed by James Roberts,* 1600.
   Copies in Capell's Collection, Bodleian Library, and the British Museum. Reprinted by Steevens in 1766, partially collated with the first edition.

3. —— The merry conceited humors of Bottom the Weaver, 4to. Lond. 1661.
   Reprinted in Kirkman's "Wits, or sport upon sport."

4. —— The Fairy Queen, altered from the Midsummer Night's Dream, 4to. Lond. 1692.

5. —— A comic masque of Pyramis and Thisbe. By Richard Leveridge, 12mo. Lond. 1716.

6. —— Pyramis and Thisbe, a mock opera. By Lampe, 8vo. Lond 1745.

7. —— The Fairies ; an opera taken from A Midsummer Night's Dream, by D. Garrick, 8vo. Lond. 1755.

8. —— Altered by D. Garrick, 8vo. Lond. 1763.

9. —— The Fairy Tale, taken from A Midsummer Night's Dream, by George Colman, 4to. Lond. 1763.

10. —— With alterations, additions, and new songs. By F. Reynolds, 8vo. Lond. 1816.

11. —— With alterations (by J. R. Planché, Esq.) 12mo. Lond. 1840.

VIII. LOVE'S LABOUR LOST.

1. A pleasant conceited comedie called Loves Labors Lost. As it was presented before her Highnes this last Christmas. Newly corrected and augmented by W. Shakespere, 4to. London, *Imprinted by W. W. for Cuthbert Burby,* 1598.
   Bibl. Heber. Pt. 2, No. 5448, £40. Copies in Capell's Collection and the Bodleian Library.

2. —— 4to. London, *Printed by W. S. for John Smethwicke,* 1631.
   Bibl. Heber. Pt. 2, No. 5449, 10s. 6d. Copies in Capell's Collection, Bodleian Library, and the British Museum.

8

3. The Students, a comedy, altered from Loves Labour Lost, 8vo. Lond. 1762.

IX. THE MERCHANT OF VENICE.

1. The most excellent historie of the Merchant of Venice. With the extreame crueltie of Shylocke the Jewe towards the sayd merchant, in cutting a just pound of his flesh: and the obtayning of Portia by the choyse of three chests, 4to. London, *Printed by I. R. for Thomas Heyes*, 1600.
Bibl. Heber. Pt. 2, No. 5446, £33. 10s. Strettell's sale, May, 1841, £16. 16s. Copies in Capell's Collection, Bodleian Library, and the British Museum.

2. —— 4to. London, *Printed by J. Roberts*, 1600.
Reprinted by Steevens in 1766, and collated with the three other early editions. Bibl. Heber. Pt. 2, No. 5447, £12. Strettell's sale, May, 1841, £10. Copies in Capell's Collection, Bodleian Library, and the British Museum.

3. —— 4to. London, *Printed by M. P. for Laurence Hayes*, 1637.
Copies in Capell's Collection and the British Museum.

4. —— 4to. London, *Printed for William Leake*, 1652.
Copies in Capell's Collection and the British Museum.

5. —— 4to. By George Granville. Lond. 1701.

6. —— 8vo. Lond. 1713.

7. —— 8vo. Lond. 1795.

8. —— altered by Valpy, 8vo. Reading 1802.

9. —— With the notes and illustrations of various commentators, and remarks by the editor (Ambrose Eccles), 8vo. Dublin, 1805.

X. AS YOU LIKE IT.

1. Altered by C. Johnson, under the title of "Love in a Forest," 8vo. Lond. 1723.

2. —— Altered, under the title of "The Modern Receipt, or, A Cure for Love," 8vo. Lond. 1739.

3. —— Revised by J. P. Kemble, 8vo. Lond. 1810.
An additional scene to this play, written by Mr. Moser, was printed in "The European Magazine," 1809.

XI. ALL'S WELL THAT ENDS WELL.

1. Altered by J. P. Kemble, 8vo. Lond. 1793.

XII. THE TAMING OF A SHREW.

1. A wittie and pleasant comedie called The Taming of the Shrew, 4to. London, *Printed by W. S. for John Smethwicke*, 1631.
Copies in Capell's Collection and the British Museum. Reprinted by Steevens in 1766. Another play under the same title was published in 1594, and again in 1607, which is supposed to be the original of this drama, as the plot and scenery are nearly similar.

2. —— By John Lacy, 4to. Lond. 1698.

3. —— A Cure for a Scold, a ballad farce; founded upon Shakespeare's Taming of a Shrew. By J. Worsdale, 8vo. Lond. (1735.)

4. —— Catherine and Petruchio: a comedy in three acts, altered from " The Taming of a Shrew," by D. Garrick, 8vo. Lond. 1756.

XIII. A WINTER'S TALE.

1. Florizel and Perdita; or, The Sheepshearing. Altered from the *Winter's Tale*, 8vo. Lond. 1754.

2. —— Florizel and Perdita. Altered from the *Winter's Tale*, by D. Garrick, 8vo. Lond. 1756.

3. —— Altered by C. Marsh, 8vo. Lond. 1756.

4. —— Altered by J. P. Kemble, 8vo. Lond. 1802.

XIV. THE COMEDY OF ERRORS.

1. Two sheets of this play, with notes by Joseph Ritson, 12mo. 1787.

2. —— Altered by Thomas Hull, 8vo. Lond. 1793.

XV. MACBETH.

1. Macbeth, a tragedy, with alterations, additions, and new songs, by Sir W. D'Avenant, 4to. Lond. 1674.

2. —— 4to. Lond. 1710.

3. —— Altered by Mr. Lee, 8vo. Edinburgh, 1753.

4. —— Collated with the old and modern editions, by Charles Jennens, 8vo. Lond. 1773.

5. —— With notes and emendations by Harry Rowe, 8vo. York, 1797. Second edition, 1799.

6. —— German, Von Schiller, 12mo. Tub. 1801.

7. —— Revised by J. P. Kemble, 8vo. Lond. 1803.
8. —— With selected and original anecdotes and annotations, biographical, explanatory, critical, and dramatic, 8vo. Lond. 1807.

XVI. KING JOHN.

1. Altered by R. Valpy, 8vo. Lond. 1800.
2. Altered by J. P. Kemble, 8vo. Lond. 1800.
3. Revised by J. P. Kemble, 8vo. Lond. 1804.

XVII. KING RICHARD THE SECOND.

1. The tragedie of King Richard the Second. As it hath beene publikely acted by the Right Honourable the Lord Chamberlaine his Servants, 4to. London, *Printed by Valentine Simmes for Andrew Wise,* 1597.
   A copy in Capell's Collection.
2. —— 4to. London, *Printed by Valentine Simmes for Andrew Wise,* 1598.
   Bibl. Heber. Pt. 2, No. 5453, £1. 1s. Copies in the Bodleian Library and the British Museum.
3. —— 4to. London, *Printed by W. W. for Matthew Law,* 1608.
   A copy in the Bodleian Library.
4. —— 4to. London, *Printed for Matthew Law,* 1615.
   Bibl. Heber. Pt. 2, No. 5154, £2. Copies in Capell's Collection, Bodleian Library, and the British Museum.
5. —— Port. 4to. London, *Printed by John Norton,* 1634.
   Copies in Capell's Collection and the British Museum.
6. —— By Tate, 4to. Lond. 1681.
7. —— Altered under the title of "The Sicilian Usurper," 4to. Lond. 1691.
8. —— Altered by Lewis Theobald, 8vo. Lond. 1720.
9. —— Altered from Shakespeare and the style imitated, by James Goodhall, 8vo. Manchester, 1772.

XVIII. KING HENRY IV.—First Part.

1 The Historie of Henrie the Fourth; with the Battell at Shrewsburie, betweene the King and Lord Henry Percy surnamed Henrie Hotspur of the North. With

the humorous conceits of Sir John Falstalfe, 4to. London, *Printed by P. S. for Andrew Wise*, 1598.
A copy in Capell's Collection.

2. —— 4to. London, *Printed by S. S. for Andrew Wise*, 1599.
Bibl. Heber. Pt. 2, No. 5455, *Imp.*, £1. 1s. Copies in Capell's Collection, Bodleian Library, and the British Museum.

3. —— 4to. London, *Printed by Valentine Simmes for Matthew Law*, 1604.
Fragment in Capell's Collection and a perfect copy in the Bodleian Library.

4. —— 4to. London, *Printed for Matthew Law*, 1608.
Bibl. Heber. Pt. 2, No. 5456, £12. 12s.

5. —— 4to. London, *Printed by W. W. for Matthew Law*, 1613.
Bibl. Heber. Pt. 2, No. 5457, £3. Copies in Capell's Collection and the Bodleian Library. Reprinted by Steevens in 1766.

6. —— 4to. London, *Printed by T. P. for Matthew Law*, 1622.
Bibl. Heber. Pt. 2, No. 5458, £3. 13s. 6d. Copies in Capell's Collection and the British Museum.

7. —— 4to. London, *Printed by John Norton*, 1632.
Copies in Capell's Collection and the British Museum.

8. —— 4to. London, *Printed by John Norton*, 1639.
Bibl. Heber. Pt. 2, No. 5459, £1. 1s. Copies in Capell's Collection, Bodleian Library, and the British Museum.

9. —— Revived, with alterations, by Thomas Betterton, 4to. Lond. 1700.

10. —— Revised by J. P. Kemble, 8vo. Lond. 1804.

11. —— King Henry the Fourth, being a specimen of Shakespeare's plays, furnished (in imitation of the Waverley Novels) with the manners and customs of the age in which the drama's plot is laid, 2 vols. 8vo. Lond. 1826.

XIX. KING HENRY IV.—Second Part.

1. The second part of Henrie the Fourth, continuing to his death, and coronation of Henrie the Fift, with the humours of Sir John Falstaffe, and swaggering Pistoll, 4to. London, *Printed by V. S. for Andrew Wise and William Aspley*, 1600.
Bibl. Heber. Pt. 2, No. 5460, £40. : and No. 5460*, *the last leaf supplied by M. S.*, £2. 10s. Copies in Capell's Collection, Bodleian Library, and the British Museum.

2. —— 4to. London. *Printed by V. S. for Andrew Wise and William Aspley*, 1600.
Copies in the Bodleian Library and the British Museum. Reprinted by Steevens in 1766.

3. —— Altered by Thomas Betterton, 8vo. Lond. *n. d.*

4. —— Altered by Dr. Valpy, 8vo. Reading, 1801.

5. —— Revised by J. P. Kemble, 8vo. Lond. 1804.

XX. HENRY THE FIFTH.

1. The Chronicle History of Henry the Fift, with his battell fought at Agin Court in France. Together with Auntient Pistoll, 4to. London, *Printed by Thomas Creede for Th. Millington and John Busby*, 1600.
Bibl. Heber. Pt. 2, No. 5461, £24. 3s. Copies in Capell's Collection, Bodleian Library, and the British Museum.

2. —— 4to. London, *Printed by Thomas Creede for Thomas Pavier*, 1602.
A copy in Capell's Collection.

3. —— 4to. London, *Printed for T. P.*, 1608.
Bibl. Heber. Pt. 2, No. 5462, £4. 5s. Copies in Capell's Collection, Bodleian Library, and the British Museum.

4. —— Altered by James Wrighten, 4to. Lond. 1789.

5. —— Altered by J. P. Kemble, 8vo. Lond. 1801.

6. —— Revised by J. P. Kemble, 8vo. Lond. 1806.

XXI. HENRY VI.—FIRST PART.

1. Henry VI, the first part, with the murder of Humphrey, Duke of Gloucester. Altered by J. Crowne, 4to. Lond. 1681.

XXII. HENRY VI.—SECOND PART.

1. The first part of the Contention betwixt the two famous houses of Yorke and Lancaster, with the death of the good Duke Humphrey, and the Banishment and death of the Duke of Suffoelk, and the tragicall end of the proud Cardinall of Winchester, with the notable rebellion of Jack Cade, and the Duke of Yorkes first claime unto the crowne, 4to. London, *Printed by Thomas Creede for Thomas Millington*, 1594.
Bibl. Heber. Pt. 2, No. 5479, £64.

2. —— 4to. London, *Printed by W. W. for Thomas
Millington*, 1600.
Bibl. Heber. Pt. 2, No. 5481, £2. 2s. Copies in Capell's Collection and the Bodleian Library.

3. —— 4to. London, *Printed by Valentine Simmes for
Thomas Millington*, 1600.
Fragment in Capell's Collection. Not mentioned by Lowndes.

4. —— 4to. London, *Printed for T. P.* [1619.]
Bibl. Heber. Pt. 2, No. 5480, £6. 6s. Copies in Capell's Collection, Bodleian Library, and the British Museum. Reprinted by Steevens in 1766.

5. —— Altered by J. Crowne, 4to. Lond. 1681.

XXIII. HENRY VI.—THIRD PART.

1. The true tragedie of Richard Duke of Yorke, and the
death of good King Henry the Sixt, with the whole
contention betweene the two houses Lancaster and
Yorke, 4to. London, *Printed by P. S. for Thomas
Millington*, 1595.

2. —— 4to. London, *Printed by W. W. for Thomas
Millington*, 1600.
A copy in the British Museum.

3. —— 4to. London, *Printed for T. P.* [1619.]
This was published with the second part of Henry VI, under the the title of "The Whole Contention betweenc the two Famous Houses, Lancaster and Yorke." Two copies in the British Museum. See above.

XXIV. RICHARD THE THIRD.

1. The tragedy of King Richard the Third. Containing
his treacherous plots against his brother Clarence:
the pittiefull murther of his innocent nephewes: his
tyrannicall usurpation: with the whole course of his
detested life, and most deserved death, 4to. London,
Printed by Valentine Sims for Andrew Wise, 1597.
Bibl. Heber. Pt. 2, No. 5463, £41. 9s. 6d. Copies in Capell's Collection and the Bodleian Library.

2. —— 4to. London, *Printed by Thomas Creede for
Andrew Wise*, 1598.
Bibl. Heber. Pt. 2, No. 5464, £17. Copies in Capell's Collection and the British Museum.

3. —— Newly augmented by William Shake-speare, 4to.
London, *Printed by Thomas Creede for Andrew
Wise*, 1602.
Copies in Capell's Collection and the British Museum.

c

4. —— 4to. London, *Printed by Thomas Creede, and are to be sold by Matthew Lawe*, 1612.
Copies in Capell's Collection, Bodleian Library, and the British Museum. Reprinted by Steevens in 1766.

5. —— 4to. London, *Printed by Thomas Purfoot, and sold by Matthew Law*, 1621.

6. —— 4to. London, *Printed by Thomas Purfoot*, 1622.
Copies in Capell's Collection and the British Museum.

7. —— 4to. London, *Printed by John Norton*, 1629.
Copies in Capell's Collection and the British Museum.

8. —— 4to. London, *Printed by John Norton*, 1634.
Copies in Capell's Collection and the British Museum.

9. —— Altered by Colley Cibber, 4to. Lond. 1700.

10. —— Revised by J. P. Kemble, 8vo. Lond. 1810.

11. —— Adapted to the stage by R. Wroughton, 8vo. London, 1815.

12. —— *Italian*, 8vo. Pis. 1815.

XXV. HENRY VIII.

1. Henry VIII; in which are interspersed historical notes, moral reflections, &c. in respect to the unhappy fate Cardinal Wolsey met with. By Joseph Grove, 8vo. Lond. 1758.

2. —— Altered by J. P. Kemble, 8vo. Lond. 1804.

XXVI. TROILUS AND CRESSIDA.

1. The famous historie of Troylus and Cresseid. Excellently expressing the beginning of their loues, with the conceited wooing of Pandarus Prince of Licia, 4to. London, *Imprinted by G. Eld for R. Bonian and H. Walley*, 1609.
Bibl. Heber. Pt. 2, No. 5465, £16. Copies in Capell's Collection and the Bodleian Library. Reprinted by Steevens in 1766.

2. —— 4to. London, *Imprinted by G. Elde*, 1609.
In this second edition, the word "famous" is omitted on the title-page.

3. —— Altered by John Dryden, 4to. Lond. 1679.

XXVII. TIMON OF ATHENS.

1. Altered by Thomas Shadwell, 4to. Lond. 1678.

2. —— Altered by Dance, 8vo. 1768.

3. —— Altered by Richard Cumberland, 8vo. Lond. 1771.

XXVIII. CORIOLANUS.

1. Altered by John Dennis, 8vo. Lond. 1721.

2. —— Altered by Thomas Sheridan, 8vo. Lond. 1755.

3. —— Altered by J. P. Kemble, 8vo. Lond. 1789, 1806.

XXIX. JULIUS CÆSAR.

1. Julius Cæsar, 4to. Lond. 1691.

2. —— Altered by Davenant and Dryden, 12mo. Lond. 1719.

3. —— Collated with the old and modern editions, by Charles Jennens, 8vo. Lond. 1773.

4. —— *Italian*, 8vo. Mil. 1811.

5. —— *Italian*, 8vo. Pisa, 1815.

XXX. ANTONY AND CLEOPATRA.

1. Altered by Sir Charles Sedley, 4to. Lond. 1677.

2. —— Altered by Capell, 8vo. Lond. 1758.

XXXI. CYMBELINE.

1. Altered by Charles Marsh, 8vo. Lond. 1755.

2. —— Altered by W. Hawkins, 8vo. Lond. 1759.

3. —— Altered by D. Garrick, 12mo. Lond. 1761.

4. —— Altered by Henry Brooke, 8vo. Lond. 1778.

5. —— Altered by Eccles, 8vo. Lond. 1793.

6. —— Altered by J. P. Kemble, 8vo. Lond. 1801, 1810.

XXXII. TITUS ANDRONICUS.

1. The first edition of this play is said by Langbaine, who appears to have seen it, to have been printed in 1594, and it was certainly entered at Stationers' Hall on Feb. 6th in that year, under the title of " A booke entitled A noble Roman historie of ' Titus Androni- cus.'" No copy is now known to exist.

2 —— 4to. London, *Printed by J. R. for Andrew White,* 1600.

3. —— 4to. London, **Printed for Eedward White,** 1611.
Copies in Capell's Collection, Bodleian Library, and the British Museum. Reprinted by Steevens in 1766.

4. —— Altered by E. Ravenscroft, 4to. Lond. 1687.

XXXIII. PERICLES.

1. The late and much admired play, called Pericles, Prince of Tyre. With the true relation of the whole historie, adventures and fortunes of the said prince : As also the no lesse strange and worthy accidents, in the birth and life of his daughter Mariana, 4to. London, *Imprinted for Henry Gosson,* 1609.
Bibl. Heber. Pt. 2, No. 5474, £18. 4s. Copies in Capell's Collection and the British Museum.

2. —— 4to. London, *Printed for S. S.,* 1611.

3. —— 4to. London, *Printed for T. P.,* 1619.
Bibl. Heber. Pt. 2, No. 5475, £4. 4s., and No. 5476, £1. 18s. Copies in Capell's Collection and the British Museum.

4. —— 4to. London, *Printed by I. N. for R. B.,* 1630.
Copies in Capell's Collection and the British Museum.

5. —— 4to. London, *Printed by I. N., for R. B.,* 1639.
Bibl. Heber. Pt. 2, No. 5477, £1 2s.

6. —— 4to. London, *Printed by Thomas Cotes,* 1635.
Copies in Capell's Collection and the British Museum.

XXXIV. KING LEAR.

1. M. William Shak-speare : His true chronicle historie of the life and death of King Lear and his three daughters. With the unfortunate life of Edgar, sonne and heire to the Earle of Gloster, and his sullen and assumed humor of Tom of Bedlam : As it was played before the Kings Maiestie at Whitehall upon S. Stephan's night in Christmas Hollidayes. By his Maiesties seruants playing vsually at the Gloabe on the Bancke-side, 4to. London, *Printed for Nathaniel Butter,* 1608.
Bibl. Heber. Pt. 2, No. 5450, £32. Copies in Capell's Collection, Bodleian Library, and the British Museum.

2. M. William Shake-speare, His true chronicle history of the life and death of King Lear, and his three

daughters, 4to. London, *Printed for Nathaniel Butter*, 1608.

Two copies of this edition, with a few typographical variations, are in the British Museum. Bibl. Heber. Pt. 2, No. 5451, £3. 16s. Copies also in Capell's Collection and the Bodleian Library. Reprinted by Steevens in 1766.

3. —— 4to. London, *Printed by Jane Bell*, 1655.

Bibl. Heber. Pt. 2, No. 5452, £2. 2s. A copy in Capell's Collection.

4. —— Revived with alterations, by Nahum Tate, 4to. London, 1681., and 12mo. Lond. 1759. Revised by J. P. Kemble, 8vo. Lond. 1808.

5. —— altered by George Colman, 8vo. Lond. 1768.

6. —— Edited by Eccles, 8vo. Dublin, 1793.

7. —— Altered by J. P. Kemble, 8vo. Lond. 1800.

XXXV. ROMEO AND JULIET.

1. An excellent conceited tragedie of Romeo and Juliet. As it hath been often (with great applause) plaid publiquely, by the right honourable the L. of Hunsdon his servants, 4to. London, *Printed by John Danter*, 1597.

Bibl. Heber. Pt. 2, No. 5466, *Imp.*, £1. 1s. Copies in Capell's Collection, Bodleian Library, and the British Museum.

2. —— 4to. London, *Printed by Thomas Creede for Cuthbert Burby*, 1599.

Bibl. Heber. Pt. 2, No. 5467, £5. 15s. 6d. Copies in the Bodleian Library and the British Museum.

3. —— 4to. London, *Printed for John Smethwicke, n. d.*

Copies in Capell's Collection and the British Museum.

4. —— 4to. London, *Printed for John Smethwicke*, 1609.

Bibl. Heber. Pt. 2, No. 5468, £1. 14s. A copy in Capell's Collection. Reprinted by Steevens in 1766.

5. —— 4to. London, *Printed by R. Young, for John Smethwicke*, 1637.

Copies in Capell's Collection, Bodleian Library, and the British Museum.

6. —— With alterations by Garrick, 8vo. Lond. *n. d.*

7. —— *Italian*, 8vo. Fir. 1814.

XXXVI. HAMLET.

1. The tragicall historie of Hamlet Prince of Denmarke, by William Shake-speare; as it hath beene diuerse times acted by his Highnesse Seruants in the Cittie

of London : as also in the two Vniversities of Cambridge and Oxford, and else-where, 4to. London, *for N. L. and Iohn Trundell,* 1603.

Only one copy is known of this edition, and that wanting the last leaf, now in the collection of the Duke of Devonshire. The play is, however, perfect to the death of Hamlet, and has been reprinted, 8vo., Lond., 1825.

2. —— Newly imprinted and enlarged to almost as much againe as it was, according to the true and perfect coppie, 4to. London, *Printed by J. R. for N. Landure,* 1604.

3. —— 4to. London, *Printed by J. R. for N. L.,* 1605.
Copies in Capell's Collection and the British Museum.

4. —— 4to. London, *Printed by W. S. for John Smethwicke, n. d.*
Bibl. Heber. Pt. 2, No. 5469, £5. 5s. Copies in Capell's Collection, Bodleian Library, and the British Museum.

5. —— 4to. London, *for John Smithwicke,* 1609.

6. —— 4to. London, *Printed for John Smethwicke,* 1611.
Bibl. Heber. Pt. 2, No. 5470, £9. 9s. Copies in Capell's Collection and the British Museum. Reprinted by Steevens in 1766.

7. —— 4to. London, *Printed by R. Young for John Smethwicke,* 1637.
Bibl. Heber. Pt. 2, No. 5471, £1. 2s. Copies in Capell's Collection, Bodleian Library, and the British Museum.

8. —— 4to. London, 1683.

9. —— 4to. London, 1695.

10. —— 4to. Lond. 1703.

11. —— Collated with the old and modern editions, by Charles Jennens, 8vo. London, 1773.

12. —— Traducida é ilustrada con la vida del autor y notas criticas por Inarco Celenio, 4to. Madrid, 1798.

13. —— Altered by J. P. Kemble, 8vo. Lond. 1800.

14. —— Italian, 8vo. Fir. 1814.

XXXVII. OTHELLO.

1. The Tragœdy of Othello, the Moore of Venice. As it hath beene diverse times acted at the Globe, and at the Black-Friers, by his Majesties servants, 4to. London, *Printed by N. O. for Thomas Walkley,* 1622.
Bibl. Heber. Pt. 2, No. 5172, £28. Strettell's sale, May, 1841, £21. Copies in Capell's Collection and the Bodleian Library. Reprinted by Steevens in 1766.

19

2. —— 4to. London, *Printed by A. M. for Richard Hawkins*, 1630.

Bibl. Heber. Pt. 2, No. 5473, £2. 9s. Copies in Capell's Collection, Bodleian Library, and the British Museum.

3. —— 4to. London, *Printed for William Leake*, 1655.

Copies in Capell's Collection and the British Museum. The last page contains a list of books "printed or sold by William Leake."

4. —— 4to. Lond. 1681.

5. —— 4to. Lond. 1687.

6. —— 4to. Lond. 1695.

7. —— 4to. Lond. 1701.

8. —— 4to. Lond. 1705.

9. —— Collated with the old and modern editions, by Charles Jennens, 8vo. London, 1773.

10. —— Revised by J. P. Kemble, 8vo. Lond. 1804.

11. —— *Italian*, 8vo. Fir. 1814.

12. —— *French*, 8vo. Paris, 1830.

COMMENTARIES, ESSAYS, &c.

1. The tragedies of the last age, considered and examined by the practice of the ancients, and by the common sense of all ages, in a letter to Fleetwood Shepheard, Esq., by Mr. Rymer, 8vo. Lond. 1678. Second edition, 1692.

2. A short view of tragedy; its original excellency, and corruption, with some reflections on Shakespear, and other practitioners for the stage. By Mr. Rymer, 8vo. Lond. 1693.

3. Some reflections on Mr. Rymer's "Short view of tragedy," and an attempt at a vindication of Shakespeare. By Charles Gildon.
   Printed in the "Miscellaneous Letters and Essays," 8vo. Lond. 1694.

4. The Impartial Critic ; or, some observations on Mr. Rymer's late book, entitled "A Short view of tragedy." By John Dennis, 4to. Lond. 1693.

5. Remarks on the plays of Shakespeare. By C. Gildon, 8vo. [Printed at the end of the seventh volume of Rowe's Shakespeare, 1710.]

6. Shakespeariana, a collection of passages from Shakespeare. By Charles Gildon.
   Printed at the end of "The Complete Art of Poetry," 12mo. Lond. 1718.

7. An essay on the genius and writings of Shakespear, with some letters of criticism to the Spectator. By John Dennis. 8vo. Lond. 1712.

8. Shakespear restored, or specimens of blunders committed and unamended in Pope's edition of this poet. By Lewis Theobald, 4to. Lond. 1726.

9. An answer to Mr. Pope's preface to Shakespear, being a vindication of the old actors who were the publishers and performers of that author's plays. By a strolling player [John Roberts], 8vo. Lond. 1729.

10. Some remarks on the tragedy of Hamlet Prince of Denmark, written by William Shakspeare, 8vo. Lond. 1736.

11. Explanatory and Critical Notes on divers passages of Shakespeare. By Francis Peck, M. A.
    Printed in the "Memoirs of Milton," 4to. Lond. 1740.

12. Miscellaneous Observations on the Tragedy of Macbeth, with Remarks on Sir T[homas] H[anmer's] edition of Shakespear: to which is affixed Proposals for a new edition of Shakespear, with a specimen. [By Samuel Johnson] 12mo. Lond. 1745.

13. A word or two of advice to William Warbuton, a dealer in many words, by a Friend [Zach. Grey], 8vo. Lond. 1746.

14. An answer to certain passages in Mr. W[arbuton's] Preface to his edition of Shakespear; together with some remarks of the many errors and false criticisms in the work itself, 8vo. Lond. 1748.

15. Critical Observations on Shakespere. By John Upton, 8vo. Lond. 1746. Second edition, 1748.

16. An Enquiry into the Learning of Shakespeare, with remarks on several passages of his plays, in a Conversation between Eugenius and Neander. By Peter Whalley, A. B., 8vo. Lond. 1748.

17. The Canons of Criticism and Glossary; being a supplement to Mr. Warburton's Edition of Shakespeare, collected from the Notes in that celebrated work, and proper to be bound with it. By Thomas Edwards, 8vo. Lond. 1748.
    Very frequently reprinted. The best edition is the seventh, which was published with additions in 1765. At the end of this edition are printed Mr. Roderick's Remarks on Shakspeare.

18. An attempte to rescue that aunciente English Poet and Playwrighte, Maistre William Shakespere, from the many errours falsely charged on him by certaine new-

D

fangled wittes, and to let him speak for himself, as right well he wotteth, when freede from the many careless mistakings of the heedless first imprinters of his workes, by a gentleman, formerly of Gray's Inn [John Holt], 8vo. Lond. 1749.

19. Remarks on the Tempest; or, an attempt to rescue Shakspeare from the many errors falsely charged on him by his several editors, &c. [By Mr. Holt], 8vo. London, 1750.

20. A free and familiar letter to that great refiner of Pope and Shakspeare, the Rev. Mr. Wm. Warburton [By Dr. Grey], 8vo. Lond. 1750.

21. Remarks upon a late [Warburton's] edition of Shakespear, with a long string of emendations, borrowed by the celebrated editor from the Oxford edition without acknowledgement; to which is prefixed a defence of the late Sir Thomas Hanmer, Bart. [By Dr. Grey], 8vo. Lond. 1751.
This work was reprinted in the following year [1752] under the title of " Examination of a late edition of Shakespear."

22. A poetical epistle from Shakespeare in Elysium to Mr. Garrick at Drury Lane Theatre, 4to. Lond. 1752.

23. Miscellaneous Observations on the Tragedy of Hamlet, Prince of Denmark : with a preface, containing some general remarks on the writings of Shakespear, 8vo. Lond. 1752.

24. Critical, historical and explanatory notes on Shakespeare, with emendations of the text and metre. By Zachary Grey, LL. D., 2 vols. 8vo. Lond. 1752. *Second edition*, 1754. ***Third edition***, 1755.

25. The Beauties of Shakespear, regularly selected from each play. By William Dodd, B. A., 2 vols. 12mo. Lond. 1752.
Frequently reprinted. The sarcastic dedication to Lord Chesterfield was cancelled in most copies. The third edition, with the author's last corrections, was published in 1780, in three volumes, 12mo.

26. Shakespear illustrated ; or, the novels and histories on which the plays of Shakespeare are founded, collected and translated from the original authors ; with critical remarks. By Mrs. Charlotte Lennox, 3 vols. 12mo. Lond. 1753-4.
The dedication to the Earl of Orrery was written by Dr. Johnson; and Malone was of opinion that many of the observations throughout the work were written by him.

27. The Tomb of Shakspeare, a poetical vision. By J. G. Cooper, 4to. Lond. 1755. *Second edition,* 1755.

28. The novel from which the play of The Merchant of Venice, written by Shakespear, is taken, translated from the Italian: to which is added, a translation of a novel from the Decamerone of Bocaccio, 8vo. Lond. 1755.

29. Visionary Interview at the Shrine of Shakespear. By H. Howard, 4to. Lond. 1756.

30. Proposals for printing, by subscription, the dramatic works of W. Shakespear, corrected and illustrated by Sam. Johnson, 8vo. Lond. 1756.

31. Notes and various readings of Shakespeare. By Edward Capell, 4to. Lond. 1759. *Second edition, with additions,* 3 vols., 1779-80.

32. Ode on Shakespeare, and testimonies to the genius and merits of Skakespeare, 4to. *n. d.*

33. The castrated letter of Sir Thomas Hanmer, in the sixth volume of the Biographia Britannica, wherein is discovered the rise of the Bishop of Gloucester's quarrel with the baronet, about his edition of Shakespeare's plays, to which is added, an impartial account of the extraordinary means used to suppress the remarkable letter. By a proprietor of that work [Philip Nichols], 8vo. and fol. Lond. 1763.

34. A revisal of Shakespeare's text; wherein the alterations introduced into it by the modern editors and critics are particularly considered. By Benjamin Heath, 8vo. Lond. 1765.

35. Dr. Johnson's preface to his edition of Shakespeare's Plays, 8vo. Lond. 1765.

36. Prefaces to Shakespeare's plays by Dr. Johnson, Mr. Pope, Mr. Theobald, Sir T. Hanmer, and Dr. Warburton; with some account of the life of Shakespeare, by Mr. Rowe, 8vo. Lond. 1765.

37. A review of Dr. Johnson's new edition of Shakespeare: In which the ignorance or inattention of that editor is exposed, and the poet defended from the persecution of his commentators. By William Kenrick, 8vo. Lond. 1765.

38. An examination of Mr. Kenrick's Review of Dr. Johnson's edition of Shakespeare [By Mr. Barclay, a student of Oxford], 8vo. Lond. 1766.

39. A defence of Mr. Kenrick's Review of Dr. Johnson's Shakespeare; containing a number of curious and ludicrous anecdotes of literary biography. By a friend [W. Kenrick], 8vo. Lond. 1766.

40. Observations and conjectures on some passages of Shakespeare. By Thomas Tyrwhitt, 8vo. Oxford, 1766.

41. An essay on the learning of Shakespeare. By Richard Farmer, D. D., 8vo. Lond. 1767. *Second edition greatly enlarged*, 8vo. Cambridge, 1767. Reprinted 1789 and 1821.

42. A letter to David Garrick, Esq., concerning a glossary to the plays of Shakespeare on a more extensive plan than has hitherto appeared. To which is annexed a specimen. By Richard Warner, 8vo. Lond. 1768.
The original manuscript of this work is in the British Museum.— MS. Addit. 10,544.

43. A glossary to the plays of Shakespeare, in which are explained technical terms, words obsolete or uncommon, and common words used in an uncommon sense. By Richard Warner.
Never published. The original manuscript, consisting of seventy-one volumes in quarto and octavo, is preserved in the British Museum, MS. Addit. 10,472 to 10,542. An interleaved copy of Tonson's edition of Shakespeare, with MS. notes by Warner, is also preserved in the British Museum.

44. An essay on the writings and genius of Shakespeare, compared with the Greek and French Dramatic poets. By Mrs. Elizabeth Montagu, 8vo. 1769.
Frequently reprinted.

45. Ode upon dedicating a building and erecting a statue to Shakespeare at Stratford-upon-Avon. By David Garrick, 4to. Lond. 1769.

46. Shakespeare's Jubilee, a masque. By George Saville Carey, 8vo. Lond. 1769.

47. Shakespeare's Garland; being a collection of new songs, ballads, roundelays, catches, glees, comic serenates, &c., performed at the Jubilee at Stratford-upon-Avon, 8vo. Lond. 1769.

48. Garrick's Vagary, or England run Mad; with Particulars of the Stratford Jubilee, 8vo. 1769.

49. Judith, a Sacred Drama, as performed in the church of Stratford-upon-Avon, on occasion of the Jubilee, 4to. 1769.

50. Stratford Jubilee, a new comedy, with Scrub's Trip to the Jubilee. 1769.

51. Trinculo's Trip to the Jubilee, 4to. 1769.

52. Man and Wife; or, the Shakespeare Jubilee, 8vo. 1770.

53. Lamentable and true tragedie of M. Arden, of Feversham in Kent; with a preface in favour of its being the earliest dramatic work of Shakespeare [by Edward Jacob], 8vo. Lond. 1770.

54. Introduction to the school of Shakespeare, held on Wednesday evenings, in the Apollo, at the Devil Tavern, Temple Bar. By William Kenrick, 8vo. *n. d.*; 8vo. Lond. 1773.

55. Cursory remarks on tragedy, on Shakespeare, and on certain French and Italian poets, principally tragedians [By Edward Taylor], 8vo. Lond. 1772. *Second edition* 1774.

56. An essay on the character of Hamlet, as performed by Mr. Henderson, at the Haymarket, 8vo. *n. d.*

57. Shakespeare; containing the traits of his character, 8vo. *n. d.*

58. A philosophical analysis and illustration of some of Shakspeare's dramatic characters [By William Richardson], 8vo. Lond. 1774.
Frequently reprinted.

59. Cursory remarks on tragedy, on Shakespeare and on certain French and Italian poets, principally tragedians [By William Richardson], 8vo. Lond. 1774.

60. Shakespeare: Rara Avis in Terra. By Kenrick Prescott, 4to. Cambridge, 1774. *Privately printed.*
I copy the title of this tract from Lowndes, who says that it consists of eight leaves. It is not mentioned by Watt, nor even by Cole in his MS. Athenæ.

61. Introduction to Shakespeare's plays; containing an Essay on Oratory, 8vo. Lond. 1774.

62. The morality of Shakespeare's drama illustrated. By Mrs. Elizabeth Griffith, 8vo. Lond. 1775.

63. A lyric ode on the fairies, ærial beings, and witches of Shakespeare, 4to. Lond. 1776.

64. A letter to George Hardinge, Esq., on the subject of a passage in Mr. Steevens' preface to his impression of Shakespeare, 4to. Lond. 1771.
This tract is by some attributed to the Rev. Mr. Collins of Hertfordshire.

65. An essay on the dramatic character of Sir John Falstaff. By Maurice Morgann, 8vo. Lond. 1777. *Second edition, with preface*, 1825.

66. A letter from M. de Voltaire to the French Academy on the merits of Shakespeare, with a dedication to the Marquis of Granby, and a preface by the Editor, 8vo. Lond. 1777.

67. Discours sur Shakspeare et sur M. de Voltaire, par Joseph Baretti, 8vo. Lond. 1777.

68. Modern characters from Shakespeare, alphabetically arranged, 12mo. 1778.
Some of these characters were admirably adapted. Three, if not more, editions, appeared in 1778.

69. The Haunts of Shakespeare, a poem. By William Pearce, 4to. Lond. 1778.

70. Catalogue of Mr. Capell's Shaksperiana, presented by him to Trinity College, Cambridge, and printed from an exact copy of his own MS. 8vo. 1779. pp. 20.
Thirty copies only of this tract were printed by Mr. Steevens for the use of his friends. It has recently [1829] been reprinted in Mr. Hartshorne's " Book Rarities in the University of Cambridge." Capell's own transcripts and notes on Shakespeare are preserved with this collection in the library of Trinity College.

71. Six old plays, on which Shakespeare founded his Measure for Measure, Comedy of Errors, Taming the Shrew, King John, King Henry IV., King Henry V., and King Lear, 2 vols, 12mo. Lond. 1779.

72. Clifton : a Poem, to which is added an Ode to Shakspear, in honor of the Jubilee, by Henry Jones, 4to. Bristol, 1779.

73. A supplement to the edition of Shakespeare's plays published in 1778 ; containing additional observations by several of the former commentators. To

which are subjoined, The Genuine Poems of the same Author, and seven plays that have been ascribed to him, with notes by the editor [Malone] and others, 2 vols. 8vo. Lond. 1780.

74. The Stockton Jubilee; or, Shakespeare in his glory [By Joseph Ritson], 8vo. 1781.
Of great rarity. This pamphlet consists of extracts from Shakespeare applied to most of the principal inhabitants of that town, descriptive of their several characters.

75. A second appendix to Mr. Malone's supplement to the last edition of the plays of Shakespeare, 8vo. Lond. 1783.
Fifty copies only printed.

76. Remarks, critical and illustrative, on the text and notes of the last [Steevens'] edition of Shakespeare. By Joseph Ritson, 8vo. Lond. 1783.

77. Contes moraux tires de tragédies de Shakespeare. Par. M. Perrin, 12mo. Lond. 1783.

78. A familiar address to the curious in English poetry, more particularly to the readers of Shakespeare. By Thersites Literarius, 8vo. Lond. 1784.

79. Essays on Shakespeare's dramatic characters of Richard the Third, King Lear, and Timon of Athens; with an Essay on the Faults of Shakespeare, and additional observations on the character of Hamlet. By William Richardson, 12mo. Lond. 1784.

80. The beauties of Shakespeare, selected from his works, to which are added the principal scenes in the same author, 8vo. Third edition, Lond. 1784.
Frequently reprinted.

81. Dramatic Miscellanies, consisting of critical observations on the plays of Shakespeare, &c. By Thomas Davies, 2 vols. 8vo. Lond. 1784.

82. Comments on the last edition of Shakespeare's plays. By John Monck Mason, 8vo. Dublin, 1785; Lond. 1797.

83. Remarks on some of the characters of Shakespeare. By Thomas Whately, 8vo. Lond. 1785. Second edition, 8vo., Oxford, 1808. Third edition edited by Archbp. Whately, 12mo. Lond. 1839.

84. The Etymologist, a Comedy, dedicated to all the

commentators on Shakespeare, and particularly to G[eorge] S[teevens]. 8vo. Lond. 1785.

85. Macbeth re-considered; an essay intended as an answer to part of the remarks on some of the characters of Shakespeare. By John Philip Kemble, 8vo. Lond. 1786.

86. A fragment on Shakespeare, extracted from Advice to a young Poet, by the Rev. Martin Sherlock; and translated from the French, 8vo. Lond. 1786.

87. Imperfect hints towards a new edition of Shakespeare. By Samuel Fenton, 4to. Lond. 1787. 2nd Part 1788.

88. A concordance to Shakespeare, suited to all the editions; in which the distinguished and parallel passages in the plays of that justly admired writer, are methodically arranged: to which are added three hundred notes and illustrations entirely new. By Andrew Becket, 8vo. Lond. 1787.

89. Ueber W. Shakespeare, J. Z. Eschenburg. *Port.* 8vo. Zurich, 1787. Repr. 1806.

90. A catalogue of pictures in the Shakespeare Gallery, 8vo. 1787, &c.

91. Essay on the character of Hamlet. By the Rev. Thomas Robertson, 4to. Lond. 1788.

92. The Quip Modest; a few words by way of supplement to remarks critical and illustrative, on the text and notes of the last edition of Shakespeare. By Joseph Ritson, 8vo. Lond. 1788.

93. Essay on the character of Hamlet. By the Rev. T. Robertson, 4to. Lond. 1788.

94. Cursory remarks on some of the ancient English poets. By Philip Neve, 8vo. Lond. 1789.

95. The Bee; or a comparison to the Shakespeare Gallery, 8vo. *n. d.*

96. An index to remarkable passages and words made use of by Shakespeare. By Samuel Ayscough, 8vo. Lond. 1790; Dublin, 1791; Lond. 1807; Lond. 1827.

97. Remarks upon a late edition of Shakespeare; with a long string of emendations borrowed by the celebrated

editor from the Oxford edition without acknowledgement, 8vo. *n. d.*

98. Letter on Boydell's edition of Shakespeare's works. By George Nicol, 4to. Lond. 1791.

99. Sonnets [40] from Shakespeare, by Albert [the Rev. John Armstrong], 8vo. Lond. 1791.
These sonnets appeared originally in the Gazetteer and Morning Chronicle.

100. Cursory criticisms on the edition of Shakespeare published by Edmond Malone. By Joseph Ritson, 8vo. Lond. 1792.

101. A select collection of the beauties of Shakespeare, with some account &c. of the life of Shakespeare [By John Croft], 8vo. York, 1792.

102. Letter to Dr. Farmer relative to the edition of Shakespeare published in 1790. By E. Malone, 8vo. Lond. 1792.

103. Cursory remarks upon the arrangement of the plays of Shakespeare, occasioned by reading Mr. Malone's essay on the chronological order of those celebrated pieces. By James Hurdis, M. A., 8vo. Lond. 1792.

104. Prospectus of an intended edition of Shakespeare, in 15 vols., royal 8vo. By E. Malone, 4to. Lond. 1792.

105. A dissertation on the three parts of Henry VI. By E. Malone, 8vo. Lond. 1792.

106. Shakespeare Gallery, containing a select series of scenes and characters, with criticisms and remarks. By C. Taylor, 4to. 1792.

107. The genius of Shakespeare, a summer dream, 4to. Lond. 1793.

108. The whole historical dramas of William Shakespeare, illustrated by an assemblage of portraits of the royal, noble, and other persons mentioned, together with those of commentators, actors, and views of castles, towns, &c. [engraved by Harding], with short biographical and topographical accounts, 2 vols., 4to., and imperial 8vo., 1793. *Second edition*, 1811.

109. Essay on the origin of the English Stage, particularly the historical plays of Shakspeare. By Thomas Percy, 8vo. Lond. 1793.

E

110. Proposals for engraving the Felton Portrait of Shakespeare. By W. Richardson, 8vo. Lond. 1794.

111. The Infant Vision of Shakespeare, and other poems.
By Mr. Harrison, 4to. Lond. 1794.

112. Shakespearian Museum, with portraits and plates, 4to.
Lond. 1794.

113. A specimen of a commentary on Shakespeare; containing, 1st., Notes on As you like it; 2ndly, An
attempt to explain and illustrate various passages, on
a new principle of criticism, derived from Mr.
Locke's doctrine of the association of ideas [By Walter
Whiter], 8vo. Lond. 1794.

114. Proposals of an intended edition of Shakespeare, in
20 vols., royal 8vo. By E. Malone, fol. Lond. 1795.

115. The story of the Moor of Venice, translated from the
Italian, with two essays on Shakespeare, and pre-
liminary observations. By Wolstenholme Parr, A. M.,
8vo. Lond. 1795.

116. Shakespeare's Jests, or Jubilee Jester, 8vo. 1795.

117. Miscellaneous papers and legal instruments, under the
hand and seal of William Shakespeare, from the
original manuscripts in the possession of Samuel
Ireland, of Norfolk Street. *With fac-similes, &c.*,
fol. Lond. 1796. *Second edition*, 8vo. 1796.

118. A letter to George Steevens, Esq., containing a critical
examination of the papers of Shakespeare, published
by Mr. Samuel Ireland, with extracts from Vortigern.
By James Boaden, 8vo. Lond. 1796.

119. Familiar verses from the ghost of Willy Shakespeare
to Sammy Ireland. To which is added Prince Robert,
an auncient ballad [By G. M. Woodward, the
caricaturist], 8vo. Lond. 1796.

120. A comparative review of the opinions of Mr. James
Boaden [Editor of the Oracle], in February, March,
and April, 1795; and of James Boaden, Esq. [Author
of Fontainville Forest, and of a letter to George
Steevens, Esq.], in February, 1796, relative to the
Shakespeare manuscripts. By a Friend to Consistency
[Mat. Wyatt], 8vo. *n. d.*

121. Vortigern under consideration, with general remarks
on Mr. James Boaden's letter to George Steevens, Esq.

relative to the manuscripts, drawings, seals, &c., ascribed to Shakespeare, and in possession of S. Ireland, Esq. [By W. C. Oulton], 8vo. Lond. 1796.

122. An inquiry into the authenticity of certain miscellaneous papers, published Dec. 24, 1795, and attributed to Shakespeare, Queen Elizabeth, and Henry, Earl of Southampton. By Edmund Malone, Esq., 8vo. Lond. 1796.

123. Authentic account of the Shakespearian manuscripts. By W. H. Ireland, 8vo. Lond. 1796.

124. Sir John Falstaff's letters, dedicated to Sammy Ireland, 12mo. Lond. 1796.

125. Mr. Ireland's vindication of his conduct respecting the publication of the supposed Shakespeare manuscripts; being a preface or introduction to a reply to the critical labours of Mr. Malone, 8vo. Lond. 1796.

126. Observations on Hamlet, and the motives which induced Shakespeare to fix on the story of Amleth. By James Plumptre, M. A., 8vo. Cambridge, 1796.

127. Shakespeare's manuscripts in the possession of Mr. Ireland examined, respecting the internal and external evidences of their authenticity. By Philalethes [Col. F. Webb], 8vo. Lond. 1796.

128. Free reflections on miscellaneous papers and instruments, under the hand and seal of Shakespeare, in the possession of Samuel Ireland, of Norfolk Street. By Francis Godolphin Waldron, 8vo. Lond. 1796.
Waldron is said to have been assisted by Steevens in preparing this volume for the press.

129. Original letters, &c. of Sir John Falstaff; selected from genuine MSS., which have been in the possession of Dame Quickly and her descendants, 12mo. Lond. 1797.

130. Remarks on Shakespeare's Tempest. By Charles Dirrill, Esq. [Richard Sill], 8vo. Lond. 1797,

131. An investigation of Mr. Malone's claim to the character of scholar or critic; being an examination of his " Inquiry into the authenticity of the Shakespeare manuscripts." By Samuel Ireland, 8vo. Lond. [1797].

132. An apology for the believers in the Shakespeare papers, which were exhibited in Norfolk Street, London. By George Chalmers, 8vo. Lond. 1797.

133. An appendix to observations on Hamlet; being an attempt to prove that Shakespeare designed that tragedy as an indirect censure on Mary, Queen of Scots. By James Plumptre, M. A., 8vo. Lond. 1797.

134. Additional comments on the plays of Shakespeare, extended to the late editions of Malone and Steevens. By John Monck Mason, 8vo. 1798.

135. Passages, selected by distinguished personages, on the great literary trial of Vortigern and Rowena, a Comi-Tragedy; "Whether it be or be not from the immortal pen of Shakespeare," 4 vols., 12mo. *n. d.*

136. The Wreath; to which are added Remarks on Shakespeare. By Edward Dubois, 8vo. Lond. 1799.

137. Vortigern, an Historical Tragedy, represented at the Theatre Royal, Drury Lane; and Henry the Second, an Historical Drama, supposed to be written by the Author of Vortigern, 8vo. [1799.]
Vortigern was republished in 1832, by W. H. Ireland, with an original preface and a fac-simile of the forgery.

138. A supplemental apology for the believers in the Shakespeare papers. By George Chalmers, 8vo. Lond. 1799.

139. An appendix to the supplemental apology for the believers in the supposititious Shakespeare papers. By George Chalmers, 8vo. Lond. 1800.

140. Chalmeriana; a collection of papers occasioned by reading Chalmer's supplemental apology, 8vo. Lond. 1800.

141. Another essence of Malone; or, the beauties of Shakespeare's editor. In two parts. By George Hardinge, 8vo. Lond. 1801.

142 Catalogue of the books, paintings, &c., of the late Samuel Ireland, Esq., 8vo. Lond. 1801.
This catalogue contains a complete list of the Shakesperian forgeries.

143. Chronology of Shakespeare's plays. By Edmund Malone, 18mo. *n. d.*

144. School for Satire; containing "Capell's Ghost, to Edmund Malone, Esq., editor of Shakespeare," a parody, 8vo. Lond. 1802.

145. The Shakesperian Miscellany. By F. G. Waldron, 4to. Lond. 1802.

146. Remarks on Mr. John Kemble's performance of Ham-. let and Richard III., 8vo. Lond. 1802.

147. An attempt to illustrate a few passages in Shakespeare's works. By J. T. Finegan, 8vo. Bath, 1802.

148. Michel Ange en rapport avec Shakespeare, 8vo. Lond. 1802.

149. A complete verbal index to the plays of Shakespeare. By Francis Twiss, 2 vols., 8vo. Lond. 1805.
     Rare, the greater part of the impression having been destroyed by fire.

150. Notes upon some of the obscure passages in Shakespeare's plays. By Lord Chedworth, 8vo. Lond. 1805.
     Privately printed. See Martin's Catalogue of Privately Printed Books, p. 100.

151. Remarks, critical, conjectural, and explanatory, upon the plays of Shakespeare. By E. H. Seymour, 2 vols., 8vo. Lond. 1805.

152. The confessions of William Henry Ireland; containing the particulars of his fabrication of the Shakespeare manuscripts, together with anecdotes and opinions (hitherto unpublished) of many distinguished persons in the literary, political, and theatrical world, 8vo. Lond. 1805.

153. History and antiquities of Stratford-upon-Avon; comprising a description of the collegiate church, the life of Shakespeare, &c. By R. B. Wheler, 8vo., n. d.

154. Illustrations of Shakespeare, and of ancient manners, with dissertations on the clowns and fools of Shakespeare, on the Gesta Romanorum, and on the English Morris dance. By Francis Douce, 2 vols., 8vo. Lond. 1807. Reprinted, 1 vol. 8vo. Lond. 1839.

155. Comments on the several editions of Shakespeare's plays. By J. Monck Mason, 8vo. Dublin, 1807.

156. Comments on the commentators of Shakespeare. By Henry James Pye, 8vo. Lond. 1807.

157. Tales from Shakespeare. By Charles Lamb, 2 vols., 12mo. Lond. 1807. Reprinted 1816, 1822, and 1828.

158. Short notes on Shakespeare, by way of supplement to Johnson, Steevens, Malone, and Douce. By S. Weston, 8vo. Lond. 1808.
     Privately printed.

159. An examination of the charges maintained by Messrs. Malone, Chalmers, and others, of Ben. Jonson's enmity, &c., towards Shakespeare. By O. Gilchrist, Esq., 8vo. Lond. 1808.

160. An account of the incidents from which the title and part of the story of Shakespeare's Tempest were derived, and its true date ascertained. By Edmund Malone, 8vo. Lond. 1808.
    Eighty copies only printed for private distribution.

161. Appendix to the above tract, 8vo. Lond. 1809.
    It is said that only twenty copies of this tract were printed.

162. Studies of Shakespeare, No. 1, 12mo. Lincoln, 1809.

163. Annotations on plays of Shakespeare, Johnson and Steevens' edition [By John Croft], 8vo. York, 1810.
    " This pamphlet," observes Mr. Hunter, " consists of twenty-four closely printed pages, and I venture to say contains more valuable remark than is to be found in the volumes of Zachary Jackson and Andrew Becket, or even those of John Lord Chedworth and Henry James Pye." This little book being very rare and difficult to meet with, I may mention that a copy is in the library of the Society of Antiquaries.

164. Aphorisms from Shakespeare. By Capel Lofft, 8vo. Bury, 1812.

165. Proposals for printing by subscription, in two large vols. 8vo., " Shakespeare set free ; or, the language of the poet asserted" [By A. Becket], 8vo. Lond. 1812.

166. Explanations and emendations of some passages in the text of Shakespeare, and of Beaumont and Fletcher. By Martinus Scriblerus, 8vo. Edinburgh, 1814.

167. Shakespeare's Jest-Book ; viz. Tales and Quick Answers, very merry and pleasant to rede, 3 parts, 8vo. Chiswick, 1814-15.

168. The Tragical History of Macbeth, a new Song, 8vo. 1815.

169. An inquiry into the incidents from which the title and a part of the story of Shakespeare's Tempest were derived, and its true era ascertained. By George Chalmers, 8vo. Lond. 1815.
    Only forty copies printed for private circulation.

170. Shakespeare's Himself Again ; or, the language of the poet asserted : being a full but dispassionate examin

of the readings and interpretations of the several
editors. By Andrew Becket, 2 vols., 8vo. Lond. 1815
A work of very little value.

171. Lectures on Dramatic Art and Literature by Augustus
William Schlegel, translated by John Black, 2 vols.
8vo. Lond. 1818. Reprinted in 2 vols. fcp. 8vo.
Lond. 1840.

172. Remarks on the Monumental Bust of Shakespeare, at
Stratford-upon-Avon. By J. Britton, 8vo., 1816.

173. Essay on Macbeth and Richard III. By John Philip
Kemble, 8vo. Lond. 1817.

174. Characters of Shakespeare's plays. By William Haz-
litt, 8vo. Lond. 1817.

175. Observations on Mr. Kemble in the Characters of
Cato, Wolsey, and Coriolanus, 8vo. Lond. 1817.

176. Shakespeare and his Times ; including the biography
of the poet, criticisms on his genius and writings, &c.,
and a history of the manners, customs and amusements, superstitions, poetry, and elegant literature of
his age. By Nathan Drake, M. D., 2 vols., 4to.
Lond. 1817.

177. Remarks on the life and writings of William Shakespeare. By John Britton, 8vo. 1818.
Fifty copies printed for private circulation.

178. The progress of human life : Shakespeare's seven ages
of man, illustrated by a series of extracts in prose
and poetry ; introduced by a brief memoir of Shakespeare and his writings. By John Evans, A. M.,
8vo. Chiswick, 1818. *Second edition.* Lond. 1820.

179. A few concise examples of errors corrected in Shakespeare's plays, 8vo. Lond. 1818.
Two editions of this pamphlet were published in the same year.

180. Shakespeare's genius justified ; being restorations and
illustrations of seven hundred passages in Shakespeare's plays. By Z. Jackson, 8vo. Lond. 1819.

181. Hamlet, and As You Like It, a specimen of an edition
of Shakespeare. By T. Caldecott, 8vo. Lond. 1819.
Second edition, privately printed, 1832.

182. Annotations on the plays of Shakespeare, 2 vols., 8vo.
Lond. 1819.

183. Analysis of the Illustrated Shakespeare of Thomas Wilson, fol., 1820.

184. A Glossary ; or, a collection of words, phrases, names, and allusions to customs, proverbs, &c., which have been thought to require illustration in the works of English authors, particularly Shakespeare and his contemporaries. By Archdeacon Nares, 4to. Lond. 1822.

185. The school of Shakespeare, or plays, and scenes from Shakespeare illustrated for the use of schools. With glossarial notes selected from the best annotators, by J. R. Pitman, 8vo. Lond. 1822.

186. A letter to the editor of the British Critic, occasioned by the censure pronounced in that work on the editions of Shakespeare by Johnson, Pope, Bowdler, Warburton, Theobald, Steevens, Reed and Malone, et hoc genus omne, all the herd of these and Mei-Cominses of the British School. By T. Bowdler, 8vo. Lond. 1823.

187. The costume of Shakespeare's Historial Tragedies. By J. R. Planché, 12mo. Lond. 1823-5.

188. The first sitting of the committee on the proposed monument to Shakespeare ; taken in short-hand by Zachary Croft [C. Kelsall], 8vo. Cheltenham, 1823.

189. Life of Shakespeare ; Inquiries into the originality of his dramatic plots and characters ; and essays on the ancient Theatres and theatrical usages. By Augustine Skottowe, 2 vols., 8vo. Lond. 1824.

190. Vindicatio Shakesperiana ; or, supplementary remarks on the editions of Shakespeare, by Reed and others ; with occasional illustrations of some obscure and disputed passages. By John Sherwin, M. D., 2 vols. 4to.
Never printed. The original manuscript is preserved in the library of the Literary Institution of Bath.

191. An inquiry into the authenticity of various pictures and prints which have been offered to the public as portraits of Shakespeare. By J. Boaden, Esq., 8vo. 1824.

192. A dictionary of quotations from Shakespeare, 12mo. Lond. 1824.

193. Historical and Descriptive account of the birth-place of Shakespeare. By R. B. Wheeler. With lithographic illustrations by C. F. Green, 8vo. Stratford-upon-Avon, 1824.

194. Views of Stratford-upon-Avon church, in Warwickshire; containing the monument of the immortal Shakespeare. By J. P. Neale, 8vo. Lond. 1825.

195. Mr. Wivell's account of his portrait of Shakespeare, from the Stratford Bust, 8vo. Lond. 1825.

196. Shakespeare's Romances, collected and arranged by Shakespeare II., 2 vols., post 8vo. Lond. 1825.

197. A Catalogue of some Books in the possession of H. Jadis, Esq., in Bryanstone Square, royal 8vo. Privately printed. Lond. 1826.

   pp. 37—48 comprises " Shakespeariana, a complete collection of the Books and Pamphlets relative to Shakespeare."

198. Correct detail of the ceremonies attending the Shakespearian Gala, celebrated at Stratford-upon-Avon, on Monday, Tuesday, and Wednesday, April 23, 24, and 25, 1827; together with some account of Garrick's Jubilee in 1769. By J. Jarvis, 8vo. Stratford-upon-Avon [1827].

199. An Historical Account of the Monumental Bust of William Shakspeare in the church of Stratford-upon-Avon, with critical remarks on the authors who have written on it. By Abraham Wivell, 8vo. Lond. 1827.

   Reprinted in the following article.

200. Historical account of all the portraits of Shakespeare that have been generally considered the most genuine, together with every particular which can be collected respecting them, &c. By Abraham Wivell, 8vo. Lond. 1827.

201. Shaksperiana. Catalogue of all the books, pamphlets, &c., relating to Shakspeare, 8vo. Lond. 1827.

202. A Supplement to an Inquiry into the History, &c., of the Shakspeare Portraits. By Abraham Wivell, 8vo. Lond. 1827.

203. The spirit of the plays of Shakespeare, exhibited in a series of outline plates illustrative of the story of each play. Drawn and engraved by Frank Howard, with quotations and descriptions, 5 vols., 8vo. and 4to. Lond. 1827-33.

204. Essais Littéraires sur Shakspeare on analyse raison-
née, scène par scène, de toutes les pieces de cet au-
teur. Par M. Paul Duport, 2 vols., 8vo. Paris, 1828.

205. Selections from Shakspeare. By Benjamin Oakley,
8vo. Lond. 1828.

206. Memorials of Shakespeare. By Nathan Drake, 8vo.
Lond. 1828.

207. Views in Stratford-upon-Avon and its vicinity, illustrative of the biography of Shakespeare, accompanied
with descriptive remarks. By William Rider, folio.
Warwick and Leamington, 1828.

208. A descriptive account of the second Royal Gala Fes-
tival in commemoration of the natal day of Shakespeare, 8vo. Stratford-upon-Avon, 1830.

209. Shaksperian Anthology : comprising the choicest passages and entire scenes selected from the most correct
editions, post 8vo. Lond. 1830.

210. Literary and graphical illustrations of Shakespeare
and the British Drama, 8vo. Lond. 1831.

211. The Shakesperian Dictionary, forming a general index
to popular expressions and striking passages in Shakespeare. By Thomas Dolby, 8vo. Lond. 1832.

212. Illustrations of Aristotle, on men and manners, from
the works of Shakespeare. J. E. Riddle, 8vo. Oxford, 1832.

213. A letter on Shakespeare's authorship of the " Two
Noble Kinsmen," a drama commonly ascribed to
John Fletcher [by W. Spalding], 8vo. Edinburgh,
1833.

214. An essay on Shakespeare's character of Shylock. By
George Farren, 8vo. Lond. 1833.

215. Citation and examination of William Shakespeare,
&c., touching deer-stealing, 12mo. Lond. 1834.

216. A parallel of Shakespeare and Scott, 12mo. Lond.
1835.

217. New facts regarding the works of Shakespeare. By
J. P. Collier, 8vo. Lond. 1835.

218. New particulars regarding the writings of Shakespeare. By J. P. Collier, 8vo. Lond. 1836.

219. On the sonnets of Shakespeare, identifying the persons to whom they are addressed, and elucidating several points in the poet's history. By James Boaden, 8vo. Lond. 1837.

220. The Wisdom and Genius of Shakspeare, comprising Moral Philosophy, Delineations of Character, Paintings of Nature and the Passions, with 700 Aphorisms and Miscellaneous Pieces, with select and original Notes and Scriptural References. By the Rev. Thomas Price, fcp. 8vo. Lond. 1838.

221. Shakespeare's Will, faithfully copied from the original in the Prerogative Court of Canterbury; with facsimiles of the three original autographs annexed, 8vo. Lond. 1838.

222. Observations on an autograph of Shakespeare, and the orthography of his name. By Sir Frederick Madden, 8vo. Lond. 1838.
  Reprinted from the Archæologia, vol. 27, with some corrections.

223. Traditionary anecdotes of Shakespeare, collected in Warwickshire, in the year 1693. Now first printed from the original manuscript, 8vo. Lond. 1838.

224. Letters on the natural history of the Insects mentioned in Shakespeare's plays. By R. Patterson, 12mo. Lond. 1838.

225. Shakespeare's Autobiographical Poems. By C. A. Brown, 8vo. Lond. 1838.

226. A disquisition on the scene, origin, date, &c., &c., of Shakespeare's Tempest. In a letter to Benjamin Heywood Bright, Esq., from the Rev. Joseph Hunter, F. S. A., 8vo. Lond. 1839.

227. Shakespearian Readings, by B. H. Smart, 12mo. Lond. 1839.

228. Diary of the Rev. John Ward, A. M., Vicar of Stratford-upon-Avon, extending from 1648 to 1679, edited by Charles Severn, M. D., 8vo. Lond. 1839.

229. An Essay on the Play of the Tempest. By P. Macdonnell, 8vo. Lond. 1840.

230. Further particulars regarding the writings of Shakespeare. By J. P. Collier, 8vo. Lond. 1840.

231. Shakespeare's Library: a collection of the stories,

novels, and tales, used by Shakespeare as the foundation of his plays. Edited by J. P. Collier, 8vo.
Lond. 1840-1.

232. An introduction to Shakespeare's Midsummer Night's
Dream. By James Orchard Halliwell, Esq., F.R.S.,
&c., 8vo. Lond. 1841.

233. Memoirs of Edward Alleyn, founder of Dulwich College: including some new particulars respecting
Shakespeare, Ben Jonson, Massinger, Marston, Dek-
ker, &c. By J. Payne Collier, Esq., F. S. A., 8vo.
Lond. 1841.

POEMS.

VENUS AND ADONIS.

1. —— 4to. London, *by Richard Field*, 1593.
This poem was entered on the Stationers' Register, 13th April,
1593. A copy of this edition is in the Bodleian Library. A copy, the
only other known, sold in Strettell's sale, May, 1841, for £40. 8s. 6d.;
it had successively belonged to Dr. Chauncey, Steevens, and Bindley.

2. —— 4to. London, *by Richard Field*, 1594.

3. —— 16mo. London, *Imprinted by R. F. for John
Harrison*, 1596.

4. —— 24mo. London, *by J. H. for John Harrison*,
1600.

5. —— 16mo. London, *by William Leake*, 1602.

6. —— Edinburgh, *by John Wreittoun*, 1607.

7. —— 8vo. London, 1617.

8. —— 8vo. London, 1620.

9. —— 8vo. London, 1630.

10. —— 8vo. London, 1636.

11. —— 8vo. London, 1675.

LUCRECE.

1. —— 4to. London, *Printed by Richard Field for John
Harrison*, 1594.
Copies are in the Bodleian Library and Lion College.

2. —— 4to. Lond. 1596.

3. —— 4to. Lond. 1598.

4. —— 8vo. London, *by J. H. for John Harrison*, 1600.

5. —— Lond. 1607.

6. —— 4to. London, 1616.

7. —— 12mo. Lond. 1620.

8. —— 12mo. Lond. 1632.

9. —— 12mo. Port. Lond. 1655.

COLLECTED POEMS.

1. The Passionate Pilgrim, 8vo. London, *for William Jaggard*, 1599.
   A copy of the third edition, published in 1612, is in the Bodleian Library. It is not known when the second edition was published.

2. Poems : written by Wil. Shake-speare, Gent., 12mo. London, *Printed by Thomas Cotes*, 1640.
   This edition principally consists of translations which never proceeded from Shakespeare's pen.

3. Poems, 8vo. London, *for Lintot*, 1710.

4. —— 12mo. Lond. 1728.

5. —— 12mo. Dublin, 1771.

6. —— 12mo. Lond. 1774.

7. —— 8vo. Lond. 1775.

8. —— 12mo. Lond. 1804.

9. —— With life of Shakespeare by the Rev. Alexander Dyce, 8vo. Lond. 1826.

SONNETS.

1. Shake-speare's Sonnets. Never before imprinted, 4to. London, *by G. Eld for T. T.*, 1609.
   Reprinted by Steevens in 1766.

COLLECTED EDITIONS

OF

SHAKESPEARE'S PLAYS.

1. Mr. William Shakespeare's Comedies, Histories and Tragedies. Published according to the true originall copies, fol. London, *Printed by Isaac Jaggard and Edward Blount*, 1623.

   Reprinted very incorrectly in 1807, fol. Copies of the first edition are very valuable, as much as *two hundred guineas* having lately been given for a copy. One copy is in existence bearing the date of 1622.

2. —— fol. London, *Printed by Tho. Cotes for Robert Allot*, 1632.

3. —— fol. London, *Printed for P. C.*, 1664.

   Contains seven additional plays.

4. —— fol. London, 1685.

5. —— Revised and corrected, with an account of his life and writings by N. Rowe, 7 vols. 8vo. 1709-10. 2nd edition, 9 vols. 1714.

6. —— Collated and corrected by the former editions, by Alexander Pope, 6 vols. 4to., Lond. 1725; 10 vols. 12mo., 1728; 8 vols. 16mo., Glasgow, 1766; 9 vols. 12mo., Birmingham, 1768.

7. —— Collated with the oldest copies, and corrected, with notes, by Lewis Theobald, 7 vols. 8vo., Lond. 1733; 8 vols. 12mo., Lond. 1740; 8 vols. 12mo., Lond. 1752; 8 vols. 8vo., Lond. 1757; 8 vols. 8vo., Lond. 1762; 8 vols. 8vo., Lond. 1773.

8. —— 12mo. 8 vols. London, Tonson, 1735.

9. —— Revised and corrected by the former editions, by Sir Thomas Hanmer, 6 vols. 4to., Oxford, 1744; 6 vols. 4to., Oxford, 1770-1. Hanmer's text was used for several editions of Shakespeare about this period.

10. —— With a comment and notes by Pope and Warburton, 8 vols. 8vo. Lond. 1747.

11. —— With the corrections and illustrations of various commentators : to which are added notes by Samuel Johnson, 8 vols. 8vo. Lond. 1765.

12. —— Edited by Edward Capell, 10 vols. 8vo. Lond. 1768.

13. —— Twenty of the plays of Shakespeare, being the whole number printed in quarto during his life-time, or before the Restoration ; collated where there were different copies, and publish'd from the originals, by George Steevens, Esq., 4 vols. 8vo. Lond. 1766.

14. —— With the beauties pointed out, a life, glossary, &c. Edited by Dr. Hugh Blair, 8 vols. 12mo. Edinburgh, 1771.

15. —— From the text of Dr. S. Johnson, with the prefaces, notes, &c., of Rowe, Pope, Theobald, Hanmer, Warburton, Johnson, and select notes from many other critics : also, the introduction of the last editor Mr. Capell ; and a table, showing his various readings, 12 vols. 12mo. Dublin, 1771.

16. —— With the corrections and illustrations of various commentators ; to which are added notes by Samuel Johnson and George Steevens, with an appendix, 10 vols. 8vo., Lond. 1773 ; Revised and augmented, 1778 ; by Isaac Reed, 1785 ; 15 vols. 8vo, Lond. 1793 ; 5th edition, 21 vols. 8vo., Lond. 1813.

17. —— As they are now performed at the Theatres Royal in London, 8 vols. 12mo. 1774-5.

18. —— By Ayscough, 8vo. Lond. 1784. In one volume.

19. —— With notes by the Rev. Jos. Rann, 6 vols. 8vo. Oxford, 1786-94.

20. —— Bell's edition, 20 vols. 18mo. Lond. 1788.

21. —— With explanatory notes. Two volumes in one, 8vo. Lond. 1790.

22. —— Collated verbatim with the most authentic copies, and revised : with the corrections and illustrations of various commentators ; to which are added, an essay on the chronological order of his plays ; an essay relative to Shakespeare and Jonson ; a dissertation on the three parts of King Henry VI ; an historical account of the English stage, and notes, by Edmund Malone, 10 vols. 8vo., Lond. 1790. 16 vols. 12mo., Dublin, 1794.

23. —— From the text of Malone, with select explanatory notes [by John Nichols], 7 vols. 12mo. Lond. 1790.

24. —— Bellamy's edition, 8 vols. 8vo. Lond. 1791.

25. —— From the text of Steevens, with a selection of the most important notes [by John Nichols], 9 vols. 18mo. Lond. 1798.

26. —— With corrections and illustrations of various commentators, 23 vols. 8vo. Basil, 1800-2.

27. —— With Life by Rowe, published by C. Wagnen, 8 vols. 8vo. Brunswick, 1801.

28. —— Boydell's edition, with engravings, 9 vols. fol. Lond. 1802.
An additional series of engravings was published by Messrs. Boydell in 1802-3, in two volumes, atlas folio, from designs by Fuseli, Northcote, Opie, Hamilton, and Stothard, which are frequently found with this edition.

29. —— 10 vols. 8vo. Lond. 1803-5.

30. —— By Alexander Chalmers, 9 vols. 8vo., Lond. 1805 ; 8 vols. 8vo., Lond. 1823.

31. —— 2 vols. 8vo. Lond. 1806.

32. —— Edited by Manley Wood, 14 vols. 8vo. Lond. 1806. With plates.

33. —— Ballantyne's edition, 12 vols. 8vo. Lond. 1807.

34. —— 6 vols. 4to. Lond. 1807.

35. —— The Family Shakespeare, 4 vols. 8vo. Bath, 1807.

36. —— Embellished with 230 wood engravings. To which is prefixed a life of Shakespeare, by John Britton, 7 vols. 8vo. Chiswick, 1814-15.

37. —— The Family Shakespeare. By Thomas Bowdler, 10 vols. 18mo. Lond. 1818.
Frequently reprinted.

38. —— Malone's edition, by James Boswell, 21 vols. 8vo. Lond. 1821.

G

39. —— Complete in one pocket volume, 12mo. Chiswick, 1823.
40. —— Edited, with life of the author, by the Rev. William Harness, 8 vols. 8vo. Lond. 1825.
41. —— With memoir by W. Harvey, 8vo. Lond. 1825.
42. —— 9 vols. 48mo. London, by Corrall, 1826.
   The smallest edition ever printed.
43. —— With notes, original and selected, by Samuel Weller Singer, and a life of the poet, by Charles Symmons, D. D., 10 vols. fcp. 8vo. Chiswick, 1826.
44. —— 8 vols. 32mo. Lond. 1827.
   An elegant edition from the Chiswick press.
45. —— Edited by A. J. Valpy, 15 vols. 12mo. Lond. 1832-4.
46. —— With life by Thomas Campbell, 8vo. Lond. 1838.
47. —— Pictorial edition of the works of Shakspere, edited by Charles Knight, royal 8vo. Lond. 1839-41.

SHAKESPEARE'S WORKS IN 1598.

The following is extracted from a rare little volume entitled " PALLADIS TAMIA. Wits Treasury, being the second part of Wits Commonwealth. By Francis Meres, Maister of Artes of both Vniuersities," 12mo. London, 1598. This is the most important evidence we possess in the question of the chronological order of Shakespeare's plays, and is frequently referred to by the critics.—

Fol. 281, 282.

" As the soule of *Euphorbus* was thought to liue in *Pythagoras :* so the sweete wittie soule of *Ouid* liues in mellifluous and honytongued *Shakespeare,* witnes his *Venus* and *Adonis,* his *Lucrece,* his sugred Sonnets among his priuate friends, &c.

" As *Plautus* and *Seneca* are accounted the best for Comedy and Tragedy among the Latines : so *Shakespeare* among the English is the most excellent in both kinds for the stage : for Comedy, witnes his *Gentlemen of Verona,* his *Errors,* his *Loue labors lost,* his *Loue labours wonne,* his *Midsummers night dreame,* and his *Merchant of Venice :* for Tragedy his *Richard the 2. Richard the 3. Henry the 4. King Iohn, Titus Andronicus,* and his *Romeo* and *Juliet.*

" As *Epius Stolo* said, that the Muses would speak with *Plautus* tongue, if they would speak Latin: so 1 say that the Muses would speak with *Shakespeares* fine filed phrase, if they would speake English."

FINIS.

AN ACCOUNT

OF

THE ONLY KNOWN MANUSCRIPT

OF

Shakespeare's Plays.

AN ACCOUNT

OF

THE ONLY KNOWN MANUSCRIPT

OF

SHAKESPEARE'S PLAYS,

COMPRISING

SOME IMPORTANT VARIATIONS AND CORRECTIONS

IN THE

Merry Wives of Windsor,

OBTAINED

FROM A PLAYHOUSE COPY OF THAT PLAY

RECENTLY DISCOVERED.

BY

JAMES ORCHARD HALLIWELL, Esq. F.R.S.

HON. M.R.I.A., F.S.A., ETC.

LONDON:

JOHN RUSSELL SMITH,

4, OLD COMPTON STREET, SOHO SQUARE.

MDCCCXLIII.

AN ACCOUNT,

&c. &c.

MR. COLLIER, in a recently published work, has justly observed that although "dramatic pieces in manuscript by Ben Jonson, Beaumont and Fletcher, Massinger, Middleton, and others, are in existence, it is a remarkable fact that not a single written fragment of any of the plays of Shakespeare has come down to us, with the exception of a few passages in some unprinted poetical miscellanies." In Shakespeare's own handwriting, it is well known that nothing has been discovered, save his autograph; but Mr. Collier refers to early copies which may be supposed to contain either authorised variations from the commonly received text, or at least conjectural emendations rendered valuable by the time at which they were made. It is reasonable to suppose that persons contemporary, or nearly so, with our great poet, were more likely to alter advisedly than modern editors, because they probably had a better knowledge of his language and allusions, if they were not so competent to judge of his excellencies.

If we had letters of Shakespeare, his mere autograph would not have sold for a hundred guineas ; and had there been autograph copies of his plays extant, the public would probably never have been asked to peruse the following pages. But in the previous absence of every evidence of the kind, it is a satisfaction to me to be the first to place before the reader's notice a brief account of the only known manuscript copy of any of Shakespeare's plays,—not a mere transcript, which would be comparatively worthless, but containing constant variations from every known printed edition.

This curious relic is a manuscript of the *Merry Wives of Windsor*, one of Shakespeare's best comedies, not contemporary with the author, but written during the time of the Commonwealth, in all probability for some private playhouse.

It is entitled " The Merry Wives of Old Windsor, written by William Shakespeare," and has the following list of *Dramatis Personæ*, not given in any edition, and was therefore probably the earliest ever made :

ROBERT SHALLOW, Esq., *A Gloc'shire Justice, vncle to Master Slender.*

Sir HUGH EVANS, *a Welch Priest : Curate and Schoolemaster at Windsor.*

Mr. GEORGE PAGE, *a rich country Gentleman, in or neer Windsor.*

Mrs. MEG PAGE, *his wife.*

Mrs. ANNE PAGE, *their daughter.*

BILLY, *their son, Schollar to Master Evans.*

Mr. FRANCIS FORD, *a rich jealous curmudgeon of Windsor.*

Mrs. ALICE FORD, *his wife.*

Mr. ABRA: SLENDER, *nephew to Justice Shallow.*
Doctor CAIUS, *a French Phisitian.*
Mr. FENTON, *an expensive Courtier.*
} *Sutors to Mrs.* ANNE PAGE, *each favord by* { FATHER. MOTHER. *Mrs.* ANNE.

Sir JOHN FALSTAFFE, *a fat old decayed leacherous Court Officer.*

BARDOLFE,
NYM,
PISTOLL.
} *His late vnder-officers, now hangers on.*

ROBIN, *his page.*

Mrs. Quickly, *Doctor Caius his house keeper, but confident to the women.*

Host of the Garter, *a merry, conceited, ranting Inn-
holder.*

John Rugby, *Dr. Caius's man.*

Peter Simple, *Man to Master Slender.*

Servants to Mrs. Ford.

Fairies.

It may be observed of this list, that it exhibits
very precise and particular knowledge not only
of this play, but of others ; and clearly shows
that its compiler, whoever he was, considered
the *Merry Wives of Windsor* subsequent to
the two parts of Henry IV., and that Falstaff
was at Windsor in his declining years, as I have
elsewhere contended. This, however, is not the
place to enter into any discussion of the kind. I
shall merely, therefore, take a few extracts from
Malone's edition of the *Merry Wives*, and
compare them with the manuscript, where it
differs from all the early editions, so that each
reader will be enabled to judge for himself as to
the value of the variations, and consequently of
the critical worth of the manuscript, independently of its curiosity.

It is not my intention to attempt a notice of
all, or nearly all the variations in the manuscript ; for in order to do so, it would be necessary to reprint the greater part of the play.   I
merely offer the following as a specimen of the
variations with which the manuscript abounds.*

Act I.— Sc. 1.

" *Shal.* The luce is the fresh fish ; the *salt fish* is an old
coat.
   Slen. I may quarter, coz.
   Shal. You may, by marrying.
   Eva. It is marring, indeed, if he quarter it."

The manuscript reads " the *salt-water fish* is
an old coat," which may serve to confine the
conjectures of the commentators on this very
difficult passage within narrower bounds.   At all
events, this reading appears to overthrow the
conjecture of " A Lover of Heraldry," given in
Knight's Library Shakespeare, vol. iii. p. 41.

* It ought to be mentioned that the MS. is in the author's
possession, having been purchased by him in March, 1842,
of Mr. Proctor, who, I believe, had obtained it from Mr.
Rodd.   It was but recently that the fact of its being an independent text was discovered.   Hence its value.

In Slender's speech, the manuscript reads *uncle* instead of *coz*, an obviously correct emendation, and also made in several other places in the manuscript. A little further onwards the manuscript reads " 1700 *li*," instead of " seven hundred pounds," in three places.

Act I.—Sc. 1.

" *Fal.* I will answer it straight ;—I have done all this : — That is now answered.

Shal. The council shall know this.

Fal. 'Twere better for you if it were known in counsel ; you'll be laughed at."

The manuscript reads " if it were *not* known in council," which appears to be a better reading, and more congenial to sense.

Act I.—Sc. 1.

" *Nym.* Slice, I say! *pauca, pauca :* slice ! *that's* my humour.

Slen. Where's Simple, my man ?—*can you tell, cousin ?*"

In Nym's speech, the manuscript reads " *that is* my humour," and the next, " *He can tell you, uncle*," which is certainly preferable to the commonly received reading.

Act I.—Sc. 4.

" *Fent.* Well, I shall see her to-day ; Hold, there's money for thee ; let me have thy voice in my behalf : if thou seest her before me, commend me.

Quick. Will I ? i'faith, that *we* will ; and I will tell your worship more of the wart, the next time we have confidence ; and of the wooers."

The manuscript reads ," that I will," and thus corrects a very evident error that has passed through all the editions. In a few lines, previously, the manuscript reads, " it is not *a* good you tarry here," instead of " it is not good you tarry here."

Act II.—Sc. 1.

" *Mrs. Page.* Letter for letter ; but that the name of Page and Ford differs !—To thy great comfort in this mystery of ill opinions, here's the twin-brother of thy letter : but let thine inherit first ; for, I protest, mine never shall. I warrant he hath a thousand of these letters, writ with blank space for different names, (*sure more,*) and these are of the second edition."

The second folio reads " *sue more*," but the manuscript has "*shuh! more*," which is much more likely to be right. And here I pause a moment to make one observation on Mr. Knight's note on

the common word *precisian*, occurring just before,
and ask why Johnson's definition is not sufficient
for its explanation. If any doubt be entertained
on this point, let the reader compare the fifth
jest in " Jests to Make you Merrie," 4to. Lond.
1607, which unfortunately is not of a character
to be quoted.

Act II.—Sc. 1.

" *Mrs. Ford.* Trust me, I thought on her : she'll fit it.
Mrs. Page. You are come to see my daughter Anne ?"

The manuscript inserts the words, " Now,
Mistress Quickly," at the commencement of the
second speech ; which appears to be an evident
improvement.

Act II.—Sc. 2.

" *Fal.* Not a penny. I have been content, sir, you should
lay my countenance to pawn : I have grated upon my good
friends for three reprieves for you and your coach-fel-
low, Nym; or else you had looked through the grate, like a
geminy of baboons. I am damned in hell for swearing to
gentlemen my friends *you were good soldiers and tall fellows ;*
and when mistress Bridget lost the handle of her fan, I took't
upon mine honour thou hadst it not."

The manuscript reads " *that* you were good

soldiers and *stout* fellows," and other variations
in the same speech, such as " *my*" for " mine," &c.
In the next line, the manuscript reads, " Didst
thou not share."

ACT II.—Sc. 2.

" *Fal.* * * * I myself sometimes, leaving the fear of heaven
on the left hand, and hiding mine honour in my necessity,
am fain to shuffle, to hedge, and to lurch ; and yet you,
rogue, will ensconce your rags, your cat-a-mountain looks,
your red-lattice phrases, and your *bold-beating* oaths, under
the shelter of your honour !"

The manuscript reads " *blunderbust* oaths,"
which is a very curious variation, and well worthy
of notice. In the same speech, the manuscript
reads " term," instead of " terms," agreeing in
this with the second folio.

ACT II.—Sc. 2.

" *Pist.* This punk is one of Cupid's carriers :—
 Clap on more sails ; pursue, up with your *fights ;*
 Give fire ; she is my prize, or ocean whelm them all."

The manuscript reads, " up with your *flags*,"
which seems much more intelligible. If Mr.
Knight had referred to Cole, he would not have
given so imperfect a definition of *fights,* which
the latter author defines to be, " coverts, any

laces where men may stand unseen and use their
rms in a ship." See his *English Dictionary,*
vo. Lond. 1676.

Act II.—Sc. 2.

" *Ford.* Troth, and I have a bag of money here troubles
e : if you will help to bear it, Sir John, take all, or half,
ir easing me of the carriage."

The manuscript reads, " if you will help *me*
) bear it."

Act II.—Sc. 2.

" *Ford.* There is a gentlewoman in this town, her husband's
ame is Ford.

Fal. Well, sir.

Ford. I have long loved her, and I protest to you, bestowed
uch on her."

The conduct of this is entirely changed in the
manuscript, which reads as follows :—

" *Ford.* There is a gentleman in this town, his name is
'ord, whose wife I have long loved.

Fal. Well, sir.

Ford. And, I protest to you, bestowed much on her."

Act. II.—Sc. 2.

" *Fal.* I will use her as the key *of* the cuckoldy rogue's
offer ; and there's my harvest-home."

The manuscript reads, " the key *to* the cuckoldy rogue's coffer."

ACT II.—Sc. 2.

" Fie, fie, fie! cuckold ! *cuckold !* cuckold !"

These are the last words of this scene, and the manuscript reads " wittol," instead of the second " cuckold," and I have little doubt the manuscript is right; for it agrees with the same exclamation in the former part of the speech.

ACT II.—Sc. 3.

" *Host.* And moreover, bully. — But first, master guest, and master Page, and eke Cavalero Slender, go through the town to Frogmore."

The manuscript here inserts a very necessary word, in reading " Master *Justice* Guest," which is peculiar to this copy.

ACT III.—Sc. 1.

" *Eva.* Bless my soul! how full of cholers I am, and trempling of mind !—I shall be glad if he have deceived me : —how melancholies I am."

It may be remarked of this manuscript that all Evans's speeches are very carefully spelt to indicate his peculiar phraseology, much more so than

the printed editions ; and this is one evidence
that it was a playhouse copy. Thus, in the present speech, the manuscript reads,—" Plesse my
soul : how full of chollers I am, and trempling
of mind : I shall pe glat if he hafe deccivet me :
how melanchollies I am? I will knog his vrinalls
apout his knaves costart, when I hafe goot oppor-
tunities for the 'orke : Plesse my soul : (*sings*)

> " To shallow rifers to whose falls :
> Melotious birts sing matricalls :
> There will we make our peds of roses,
> And a thousand fragrant posies."

Surely there is more humour in this than in
the printed editions, where the spelling is not
uniform. In the first folio, it is " *sings* madri-
galls," which reading is not, however, adopted by
Mr. Knight.

ACT III.—Sc. 1.

" *Page.* I warrant you, he's the man should fight with
him."

The manuscript reads, " the man *that* should
fight with him."

ACT III.—Sc. 1.

" *Host.* Peace, I say, Gallia and *Gaul ;* French and Welsh ;
soul-curer and body-curer."

The manuscript reads "Gallia and *Wallia*," which seems to confirms Hanmer's very sensible emendation.

Act III.—Sc. 2.

" *Ford.* A man may hear this shower sing in the wind!—and Falstaff's boy with her!—Good plots!—*they are* laid; and our revolted wives share damnation together."

The manuscript reads " *and well* laid," which appears to be a most sensible emendation.

Act III.—Sc. 2.

" *Page.* Not by my consent I promise you. The gentleman is of no having; he kept company with the wild Prince and Poins; he is of too high a region, he knows too much. No, he shall not knit a knot in his fortunes with the finger of my substance."

After the word "fortunes," the manuscript adds "with my money."

Act III.—Sc. 3.

" *Fal.* I see what thou wert, if Fortune thy foe were not, *Nature* thy friend: Come, thou canst not hide it."

This passage has puzzled the commentators, and Mr. Knight is not of opinion that a perfect sense can be made of the passage as it stands.

The reading of the manuscript renders the matter quite clear, and partially confirms Pope's conjecture. It is, " *Nature's* thy friend." This single emendation is sufficient to stamp a value on the manuscript. Throughout this scene are a variety of alterations. At p. 79, the manuscript reads, " I *am* come before to tell you," which is an improvement. The printed editions omit the word "am." The manuscript also reads, " *Why, your* husband's *a* coming hither, woman," the two words in italics being omitted in the printed copies. It would be impossible to notice all variations of this kind, without reprinting the play. These instances are merely given as examples taken at random to show that the manuscript is an independent text.

ACT III.—Sc. 3.

" *Mrs. Page.* What a taking was he in, when your husband asked *who* was in the basket.

Mrs. Ford. I am half afraid he will have need of washing ; so throwing him into the water will do him a *benefit.*"

The manuscript here affords a most important emendation, reading " *what* was in the basket." It is very clear that Ford could not have asked *who* was in the basket, because had it entered his head that any one was there, he would of course have discovered the trick. That the manuscript is correct is clear from a subsequent passage, where Falstaff tells Master Broome, that the jealous knave " asked them once or twice *what* they had in their basket." The manuscript also reads " a good turn," instead of " a benefit."

Act III.—Sc. 4.

" *Slen.* No, she shall not dismay me, I care not for that, —*but that I am afeard.*"

The manuscript reads, " but—I am affeard, la!" It also adds the words, " and family frailties," after " faults," in Anne's next speech; and instead of " a hundred and fifty pounds jointure," we have " a hundred and fifty pounds *a year* jointure."

Act III.—Sc. 4.

" My daughter will I question how she loves you,
And as I find her, so am I affected ;
Till then, farewell, sir : —she must needs go in ;
Her father will be angry."

This speech leaves off abruptly, and I have

little doubt that we should read, with the manuscript.—

"Her father will be angry *else.*"

It may be mentioned that Mrs. Quickly's speech in the manuscript is entirely different from that in the printed editions, but this, with others, must be reserved for a future opportunity.

Act IV.—Sc. 2.

" *Ford.* Ay, but if it prove true, master Page, have you any way then to unfool me again.—Set down the basket, villain:—Somebody call my wife :—Youth in a basket !—O, you panderly rascals ! there's a knot, a *ging,* a pack, a conspiracy against me."

The first folio reads *gin,* but the manuscript has *gang,* which is clearly the right word. A little further on, the manuscript reads, " Here's no man *here,*" which last word is omitted in the printed editions, although necessary.

Act IV.—Sc. 5.

" *Host.* Here's a Bohemian-Tartar tarries the coming down of *thy* fat woman. Let her descend, bully, let her descend; my chambers are honourable : Fie ! privacy ? fie !"

The manuscript reads " of *that* fat woman"

which is more likely to be correct than the commonly received reading.

Act V.—Sc. 2.

"*Page.* The night is dark ; light and spirits will become it well. Heaven prosper our sport! No man means evil but the devil, and we shall know him by his horns. *Let's away ; follow me.*"

The manuscript reads, " Let's away ; come, son Slender, follow me."

With this specimen I conclude, and leave to others the question how far these emendations may be safely admitted into an edition of Shakespeare. The question, perhaps, is one rather of authority than judgment; and it may certainly be a doubt whether the manuscript is of a higher authority, as far as regards the text, than the corrections of the first folio which Mr. Collier discovered in a copy belonging to Lord Francis Egerton. But early corrections, like the corrections in the folio of 1632, must be of more authority than those made by Rowe, Pope, and subsequent editors ; and an early manuscript copy of any one of Shakespeare's plays, even though written after the poet's death, cannot but be considered a great curiosity. It would be impossible to say whether the manuscript now under consideration was taken from a contemporary copy or not. It is, however, certain that no transcript of an early edition, though carefully corrected, could possibly contain the numerous and extensive variations which are found in this manuscript of the " Merry Wives of Windsor."

And it is this last consideration which inclines me to think that it must have been copied for some private exhibition, so common, according to Kirkman, during the Commonwealth. If so, the corrections made in it were probably by some one who had seen this play acted, and had remembered the players' versions of those passages he has altered. And this, upon the whole, appears to be the most probable mode of accounting for the peculiar readings with which it abounds.

Mr. Collier attaches considerable value to a few extracts from Shakespeare's plays which he found in an early manuscript common-place book, although he confesses that it is doubtful whether the writer employed printed copies, resorted to manuscript authorities, or only recorded striking passages which he heard at the theatres. Even with this doubt, so honestly expressed, Mr. Collier tells us that " these brief extracts, never exceeding five lines, now and then throw light upon difficult and doubtful expressions." I quote this, not in the expectation of claiming for the manuscript any additional value, but for the purpose of showing how very little early written authority for the text of Shakespeare has yet been discovered, and the extreme importance given by the critics to evidence of this nature. Some of us, perhaps, are sufficiently sanguine to believe that one day or other will bring to light a copy of " Love's Labours Won," or a bundle of the original prompt copies of Shakespeare's plays, as they were exhibited within his " wooden O ;" but those who do not anticipate such wonders, whose "ultima Thule" of expectation is the sight of the first edition of " Titus Andronicus," and who recollect how com-

paratively few and unimportant the recent discoveries have been, will be more inclined to
receive the present addition to Shakespearian
criticism in a favourable light.

THE END.

AN INTRODUCTION

TO SHAKESPEARE'S

MIDSUMMER NIGHT'S DREAM

BY

JAMES ORCHARD HALLIWELL, ESQ.

F.R.S., HON. M.R.I.A., F.S.A., F.R.A.S.,

ETC.

" Such sights as youthful poets dream
On summer eves by haunted stream."

LONDON

WILLIAM PICKERING

1841

CONTENTS.

CHAPTER I.

" Ah, can I tell
The enchantment that afterwards befel ?
Yet it was but a dream : yet such a dream !"

IT remains to be seen, whether the labours of former
commentators have, as some imagine, exhausted all
that proper and useful annotation on the works of
Shakespeare, which the lapse of two centuries, and
the continual change in our language and manners,
have rendered necessary.

We shall not here pause to consider those, if any
there be, who despise even the most minute illustration
of the works of our great dramatist. The merits of
those works are beyond the reach of criticism, in the
common acceptation of the term, and an unanimous
voice has pronounced every thing relating to them
and their author, hallowed and sacred. The judgment of time has classed them amongst the noblest
productions of human genius, and nothing now remains for us, but to hail them as the immortal progeny of an immortal author.

But the high privilege to which such an author
may lay claim, by no means descends to his editors
or commentators ; and we predict, that many years
must yet elapse, ere that complete inquiry into
Shakespeare's language and allusions, without which

B

the spirit of his writings can never be fully understood or appreciated, can be presented to the view
of the general reader by means of a commentary.
It is with this conviction, that we venture to place
the following observations on one of the most remarkable of his plays before the notice of the public.

The very name of A Midsummer Night's Dream
has furnished a subject for discussion. The time of
action is on the night preceding May-day. Theseus
goes out a maying, and when he finds the lovers, he
observes :—

> " No doubt they rose up early, to observe
> The rite of May."

" I am convinced," says Coleridge, " that Shakespeare availed himself of the title of this play in his
own mind, and worked upon it as a dream throughout." Such was no doubt the case, and may we not
conclude, that the first idea of the play was conceived
on Midsummer Night? Aubrey, in a passage, which
refers perhaps to the character of Bottom the weaver,
implies that its original was a constable at Grendon,
in Buckinghamshire, and adds, " I thinke it was
Midsummer Night, that he, [i. e. Shakespeare,] happened to lye there." The title doubtlessly refers
to the whole piece, and not to any particular part
of it. The poet himself says :—

> " If we shadows have offended,
> Think but this, and all is mended ;
> That you have but slumbered here,
> While these visions did appear.
> And this weak and idle theme,
> *No more yielding but a dream,*
> Gentles, do not reprehend."

In Twelfth Night, Olivia observes of Malvolio's

seeming frenzy, that it " is a very Midsummer mad-
ness;" and Steevens thinks that as "this time was
anciently thought productive of mental vagaries, to
that circumstance it might have owed its title."
Heywood* seems to allude to a similar belief, when
he says—

> " As mad as a March hare; where madness compares,
> Are not Midsummer hares as mad as March hares?"

Malone thinks that the title of the play was suggested by the season in which it was introduced on
the stage. The misnomer, however, if it is one, does
not imply a greater anachronism than several which
the play itself presents. For instance, Theseus mar-
ries Hippolita on the night of the new moon; but
how does this agree with the discourse of the clowns
at the rehearsal?

> " *Snug.* Doth the moon shine that night we play our play?
> *Bot.* A calendar, a calendar! look in the almanack; find out
> moonshine, find out moonshine.
> *Quin.* Yes, it doth shine that night.
> *Bot.* Why, then you may leave a casement of the great cham-
> ber window, where we play, open; and the moon may shine in
> at the casement."

Again, the period of action is four days, con-
cluding with the night of the new moon. But
Hermia and Lysander receive the edict of Theseus
four days before the new moon; they fly from
Athens "to-morrow night;" they become the sport
of the fairies, along with Helena and Demetrius,
during one night only, for, Oberon accomplishes all
in one night, before "the first cock crows;" and the
lovers are discovered by Theseus the morning before

---

* Epigrammes upon Proverbes. 4to. Lond. 1567, No. 95.

that which would have rendered this portion of the
plot chronologically consistent. For, although Oberon, addressing his queen, says,

> " Now thou and I are new in amity;
> And will, *to-morrow midnight*, solemnly,
> Dance in Duke Theseus' house triumphantly."

yet Theseus, when he discovers the lovers, asks
Egeus,

> " is not this the day
> That Hermia should give answer of her choice?"

and the answer of Egeus, " It is, my Lord," coupled
with what Theseus says to Hermia in the first Act—

> " Take time to pause; and by the next new moon
> (The sealing-day betwixt my love and me,
> For everlasting bond of fellowship),
> Upon that day either prepare to die,
> For disobedience to your father's will;
> Or else to wed Demetrius, as he would;
> Or on Diana's altar to protest,
> For aye, austerity and single life."

proves that the action of the remaining part of the
play is not intended to consist of two days.

The preparation and rehearsal of the interlude
present similar inconsistencies. In Act i., Sc. 2,
Quince is the only one who has any knowledge of
the " most lamentable comedy, and most cruel death
of Pyramus and Thisbe," and he selects actors for
Thisby's mother, Pyramus's father, and Thisby's
father, none of whom appear in the interlude itself.
In Act iii., Sc. 1, we have the commencement of the
play in rehearsal, none of which appears in the piece
itself. Again, the play could have been but partially rehearsed once; for Bottom only returns in
time to advise " every man look o'er his part;" and

immediately before his companions were lamenting the failure of their " sport." How then could the " merry tears" of Philostrate be shed at its rehearsal ?

But all these merely tend to prove that Shakespeare wrote with no classical rules before him, and do not in the least detract from the most beautiful poetical drama in this or any other language. Shakespeare was truly the child of nature, and when we find Hermia, contemporary with Theseus, swearing

> " by that fire which burn'd the Carthage queen,
> When the false Trojan under sail was seen."

the anachronism is so palpable to any one of classical acquirements, that the evident conclusion is, that we must receive his works as the production of a genius unfettered by the knowledge of more philosophical canons, and of a power which enabled the bard to create, assisted only by the then barren field of his country's literature, that which " was not of an age, but for all time." This, we are convinced, must be the conclusion of all who read the works of Shakespeare in a proper spirit, unbiassed by the prejudices of a prosaic age; and it is only then that they can really hear him, as

> " Fancy's child,
> Warble his native wood-notes wild."

CHAPTER II.

Ὡς ου κρινουμαι τωνδε σοι τα πλειονα.

MALONE and Knight have assigned the composition of A Midsummer Night's Dream to the
year 1594. We suppose this play to have been written in the autumn of that year, and we believe
we can bring better evidence than has yet been
adduced.

Dr. Simon Forman, the celebrated astrologer, has
given us in MS. No. 384 in the Ashmolean Museum
at Oxford, the following important observations on
the year 1594 :—

" Ther was moch sicknes but lyttle death, moch
.fruit and many plombs of all sorts this yeare and
small nuts, but fewe walnuts. This monethes of
June and July were very wet and wonderfull cold
like winter, that the 10. dae of Julii many did syt
by the fyer, yt was so cold ; and soe was yt in Maye
and June ; and scarce too fair dais together all that
tyme, but yt rayned every day more or lesse. Yf yt
did not raine, then was yt cold and cloudye. Mani
murders were done this quarter. There were many
gret fludes this sommer, and about Michelmas,
thorowe the abundaunce of raine that fell sodeinly ;
the brige of Ware was broken downe, and at Stratford Bowe, the water was never seen so byg as yt
was ; and in the lattere end of October, the waters
burste downe the bridg at Cambridge. In Bark-

shire were many gret waters, wherewith was moch harm done sodenly."—MS. Ashm. 384, fol. 105.

Now this minute piece of meteorological information, so much more satisfactory than any yet in print, will be found to agree exactly with the complaint of Titania in the following speech addressed to Oberon :

" These are the forgeries of jealousy ;
And never, since the middle summer's spring,
Met we on hill, in dale, forest, or mead,
By paved fountain, or by rushy brook,
Or on the beached margent of the sea,
To dance our ringlets to the whistling wind,
But with thy brawls thou hast disturbed our sport.
Therefore the winds, piping to us in vain,
As in revenge, have suck'd up from the sea
Contagious fogs ; which, falling in the land,
Have every pelting river made so proud,
That they have overborne their continents :
The ox hath therefore stretch'd his yoke in vain,
The ploughman lost his sweat ; and the green corn
Hath rotted, ere his youth attain'd a beard :
The fold stands empty in the drowned field,
The crows are fatted with the murrain flock ;
The nine-men's morris is fill'd up with mud ;
And the quaint mazes in the wanton green,
For lack of tread, are undistinguishable :
The human mortals want their winter here ;
No night is now with hymn or carol blest.
Therefore the moon, the governess of floods,
Pale in her anger, washes all the air,*
That rheumatic diseases do abound.
And thorough this distemperature, we see
The seasons alter : hoary-headed frosts
Fall in the fresh lap of the crimson rose ;
And on old Hiems' chin and icy crown,
An odorous chaplet of sweet summer buds
Is, as in mockery, set. The spring, the summer,

---

* " The moone gathereth deawe in the aire, for she printeth the vertue of hir moysture in the aire, and chaungeth the ayre in a manner that is unseene, and breedeth and gendereth deaw in the upper part thereof."—*Bartholomæus by Glanville*, 1582, fol. 133.

The childing autumn, angry winter, change
Their wonted liveries; and the 'mazed world,
By their increase, now knows not which is which :
And this same progeny of evils comes
From our debate, from our dissension;
We are their parents and original."

It will be remembered that the phrase " rheumatic diseases" is not here used in its modern acceptation. Colds, coughs, &c. were included under this class of complaints, and their prevalence agrees with Forman's statement,—" ther was moch sicknes but lyttle death."

Forman's account is, indeed, altogether too remarkably similar to Shakespeare's to have been the result of chance. No one, we think, can read them both without being convinced that they relate to one and the same period. In pursuing this argument, we shall not perhaps be blamed for hinting at the possibility of the plenty of nuts, as mentioned by Forman, having suggested Titania's offer of " new nuts" to Bottom (Act iv. Sc. 1); and " new nuts" could scarcely have been procured at any other season than autumn.

" This yere," says Stowe the Chronicler, " in the month of May, fell many great showers of rain, but in the months of June and July much more; for it commonly rained every day or night till St. James' day, and two days after together most extremely; all which notwithstanding, in the month of August, there followed a fair harvest, but in the month of September fell great rains, which raised high waters, such as stayed the carriages, and broke down bridges at Cambridge, Ware, and elsewhere in many places."

Steevens has quoted the following from Churchyard's Charitie, published in 1595, although he does not seem to be aware that the author of course alludes to the preceding year :—

> " A colder time in world was never seene :
> The skies do lowre, the sun and moone wax dim ;
> Sommer scarce knowne, but that the leaves are greene.
> The winter's waste drives water ore the brim ;
> Upon the land great flotes of wood may swim.
> Nature thinks scorne to do hir dutie right,
> Because we have displeasde the Lord of Light."

Churchyard, as Steevens observes, was not enumerating, on this occasion, fictitious, but real misfortunes. He wrote the present poem to excite charity on his own behalf; and among his other sufferings very naturally dwelt on the coldness of the season, which his poverty had rendered the less supportable.

It is remarkable that Churchyard, in the preface to the above-mentioned volume, states that " a great nobleman told me this last wet sommer, the weather was too colde for poets." How singular that A Midsummer Night's Dream should have been written at such a time! Would that some of our modern poets could be induced to profit by the hint.

Chetwood, in his work entitled " The British Theatre," 12mo. Dublin, 1750, has given a list of titles and dates of the early editions of Shakespeare's Plays, among which we find " A moste pleasaunte comedie, called A Midsummer Night's Dreame, wythe the freakes of the fayries," stated to have been published in the year 1595. No copy either with this date or under this title has yet been discovered. It is, however, necessary to state, that Steevens and others have pronounced many of the titles which Chetwood has given to be fictitious.

In an old comedy called, *The Wisdome of Doctor*

Dodypoll, first printed in 1600, but known to have been written as early as 1596, occurs a passage, which is conjectured by Steevens, to have been borrowed from a similar passage in the Midsummer Night's Dream :—

> " 'Twas I that lead you through the painted meades,
> Where the light fairies daunst upon the flowers,
> *Hanging on every leaf an orient pearle*,
> Which, strooke together with the silken winde,
> Of their loose mantels made a silver chime."

There is another allusion in the Midsummer Night's Dream, which may hereafter be found to be corroborative of the date to which we have assigned its composition. But of this more particularly in another chapter.

Early in the year 1598, appeared Meres' *Wit's Treasury, being the Second Part of Wit's Commonwealth*, in which (fol. 282) he mentions A Midsummer Night's Dream of Shakespeare. It was probably not then a new performance, or it could scarcely have found its way into Meres' list. This is the only direct notice of it we possess, previously to the publication of two small quarto editions in the year 1600, one printed " for Thomas Fisher," and the other, " printed by James Roberts." We think there can be little doubt, on an examination of these editions, that Fisher's is the genuine one, and the earliest.* It was entered at Stationer's Hall on the

---

* For the sake of the bibliomaniac, we may state, that Fisher's edition is very rare and difficult to meet with. Steevens' copy, which was imperfect, sold for the sum of £25 10*s*., and Heber's copy, a remarkable fine one, produced thirty-six pounds. The edition by Roberts is comparatively common, and worth from five to ten pounds.

8th October, the same year. The play was not reprinted after 1600, till it was inserted in the folio
of 1623 ; and the text in that edition differs very
slightly from that in the preceding quartos.

CHAPTER III.

" The characters in The Midsummer Night's Dream are classical, but the costume is strictly Gothic, and shews that it was
through the medium of Romance that he drew the knowledge of
them."—*Letter on Shakespeare's authorship of the Two Noble
Kinsmen.*

CHAUCER'S Knight's Tale has long been considered as the source whence Shakespeare
derived the hint of A Midsummer Night's Dream.
We have a few general obervations to offer on the
sources of this play, at the same time expressing our
firm conviction, that the plot as a whole, was one of
the " heirs of his own invention."

Chaucer's Knight's Tale, the Legende of Thisbe of
Babylon, by the same author, and Golding's translation of Ovid's Metamorphoses, were all well known
to Shakespeare, and together furnished materials for
the basis of this play.

From the first of these, several corresponding extracts have been given by the commentators, but
they appear to have overlooked the following
passage, which occurs nearly at the end of the
Knight's Tale, and may have furnished Shakespeare
with the idea of introducing an interlude at the end
of his play :—

" ne how the Grekes play
The wake-plaies ne kepe I not to say :

> Who wrestled best naked, with oile enoint,
> Ne who that bare him best in no disjoint.
> I woll not tellen eke how they all gon
> Hom till Athenes whan the play is don."

The introduction of the clowns and their interlude was perhaps an afterthought.

Again, in the Knight's Tale, we have this passage,

> " Duke Theseus, with all his cumpany,
> Is comin home to Athenes the cité,
> With alle bliss, and grete solempnité."

which bears too remarkable a resemblance to what Theseus says in the Midsummer Night's Dream, to have been accidental :—

> " Away with us, to Athens : Three and three,
> We'll hold a feast in great solemnity."

In the Legende of Thisbe of Babylon, we read,—

> " Thus would thei saine, alas ! thou wicked wal,
> Thorough thine envie thou us lettist al."

which is certainly similar to the following line in Pyramus's address to Wall :—

> " O wicked Wall, through whom I see no bliss !"

Golding's translation of Ovid was published in 1567, and the many similarities between the tale of Pyramus and Thisbe as there related and Shakespeare's interlude, satisfactorily prove the source of the latter.   We give the whole passage, and let the reader judge for himself :—

> " Within the towne (of whose huge walles so monstrous high and
>   thicke,
> The fame is given Semiramis for making them of bricke.)
> Dwelt hard together two young folke in houses joynde so nere,

That under all one roofe well nie both twaine convayed were,
The name of him was *Pyramus*, and Thisbe called was she;
So faire a man in all the East was none alive as he,
Nor nere a woman, mayde, nor wife, in beautie like to her.
This neigh-brod bred acquaintance first, this neigh-brod first did
    ster
The secret sparkes : this neigh-brod first an entrance in did show
For love, to come to that to which it afterward did grow.
And if that right had taken place they had beene man and wife ;
But still their parents went about to let which (for their life)
They could not let. For both their hearts with equal flame did
    burne ;
No man was privie to their thoughts. And for to serve their
    turne,
Instead of talke they used signes : the closlier they supprest
The fire of love, the fiercer still it raged in their brest.
The wall that parted house from house had riven therein a cranie,
Which shroonke at making of the wall : this fault not markt of
    anie
Of many hundred yeeres before (what doth not love espie ?)
These lovers first of all found out, and made a way whereby
To talke together secretly, and through the same did go
Their loving whisprings very light and safely to and fro.
Now, as at one side *Pyramus*, and *Thisbe* on the tother,
Stood often drawing one of them the pleasant breath from other :
O thou envious wall (they sayed), why letst thou lovers thus ;
What matter were it if that thou permitted both of us
In armes each other to embrace : or if thou think that this
Were over-much, yet mightest thou at least make roome to kisse.
And yet thou shalt not finde us churles : we thinke our selves in
    det,
For the same piece of curtesie, in vouching safe to let
Our sayings to our friendly eares thus freely come and go.
Thus having where they stood in vaine complained of their wo,
When night drew neare they bad adue, and ech gave kisses
    sweete,
Unto the parget on their side the which did never meete.
Next morning with her cheerefull light had driven the starres aside,
And Phœbus with his burning beames the dewie grasse had dride,
These lovers at their wonted place by fore-appointment met,
Where, after much complaint and mone they covenanted to get
Away from such as watched them, and in the evening late
To steale out of their father's house, and eke the citie gate.
And to th' intent that in the fields they strayd not up and downe,
They did agree at Ninus Tombe to meet without the towne,
And tary underneath a tree that by the same did grow :
Which was a faire high mulberie with fruite as white as snow,

Hard by a coole and trickling spring. This bargaine pleased
    them both.
And so day-light (which to their thought away but slowly goth)
Did in the ocian fall to rest, and night from thence did rise.
As soone as darkenesse once was come, straight *Thisbe* did devise
A shift to winde her out of doores, that none that were within
Perceived her : and muffling her with clothes about her chin,
That no man might discerne her face, to Ninus Tombe she came
Unto the tree : and set her downe there underneath the same.
Love made her bold. But see the chance ; there comes be-
    smerde with blood,
About the chappes, a lyonesse all foming from the wood,
From slaughter lately made of kine, to staunch her bloody thirst
With water of the foresaid spring. Whom Thisbe spying first,
Afarre by moone-light, thereupon with fearfull steps gan flie,
And in a darke and yrkesome cave did hide herselfe thereby.
And as she fled away for haste she let her mantle fall,
The which for feare she left behinde not looking backe at all.
Now when the cruell lyonesse her thirst had staunched well,
In going to the wood she found the slender weede that fell
From Thisbe, which with bloodie teeth in peeces he did teare :
The night was somewhat further spent ere Pyramus came there,
Who seeing in the suttle sand the print of lyon's paw,
Waxt pale for feare. But when also the bloodie cloke he saw
All rent and torne : one night (he sayed) shall lovers two con-
    found,
Of which long life deserved she of all that live on ground ;
My soule deserves of this mischaunce the perill for to beare.
I, wretch, have been the death of thee, which to this place of
    feare
Did cause thee in the night to come, and came not there before.
My wicked lims and wretched guts, with cruell teeth therefore,
Devoure ye, O ye Lyons all that in this rocke doe dwell.
But cowards use to wish for death. The slender weede that fell
From Thisbe up he takes, and straight doth beare it to the tree,
Which was appointed erst the place of meeting for to bee.
And when he had bewept, and kist the garment which he knew,
Receive thou my blood too (quoth he) ; and therewithall he drew
His sword, the which among his guts he thrust, and by and bie
Did draw it from the bleeding wound, beginning for to die,
And cast himselfe upon his backe, the blood did spinne on hie,
As when a conduite pipe is crackt, the water bursting out
Doth shote it selfe a great way off, and pierse the ayre about,
The leaves that were upon the tree besprinkled with his blood,
Were died black. The roote also bestained as it stood,
A deepe dark purple colour straight upon the berries cast,
Anon scarce ridded of her feare with which she was agast

For doubt of disapoynting him comes *Thisbe* forth in hast,
And for her lover lookes about, rejoycing for to tell
How hardly she had scapt that night the danger that befell.
And as she knew right well the place and facion of the tree,
(As which she saw so late before :) even so when she did see
The colour of the berries turn'd, she was uncertaine whither
It were the tree at which they both agreed to meet togither.
While in this doubt full stound she stood, she cast her eye aside,
And there beweltred in his blood hir lover she espide,
Lie sprawling with his dying lims : at which she started backe,
And looked pale as any box, a shuddring through her stracke,
Even like the sea which suddenly with whissing noyse doth move,
When with a little blast of wind it is but toucht above.
But when approching nearer him she knew it was her love,
She beate her brest, she shriked out, she tare her golden heares,
And taking him betweene her armes did wash his woundes with
            teares.
She meynd her weeping with his blood, and kissing all his face,
(Which now became as cold as yse) she cryde in wofull case,
Alas, what chaunce my *Pyramus* hath parted thee and mee.
Make answere, O my *Pyramus :* it is thy *Thisb.* even shee
Whom thou doost love most hartily that speaketh unto thee,
Give eare and raise thy heavie head. He hearing *Thisbes* name,
Lift up his dying eyes, and having seene her, closd the same.
But when she knew her mantle there, and saw his scaberd lie
Without the sworde : Unhappy man, thy love hath made thee die :
Thy love (she said) hath made thee slea thyselfe.   This hand of
            mine
Is strong inough to doe the like.   My love no lesse than thine
Shall give me force to worke my wound, I will pursue thee dead,
And wretched woman as I am, it shall of me be sed
That like as of thy death I was the onely cause and blame,
So am I thy companion eke and partner in the same.
For death which onely could alas asunder part us twaine,
Shall never so dissever us but we will meete againe.
And you the parents of us both, most wretched folke alive,
Let this request that I shall make in both our names belive,
Intreate you to permit, that we whom chaste and stedfast love,
And whom even death hath joyned in one, may as it doth behove
In one grave be together layd.   And thou unhappie tree
Which shouldest now the corse of one, and shalt anon through mee
Shroude two, of this same slaughter hold the sicker sinnes for ay,
Blacke be the colour of thy fruite and mourning like alway,
Such as the murder of us twaine may evermore bewray.
This said, she tooke the sword yet warme with slaughter of her love,
And setting it beneath her brest did to the heart it shove.
Her prayer with the Gods and with their parents tooke effect,

For when the fruite is thoroughly ripe, the berrie is bespect
With colour tending to a blacke.   And that which after fire
Remained, rested in one tombe as *Thisbe* did desire."

We may add, that most of the classical allusions
in the Midsummer Night's Dream are to be found
in the book we have just quoted. In point of fact,
classical allusions were much more general and
popular in Shakespeare's age than at the present,
and scarcely a ballad can be found of the time of
Queen Elizabeth, that does not refer to some tale of
antiquity. The fates of Pyramus and Thisbe, now
confined to the boys of public schools, was then a
subject of popular sympathy. Mr. Collier has
printed a ballad entitled " The Panges of Love and
Loves Fittes," in which the unhappy fate of the two
lovers is again deplored :—

> " What say you then to Piramus,
>   That promised his love to mete,
> And founde by fortune merveilous,
>   A bloudie cloth before his feete?
> For Tysbies sake hymselfe he slewe,
>   Ladie! Ladie!
> To prove that he was a lover trewe,
>   My dear Ladie!"

And, indeed, who can accuse Shakespeare of
having taken directly from the classic writers, when
there are, in fact, fewer classical allusions and imita-
tions in his plays than in many of those of his contemporaries? Whalley,* we believe, was the first
who pointed out the similarity between the opening
speech of Theseus :

> " Now, fair Hippolyta, our nuptial hour
>   Draws on apace ; four happy days bring in

---

* On the Learning of Shakespeare, 8vo. Lond. 1748, p. 55.
He is followed by Malone.

Another moon; but oh, methinks, how slow
This old moon wanes! she lingers my desires,
Like to a stepdame, or a dowager,
Long withering out a young man's revenue."

and the following passage in the epistles of Ovid :

—" Ut piger annus
Pupillis, quos dura premit custodia matrum :
Sic mihi tarda fluunt ingrataque tempora."

But surely the translation of this, as given by
Drant in 1567, is more similar to Shakespeare's:

" Slowe seames the yeare unto the warde
Which houlden downe must be,
In custodie of stepdame straite,—
Slowe slydes the time to me."

The word *dowager*, as Mr. Knight observes, is here
used in the original sense of a widow receiving *dower*
out of the revenue which has descended to the heir with
this customary charge. Slender, in the Merry Wives
of Windsor, Act i. Sc. 1, alludes to this custom :—
" I keep but three men and a boy yet, till my mother
be dead." Stepdames were, indeed, seldom looked
upon by the youths under their charge with any
degree of affection; their severity is thus mentioned
by Barnfeild, in his *Complaint of Poetrye*, 1598 :—

" Then, if a stony heart must thee inter,
Go find a stepdame or a usurer."

We are now proceeding to offer a new conjecture
to our readers, which was first suggested by perusing
the following old ballad, preserved, with other black-
letter broadsides, in the library of the Society of
Antiquaries. It was written, as appears from a
colophon, by T. Hedley, and " imprinted at London

by Hary Sutton, dwellyng in Poules Churchyard,"
and therefore considerably before the earliest date
that could be assigned to any of Shakespeare's plays.
It was probably reprinted.

> " *Of such as on fantesye, decree and discus*
> *On other men's works, lo, Ovid's tale thus!*

" Rude Pan wold nedes one day in companie,
Compare to mend Apollo's melodye,
And toke his homlie pipe and gan to blo ;
The gentil God, that saw his rudnes so,
Although himselfe knewe how for to excell,
Contented stode, to here his conning well.
Pan played and played boystiouslye,
Apollo played but much melodiously,
And such a tune wyth such musicke gave,
As wel became hys knowledge for to have ;
Midas stode by to judge, and to decre
Whych of them both should best in musycke be ;
And as he herde Pan playe and use hys song,
He thought it such as he had lyked long,
And wonted was to here of others oft ;
Apollo's harpe and song went very soft,
And swete and straunge, as none might sweter be,
But yet, thought Midas, thys musycke lykes not me.
And therfore strayght ful loude he cried and said,
' Pan to myne eares of both hath better plaied.'
Quoth then Apollo, ' syns thus thou demest Pan,
Me to excel, that God of connyng am,
And so doest judge of thynges thou canst no skyll,
Midas henceforth, lo ! thus to the I wyll ;
Thou shalte have eares to shewe and tell I wys,
Both what thy skyll and what thy reason is ;
Whych on thy head shall stande and wytnes be,
Howe thou haste judged thys rurall God and me.
Nay, be content, for I have it sayd.'
A full sad man stood Mydas then dismayde,
And as he felt to trye if it so was,
He found he had two eares as hath an asse,
Newly growen out wheras hys own eares stoode.
Sore chaunged then his collour and his moode,
But yet for thie, havyng no worde to say,
He shooke hys eares and sadly went hys waye.
I know no more, but thys I wot and know,
That tho the Phrigian Kyng be buryed lo,

> And both hys eares eke wyth hym hydden be,
> And so far worne that no man shall them se,
> Syns such there are that lyve at thys day yet,
> Whych have hys skyl, hys judgement, and his wit,
> And take upon them both to judge and know,
> To them I wyshe even thus, and to no mo,
> That as they have hys judgement and hys yeares,
> Even so I would they had hys fayre long eares."

We consider this tale of the transformation of the ears of Midas to have furnished Shakespeare with the notion of causing a similar change to take place in the appearance of Bottom the weaver. We would be understood not to refer to any portion of his plot, but merely to the single idea of the transformation; and even if our conjecture be right, we think it possible that Shakespeare might only have been influenced in his choice by a slight recollection of it.

The only verbal similarity is in the last line of the ballad —

> " Even so I would they had hys *fayre long eares.*"

and Titania's invitation to the Weaver—

> " Come, sit thee down upon this flowery bed,
>   While I thy amiable cheeks do coy,
> And stick musk-roses in thy sleek smooth head,
>   And kiss thy *fair large ears,* my gentle joy."

There is perhaps nothing very remarkable in this coincidence; but let us read a little further on :—

> " *Tita.* What, wilt thou hear some music, my sweet love?
>   *Bot.* I HAVE A REASONABLE GOOD EAR IN MUSIC: let us have the tongs and the bones."

How pointless is Bottom's answer taken separately, and yet how full of rich satire and humour, if the speaker be considered a second Midas ! Bottom had not, like Midas, received the asses head, as a punishment for his presumption, ignorance, and self-conceit; but, even in that point of view, the metamorphosis would have been justifiable; and, at the risk of being thought to overstep the bounds of probability, we are glad to convict our poet of one very good joke.*

The tale of Midas is of course to be found in Golding's Ovid, a book with which Shakespeare was, beyond all doubt, very intimately acquainted. The ballad we have given, moreover, if it fail to convince our readers of the correctness of the view we have taken, will serve as a striking example of the popular manner in which the mythological tales of the ancients were then made current among all classes.

Before we change the subject, we will take the opportunity of saying a few words relative to the character of Bottom the weaver. There is a connexion between this name and the trade, which the obsoleteness of the term has caused to escape the commentators. A ball of thread wound upon any cylindrical body was formerly called A BOTTOM OF THREAD. How appropriate a name then for a weaver! We can furnish our readers with an allusion to this mode of designation. It occurs in a rare little book, called *Grange's Garden*, 4to. Lond. 1577 :—

---

* L'Estrange has the following fable :—" There was a question started betwixt a cuckoo and a nightingale, which of the two had the better voice, and the better way of singing. It came at last to a trial of skill, and an ass was to be the judge; who, upon hearing both sides, gave it clearly for the cuckoo."— *Fables*, Edit. 1694, No. 414.

> " A *bottome* for your silke it seemes,
>   My letters are become,
> Whiche, with oft winding off and on,
>   Are wasted whole and some."

Nick Bottom was the name of our weaver. We suspect, from the following contemporary epigram, that the first name was common for professors of that trade:—

> " Nicke, the weaver's boy, is dead and gone,
> Surely his life was but a thrume." *

Our readers will immediately call to mind the invocation of Bottom, in the part of Pyramus, while reciting his " last dying speech:"—

> " O fates! come, come;
> Cut thread and thrum."

Bottom appears to have been of Aristotle's opinion, that the chief end of tragedy is to raise terror. " I could play Ercles rarely, or a part to tear a cat in, to make all split." This may perhaps be an allusion to Martin Slaughter's play of Hercules, now lost, but written about 1594; or it may more probably refer to a "mask of Greek worthies;" and we find, in a list † of properties for such a masque, the following entry, " a great clobb for one of them representing Hercules, 4s." It is difficult to say whether the verses which Bottom uses are an actual quotation or a burlesque, but probably the latter:—

---

* We find this in a work, entitled *Pieces of Ancient Poetry from Unpublished Manuscripts and Scarce Books*, edited by Fry, 4to. Bristol, 1814, p. 15.

† Kempe's Loseley Manuscripts, p. 87.

> " The raging rocks,
> And shivering shocks,
> Shall break the locks
> Of prison gates :
> And Phibbus' car
> Shall shine from far,
> And make and mar
> The foolish fates."

In 1581, a translation of one of Seneca's plays, entitled *Hercules,* by John Studley, was published. It is so bombastically rendered, that we are inclined to think it may be the original of the above, especially as similarities may be found.   For instance, take the commencing lines : —

> " O Lorde of ghostes ! whose fyrye flashe
> That forth thy hande doth shake,
> Doth cause the trembling lodges twayne,
> Of Phœbus' carre to shake.
> Ravgne reachlesse nowe : in every place
> Thy peace procurde I have,
> Aloffe where Nereus lookes up lande,
> Empalde in winding wave."

And again,

> " The roring rocks have quaking sturd,
> And none thereat hath pusht ;
> Hell gloummy gates I have brast oape,
> Where grisly ghosts all husht
> Have stood."—

Shakespeare, however, may allude to some production nearer his own time, and it is very possible that the burlesque may be general.

CHAPTER IV.

" Hail, bright Titania!
Why standest thou idle on these flowery banks?
Oberon is dancing with his Dryades :
I'll gather daisies, primrose, violets,
And bind them in a verse of poesy."

TYRWHITT was of opinion that the Pluto and
Proserpina of Chaucer's Merchant's Tale were
the true progenitors of Oberon and Titania; and
in this conjecture he is followed by Malone. We
believe Shakespeare to have formed his beautiful
creations out of the popular fairy mythology of the
age.

Much has been said and written on the source of
the fairy drama, as exhibited in the Midsummer
Night's Dream. Some writers have even gone to
the early literature of Wales.* We prefer confining our researches to a field that Shakespeare
himself might have had an opportunity of access.

Fairies were then so woven into the popular
belief, and were supposed to exert so wide and general an influence, that Shakespeare considered it no

---

* With all due respect for Welsh literature, we certainly must
say that the idea of its being the origin of romance and of fairy
land is not very probable. We have heard that the following note was once discovered on the side of a Welsh pedigree
roll—" About this time the world was created;" but we were
never inclined to believe the anecdote until we found the following entry in the "inventory of Mr. Morgan, shentleman," in MS.
Harl. 2127 :—" One pedigree *since before Adame* to shoe the
antiquitte of hur shentilitte."

absolute anomaly to introduce them at Athens in the
time of Theseus.   Fairies were beings that always
existed, whose presence was not confined to one
quarter or part of the world.   Would they not,
therefore, be properly introduced into a drama of
this nature?   We cannot for a moment think that
Shakespeare ever considered whether the inhabitants
of Greece believed in the existence of Fairies, or
whether the subjects of Theseus were ever haunted
by them.   No, he was writing for a people that believed, or knew that others believed in their universal
existence ; and we know enough of Shakespeare's
originals, to be convinced that he seldom, if ever,
cared for raising a substantial foundation of correct
minute facts like these.

It would answer no useful purpose, as far as we
can see, to enter into any discussion of the fairy
mythology of Greece. In what important particulars
do the fairies of Greece, as described by Allatius, or
the καλαι των ορεων of Psellus, differ from those of
England?   We do not think that we should be affording illustration to Shakespeare's play, in at-
tempting to prove the source of the latter.   The
account given by Allatius, however, agrees very remarkably with the beings of the Midsummer Night's
Dream.   They haunted especially shady trees, and
might frequently be seen dancing their rounds beside
the cool streams which watered the woody dales.
They sometimes fell in love with handsome young
men, and they were extremely fond of little children,
often carrying them away, and educating them
amongst themselves.   Many people had seen them,
sometimes dancing, at other times, two engaged in

conversation under the shade of a tree, or one or more wandering about the woods or meadows.*

One thing appears probable, that Shakespeare seems to have considered one of the fairy haunts to be in the eastern bounds of India. Titania thus taunts Oberon :—

> " Then I must be thy lady. But I know
> When thou hast stolen away from fairy land,
> And in the shape of Corin sat all day,
> Playing on pipes of corn, and versing love
> To amorous Phillida. Why art thou here,
> *Come from the farthest steep of India?*
> But that, forsooth, the bouncing Amazon,
> Your buskined mistress and your warrior love,
> To Theseus must be wedded; and you come
> To give their bed joy and prosperity."

Titania, we are told,

> " as her attendant, hath
> A lovely boy, stolen from an Indian king,"

which is not, however, very easily reconcilable with Titania' own account of the boy's mother, " in the spiced Indian air, by night."

Lane, in his Triton's Trumpet, speaks of the " land of faerie ;" and as this poem has never been printed, we may, perhaps, be justified in introducing the following extract :—

> " From Faerie Lande, I com, quoth Danus now.
> Ha ! that quoth June mee never chaunced to knowe,
> Ne could or would th'igh poet Spencer tell,
> (So farr as mote my witt this ridle spell)
> Though none that breatheth livinge aier doth knowe,

---

* See an interesting paper on the popular superstitions of modern Greece, in Frazer's Magazine for February, 1835, written by Thomas Wright, Esq. M.A., &c.

Wheare is that happie land of Faerie,
Which I so oft doe vaunt yet no wheare showe,
But vouch antequities which nobodie maie knowe.
  No marveile that, quoth Danus mirrelie,
For it is movable of Mercurie,
Which Faeries with a trice doe snatch up hence,
Fro sight and heering of the common sense ;
Yet coms on sodaines to the thoughtlesse eye
And eare (favored to heere theire minstrelsy),
Ne bootes climbe promontories yt to spie,
For then the Faeries dowt the seeinge eye.
Onlie right sold it to some fewe doth chaunce,
That (ravishd) they behold it in a traunse,
Wheare yt a furor calls, rage, extacie,
Shedd but on the poetick misterie,
Which they with serious apprehension tend,
Ells from them also yt dothe quicklie wend :
But caught ! with it they deale most secretly,
As deignes the Muse instruct them waerely.
The glorie wheareof doth but this arive,
They farr more honord dead are then alive.
But now folke vaunt by use, to call yt prittie,
Themselves theareby comparinge with (?) more wittie
Nathlesse kinges, captaines, clercks, astrologers,
And everie learnd th'ideal spirit admires.
But ah ! well fare his lines alive not dead !
Yf of his readers his reward bee bread.
Which proves, while poets thoughts up sore divine,
These fleshe flies, earth wormes, welter but in slyme.
Ha ! yet near known was, but meere poetrie,
Came to ann ancor at sadd povertie."
                              MS. Bibl. Reg. 17. B xv.

Be it where it may, the abode of Pliny's pigmies
may have originated the locus of the fairies in " the
farthest steep of India." We rest our conjecture on
the following extract from a popular work, at the same
time, not daring to hint that there ever was the slightest similarity between the men of one cubit, and the
καλαι αρχοντισαι of Shakespeare or of Greece :—

  " Pigmei be little men of a cubite long, and the Greekes call
them Pigmeos, and they dwell in mountaines of Inde, and the
sea of occean is nigh to them, as Papias sayth. And Austen
sayth in this wise, that pigmei bee unneth a cubite long, and

bee perfect of age in the thirde yeare, and ware old in the seaventh yere, and it is said, that they fight with cranes. Lib. 7. ca. 3. Plinius speaketh of Pigmeis, and sayth, that pigmei be armed in yron, and overcome cranes, and passe not theyr bounds, and dwell in temperate lande under a merrye parte of heaven, in mountains in the north side. And the fame is, that cranes pursue them, and pigmei armed, ride on goat bucks with arowes in springing time, and gather an hoast, and come to the sea and destroye their egs and birds with all their might and strength, and doe such voyages in three moneths, and except they did so, cranes should increase, and be so many, that pigmei shuld not withstand them, and they make them houses to dwell in of feathers, and with the pens of cranes, and of shells of their egges, as he sayth, and saith also, that Aristotle meaneth, that Pigmei lyve in dennes. *All the later writers affirme this to be true, they are in the uttermost mountaines of Indie.*"—*Bartholomæus de proprietatibus rerum,* fol. Lond. 1582, fol. 377.

Tarlton, in his Newes out of Purgatory, first printed in 1589, says of Robin Goodfellow, that he was " famosed in everie old wive's chronicle, for his mad merrie prankes." There is, indeed, sufficient evidence to show that there were fairy rhymes and fairy tales, of beings like those of A Midsummer Night's Dream, in circulation if not in print before that play was written.

We will here insert an anecdote from a manuscript in the Bodleian Library at Oxford, which was written in the same year to which we have assigned the composition of this play, and serves to show that common tradition at that period admitted the existence of fairy haunts, and illustrates the common opinion of the nature of those beings :—

" A farmer hired a grange commonly reported to be haunted with fairies, and paid a shrewd for it every half year. A gentleman asked him how he durst live in the house, and whether no spirits haunted him? Truth, quoth he, there be two saints in Heaven do vex me more than all the devills in hell,

namely, the Virgin Mary and Michaell the Arch-
angell, on whose daies he paied his rent."—MS.
Rawl. Poet. 66.

Mr. Collier has in his possession an unique black-
letter ballad, entitled *The Merry Puck, or Robin
Goodfellow*, which, from several passages, may be
fairly concluded to have been before the public
previously to the appearance of the Midsummer
Night's Dream. Mr. Collier reprinted, for private
circulation, twenty-five copies of this ballad, and has
not only presented us with a copy, but, with his
usual kindness and liberality, permitted it to be
inserted in this volume. It most remarkably illustrates the Puck of the Midsummer Night's Dream.

*The Merry Puck, or Robin Good-fellow : Describing his birth
and whose sonne he was, how he run away from his Mother,
how he was merry at the Bridehouse, how his Father, King
Oberon, found him, together with all his merry Prankes.
Very pleasaunt and witty.*

CHAPTER I.

Shewing his birth, and whose sonne he was.

Here doe begin the merry iests
  of Robin Good-fellow :
I'de wish you for to reade this booke,
  if you his Pranks would know.

But first I will declare his birth,
  and what his Mother was,
And then how Robin merrily
  did bring his knacks to passe.

In time of old, when Fayries us'd
  to wander in the night,
And through key-holes swiftly glide,
  now marke my story right.

Among these pretty fairy Elves
    was Oberon, their King,
Who us'd to keepe them company
    still at their revelling.

And sundry houses they did use,
    but one, above the rest,
Wherein a comely Lasse did dwell
    that pleas'd King Oberon best.

This lovely Damsell, neat and faire,
    so courteous, meek and mild,
As sayes my booke, by Oberon
    she was begot with child.

She knew not who the father was;
    but thus to all would say—
In night time he to her still came,
    and went away ere day.

The midwife having better skill
    than had this new made mother,
Quoth she, surely some fairy 'twas,
    for it can be no other.

And so the old wife rightly iudg'd,
    for it was so indeed.
This Fairy shew'd himself most kind,
    and helpt his love at need;

For store of linnen he provides,
    and brings her for her baby,
With dainty cates and choised fare,
    he serv'd her like a lady.

The Christening time then being [come,
    most merry they [did pass;
The Gossips dra[ined a cheerful cup
    as then prov[ided was.

And Robin was [the infant call'd,
    so named the [Gossips by:
What pranks [he played both day and night
    I'le tell you cer[tainly.

CHAPTER II.

Shewing how Robin Good-fellow carried himselfe, and how
he run away from his Mother.

WHILE yet he was a little lad
  and of a tender age,
He us'd much waggish tricks to men,
  as they at him would rage.

Unto his Mother they complain'd,
  which grieved her to heare,
And for these Pranks she threatned him
  he should have whipping cheare.

If that he did not leave his tricks,
  his jeering mocks and mowes:
Quoth she, thou vile, untutor'd youth,
  these Pranks no breeding shewes;

I cannot to the Market goe,
  but ere I backe returne,
Thou scof'st my neighbours in such sort,
  which makes my heart to mourne.

But I will make you to repent
  these things, ere I have done :
I will no favour have on thee,
  although thou beest my sonne.

Robin was griev'd to heare these words,
  which she to him did say,
But to prevent his punishment,
  from her he run away.

And travelling long upon the way,
  his hunger being great,
Unto a Taylor's house he came,
  and did intreat some meat :

The Taylor tooke compassion then
  upon this pretty youth,
And tooke him for his Prentice straight,
  as I have heard in truth.

CHAPTER III.

How Robin Good-fellow left his Master, and also how Oberon
told him he should be turned into what shape he could wish or
desire.

Now Robin Good-fellow, being plac't
　　with a Taylor, as you heare,
He grew a workman in short space,
　　so well he ply'd his geare.

He had a gowne which must be made,
　　even with all haste and speed ;
The maid must have 't against next day
　　to be her wedding weed.

The Taylor he did labour hard
　　till twelve a clock at night ;
Betweene him and his servant then
　　they finished aright

The gowne, but putting on the sleeves :
　　quoth he unto his man,
I 'le goe to bed : whip on the sleeves
　　as fast as ere you can.

So Robin straightway takes the gowne
　　and hangs it on a pin,
Then takes the sleeves and whips the gowne ;
　　till day he nere did lin.

His Master rising in the morne,
　　and seeing what he did,
Begun to chide ; quoth Robin then,
　　I doe as I was bid.

His Master then the gowne did take
　　and to his worke did fall.
By that time he had done the same
　　the Maid for it did call.

Quoth he to Robin, goe thy wayes
　　and fetch the remnants hither,
That yesterday we left, said he,
　　wee 'l breake our fasts together.

Then Robin hies him up the staires
and brings the remnants downe,
Which he did know his Master sav'd
out of the woman's gowne.

The Taylor he was vext at this,
he meant remnants of meat,
That this good woman, ere she went,
might there her breakfast eate.

Quoth she this is a breakfast good
I tell you, friend, indeed;
And to requite your love I will
send for some drinke with speed :

And Robin he must goe for it
with all the speed he may :
He takes the pot and money too,
and runnes from thence away.

When he had wandred all the day
a good way from the Towne,
Unto a forest then he came :
to sleepe he laid him downe.

Then Oberon came, with all his Elves,
and danc'd about his sonne,
With musick pleasing to the eare;
and, when that it was done,

King Oberon layes a scroule by him,
that he might understand
Whose sonne he was, and how hee'd grant
whate'er he did demand :

To any forme that he did please
himselfe he would translate;
And how one day hee'd send for him
to see his fairy State.

Then Robin longs to know the truth
of this mysterious skill,
And turnes himselfe into what shape
he thinks upon or will.

Sometimes a neighing horse was he,
sometimes a gruntling hog,
Sometimes a bird, sometimes a crow,
sometimes a snarling dog.

CHAPTER IV.

How Robin Good-fellow was merry at the Bridehouse.

Now Robin having got this art,
  he oft would make good sport,*
And hearing of a wedding day,
  he makes him ready for 't.

Most like a ioviall Fidler then
  he drest himselfe most gay,
And goes unto the wedding house,
  thereon his crowd to play.

He welcome was unto this feast,
  and merry they were all;
He play'd and sung sweet songs all day,
  at night to sports did fall.

He first did put the candles out,
  and being in the dark,
Some would he strike and some would pinch,
  and then sing like a lark.

The candles being light againe,
  and things well and quiet,
A goodly posset was brought in
  to mend their former diet;

Then Robin for to have the same
  did turne him to a Beare;
Straight at that sight the people all
  did run away for feare.

Then Robin did the posset eate,
  and having serv'd them so,
Away goes Robin with all haste,
  then laughing hoe, hoe, hoe!

---

* Cf. M. N. D. Act iii. Sc. 2.
  " I with the morning's love have *oft made sport*."

D

CHAPTER V.

Declaring how Robin Good-fellow serv'd an old lecherous man.

THERE was an old man had a Neece,
    a very beauteous maid;
To wicked lust her Unkle sought
    this faire one to perswade.

But she a young man lov'd too deare
    to give consent thereto;
'Twas Robin's chance upon a time
    to heare their grievous woe:

Content yourselfe, then Robin saies,
    and I will ease your griefe,
I have found out an excellent way
    that will yeeld you reliefe.

He sends them to be married straight,
    and he, in her disguise,
Hies home with all the speed he may
    to blind her Unkle's eyes:

And there he plyes his worke amaine,
    doing more in one houre,
Such was his skill and workmanship,
    than she could doe in foure.

The old man wondred for to see
    the worke go on so fast,
And there withall more worke doth he
    unto good Robin cast.

Then Robin said to his old man,
    good Unkle, if you please
To grant to me but one ten pound
    I 'le yeeld your love-suit ease.

Ten pounds, quoth he, I will give thee,
    sweet Neece, with all my heart,
So thou will grant to me thy love,
    to ease my troubled heart.

Then let me a writing have, quoth he,
    from your owne hand with speed,
That I may marry my sweet-heart
    when I have done this deed.

The old man he did give consent
    that he these things should have,
Thinking that it had bin his Neece
    that did this bargaine crave;

And unto Robin then quoth he,
    my gentle N[eece, behold,
Goe thou into [thy chamber soone,
    and I 'le goe [bring the gold.

When he into [the chamber came,
    thinking in[deed to play,
Straight Robin [upon him doth fall,
    and carries h[im away

Into the chamb[er where the two
    faire Lovers [did abide,
And gives to th[em their Unkle old,
    I, and the g[old beside.

The old man [vainly Robin sought,
    so man[y shapes he tries;
Someti[mes he was a hare or hound,
    som[etimes like bird he flies.

The [more he strove the less he sped,
    Th[e Lovers all did see;
And [thus did Robin favour them
    Full [kind and merrilie.

Thus Robin lived a merry life
    as any could enjoy,
'Mong country farms he did resort,
    and oft would folks annoy:

But if the maids doe call to him,
    he still away will goe
In knavish sort, and to himselfe
    he'd laugh out hoe, hoe, hoe!

He oft would beg and crave an almes,
    but take nought that they'd give;
In severall shapes he'd gull the world,
    thus madly did he live.

Sometimes a cripple he would seeme,
  sometimes a souldier brave :
Sometimes a fox, sometimes a hare ;
  brave pastimes would he have.

Sometimes an owle he'd seeme to be,
  sometimes a skipping frog ;
Sometimes a kirne, in Irish shape,
  to leape ore mire or bog :

Sometime he'd counterfeit a voyce,
  and travellers call astray,
Sometimes a walking fire he'd be,
  and lead them from their way.

Some call him Robin Good-fellow,
  Hob goblin, or mad Crisp,
And some againe doe tearme him oft
  by name of Will the Wispe :

But call him by what name you list,
  I have studied on my pillow,
I think the best name he deserves
  is Robin the Good Fellow.

At last upon a summer's night
  King Oberon found him out,
And with his Elves in dancing wise
  straight circled him about.

The Fairies danc't, and little Tom Thumb
  on his bag-pipe did play,
And thus they danc't their fairy round
  till almost break of day.

Then Phebus he most gloriously
  begins to grace the aire,
When Oberon with his fairy traine
  begins to make repaire,

With speed unto the Fairy land,
  They swiftly tooke their way,*

* Cf. M. N. D. Act iv. Sc. 1.

  " Then, my queen, in silence sad,
  Trip we after the night's shade :
  We the globe can compass soon,
  Swifter than the wandering moon."

And I out of my dreame awak't,
  and so 'twas perfect day.

Thus having told my dreame at full,
  I 'le bid you all farewell.
If you applaud mad Robin's prankes,
  may be ere long I 'le tell

Some other stories to your eares,
  which shall contentment give:
To gaine your favours I will seeke
  the longest day I live.

If our readers will permit us to call their attention
to the following passage, spoken by Puck, after he
had effected the transformation of Bottom, its similarity with part of the foregoing ballad will be at
once perceived :—

" I'll follow you, I'll lead you about a round,
  Through bog, through bush, through brake, through brier;
Sometime a horse I'll be, sometimes a hound,
  A hog, a headless bear, sometimes a fire;
And neigh, and bark, and grunt, and roar, and burn,
Like horse, hound, hog, bear, fire, at every turn."

So also in the ballad of Robin Goodfellow, printed
by Percy, we have the following similar account of
Robin's exploits :—

" Sometimes I meete them like a man;
  Sometimes an ox, sometimes an hound;
And to a horse I turn me can;
  And trip and trot about them round;
      But if to ride,
      My backe they stride,
  More swift than winde away I go,
      O'er hedge and lands,
      Thro' pools and ponds,
  A whirry, laughing, ho, ho, hoe!"

The name of Robin Goodfellow had, it appears,
been familiar to the English as early as the thirteenth

century, being mentioned in a tale preserved in a
manuscript of that date in the Bodleian Library at
Oxford.   It does not, however, fall in with our plan
to enter into any antiquarian discussion on the subject, but we take the opportunity of referring to
this singular fact because it affords one proof, and
that a remarkable one, of the antiquity of fairy mythology in this country of a similar nature to that
used by Shakespeare.

In the library of Lord Francis Egerton is preserved
a very curious tract, printed at London in 1628, containing a prose history of the *merry prankes* of the
same mischievous spirit, intermixed with poetry.
We have not been able to obtain a sight of this
rarity, which is supposed to be unique, but Mr. Collier has given a description of it in his catalogue of
the Bridgewater Library, and another account of it
may be found in Beloe's Anecdotes.   We suspect
that some of the metrical portions of this book are of
much earlier date, and it is possible that the following verses may be the originals of the exquisitely
beautiful Anacreontic lines spoken by Puck at the
end of the play.   We cannot, however, discover the
precise date of their composition :—

> " The moone shines faire and bright,
>   And the owle hollows :
> Mortals now take their rests
>   Upon their pillows :
> The bats abroad likewise,
>   And the night raven,
> Which doth use for to call
>   Men to death's haven.
> Now the mice peep abroad,
>   And the cats take them :
> Now doe young wenches sleepe,
>   Till their dreams wake them."

The ideas are not only similar to those of Shakespeare, but follow in precisely the same order.   But
the beautiful lines to which we have referred cannot
be too often repeated, and our conjecture will be
strengthened by a close comparison :—

> " Now the hungry lion roars,
>   And the wolf behowls the moon ;
> Whilst the heavy ploughman snores,
>   All with weary task fordone.
> Now the wasted brands do glow,
>   Whilst the scritch-owl, scritching loud,
> Puts the wretch, that lies in woe,
>   In remembrance of a shroud.
> Now it is the time of night
>   That the graves, all gaping wide,
> Every one lets forth his sprite,
>   In the churchway paths to glide :
> And we fairies, that do run
>   By the triple Hecate's team,
> From the presence of the sun,
>   Following darkness like a dream,
> Now are frolic : not a mouse
> Shall disturb this hallow'd house :
> I am sent with broom before,
> To sweep the dust behind the door."

Some similarity may also be traced between this
and the following invocation of a spirit by a very
celebrated magician.   It is taken from *The famous
history of Fryer Bacon,* edited by Mr. Thoms,
p. 44 :—

> " Now the owle is flowne abroad,
> For I heare the croaking toade,
> And the bat that shuns the day,
> Through the darke doth make her way.
> Now the ghosts of men doe rise,
> And with fearful hideous cryes,
> Seek revengement from the good
> On their heads that spilt their blood.
> Come some spirit, quicke I say,

> Night's the Devil's holyday :
> Where'ere you be, in dennes, or lake,
> In the ivy, ewe, or brake :
> Quickly come and me attend,
> That am Bacon's man and friend.
> But I will have you take no shape
> Of a bear, a horse, or ape :
> Nor will I have you terrible,
> And therefore come invisible."

Poole, in the second part of *The English Parnassus*,* has collected together several poems on the fairies, including also extracts from the Midsummer Night's Dream. "Oberon's Feast," by Herrick, appears to have been one of the most popular of poems of this nature, and others by the same writer may be found in the *Hesperides*. We prefer selecting as a specimen one which is not so generally known : it was written by Sir Simon Steward, and published in the *Musarum Deliciæ, or the Muses Recreation*, 12mo. Lond. 1656 :—

> " When the monthly horned Queen
> Grew jealous, that the stars had seen
> Her rising from Endimions armes,
> In rage, she throws her misty charmes
> Into the bosome of the night,
> To dim their curious prying light.
> Then did the dwarfish faery elves
> (Having first attir'd themselves)
> Prepare to dresse their Oberon king

---

* This was a posthumous production. The author was educated at Clare Hall, Cambridge, and a portion of the original manuscript of the work we have quoted above is still preserved in the British Museum, MS. Hargrave, 205. It may be added, that Steward's poem has been printed by Dr. Bliss, from MS. Rawl. Poet. 147, in his *Bibliographical Miscellanies*, and other MS. copies of it are in MS. Malone, 17, MS. Ashm. 38, &c. Herrick's poems on fairies are also frequently found in contemporary manuscripts.

In highest robes for revelling.
In a cobwed shirt, more thin
Then ever spider since could spin,
Bleach'd by the whitenesse of the snow,
As the stormy windes did blow
It in the vast and freezing aire;
No shirt halfe so fine, so faire.

A rich wastcoat they did bring,
Made of the trout-flies gilded wing,
At that his elveship 'gan to fret,
Swearing it would make him sweat,
Even with its weight, and needs would wear
His wastcoat wove of downy haire,
New shaven from an Eunuch's chin;
That pleas'd him well, 'twas wondrous thin.

The outside of his doublet was
Made of the four-leav'd true-love grasse,
On which was set so fine a glosse,
By the oyle of crispy mosse;
That through a mist, and starry light,
It made a rainbow every night.
On every seam, there was a lace
Drawn by the unctuous snailes slow trace;
To it, the purest silver thread
Compar'd, did look like dull pale lead.

Each button was a sparkling eye
Ta'ne from the speckled adders frye,
Which in a gloomy night, and dark,
Twinckled like a fiery spark:
And, for coolnesse, next his skin,
'Twas with white poppy lin'd within.

His breeches of that fleece were wrought,
Which from Colchos Jason brought;
Spun into so fine a yarne,
That mortals might it not discerne;
Wove by Arachne, in her loom,
Just before she had her doom;
Dy'd crimson with a maiden's blush,
And lyn'd with dandelyon push.

A rich mantle he did wear
Made of tinsel gossamere,
Be-starred over with a few
Dyamond drops of morning dew.

His cap was all of ladies love,
So passing light, that it did move,
If any humming gnat or fly
But buzz'd the ayre, in passing by;

About it was a wreath of pearle,
Drop'd from the eyes of some poor girle
Pinch'd, because she had forgot
To leave faire water in the pot.
And for feather, he did weare
Old Nisus fatall purple haire.
    The sword they girded on his thigh
Was smallest blade of finest rye.
    A paire of buskins they did bring
Of the cow-ladyes corall wing ;
Powder'd o're with spots of jet,
And lin'd with purple-violet.
    His belt was made of mirtle leaves,
Plaited in small curious threaves,
Beset with amber cowslip studds,
And fring'd about with daizy budds ;
In which his bugle horne was hung,
Made of the babbling eccho's tongue ;
Which set unto his moon-burn'd lip,
He windes, and then his faeries skip :
At that, the lazy dawn 'gan sound,
And each did trip a faery round."

The manuscript, No. 36, 37, in the Ashmolean
Museum at Oxford, contains a fairy song which does
not appear to have been printed. We take the
opportunity of inserting it here, the more especially
as such pieces are not very often met with :—

" I spied Kinge Oberon and his beuteous Queene,
    Attended by a nimble footed trayne
Of fayeryes trippinge ore the medows greene,
    And to meewards (methought) they came amayne.
    I coucht myselfe behinde a bushe to spye,
    What would betide the noble company.

" It gann to rayne, the Kinge and Queene they runne
    Under a mushroom fretted over head,
With glowormes artificially donne,
    Resemblinge much the canopy of a bedd.
    Of cloth, of silver, and such glimmeringe light
    It gave, as stars doe in a frosty night.

" The Kinge perceivinge it grew night apace,
    And that faint light was but for show alone,

Out of a box made of a fayre topace,
    Hee toke a blasinge carbuncle that showne
        Like to a flameinge barre of iron, and
        Stucke it among the glowormes with his hand.

" Like as the sunne darts forth his ruddy beames,
    Unable longer to hold up his head,
Glaunceinge his gloateinge eye upon the streames,
    Such was the lustre that this mixture bredd,
        So light it was that one might plainely see,
        What was donne under that rich canopy.

" The floore whereon they trode, it was of jett
    And mother of pearle, pollished and cutt,
Chequerd, and in most decent order sett,
    A table dyamond was theire table, butt
        To see th' reflection from the roofe to the table,
        'Twas choyce meethought and shewed admirable.

" Like to a heaven directly was that table,
    And these bright wormes they doe resemble starres,
That precious carbunckle soe invaluable,
    Lookt like a meteor with his ominous barres
        Hung out in heaven by th' allseeinge eye,
        Bidd us expect to heare a tragedye.

" Soe this great light appeard amongst the rest.
    But now it grew towards suppertyme apace,
And for to furnish out this suddaine feast,
    The servitours, who knew each one his place,
        Disperse themselves immediately, and
        Some find the choycest dayntyes on the land.

" Others dive downe to th' bottome of the deepe ;
    Another mounts up to the lofty skye,
To fetch downe hony dew of mowntaynes steepe—
    In every corner doe they serch and pry,
        Who can the best accepted present bringe,
        To please theire soe much honoured Queene and Kinge.

" One gathers grapes ripe from the lusty vine,
    And with his little hands hee squeazeth out
The juce, and then presents it up for wine ;
    And straight theire presses in among the rowt
        Another loaden with an eare of wheate,
        The whitest and the fairest hee cann gett."

We have been favoured by a friend with the following copy of the title-page of a little volume, which would doubtlessly afford some illustration of this subject,* but we have not been able to see a copy ;—" A description of the King and Queene of Fayries, their habit, fare, abode, pompe, and state, being very delightful to the sense, and full of mirth. London, printed for Richard Harper, and are to be sold at his shop at the Hospital Gate, 1635."

Mr. Thorpe, of Piccadilly, possesses an old printed ballad, entitled *The King and Queen of Fairie*, in Latin and English, commencing thus—

> " Upon a time the fairy elves,
> Having first arrayed themselves,
> Thought it meet to cloath their King,
> In robes most fit for revelling."

If we have said too much on the subject of these aerial beings, we trust that the pardon of our readers will be extended to us ; for although the minutiæ of the inhabitants of the mushroom world may be too trivial to interest some, yet it ought to be remembered that

---

* Perhaps one of the most popular fairy songs is that printed by Percy and others, commencing—

> " Come, follow, follow me," &c.

This was sung to the tune of *The Spanish Gypsie*, which began very similarly :—

> " O follow, follow me,
> For we be gipsies three."

The tune is, we are told, to be found in the *English Dancing Master*, 1651. See Thorpe's Catalogue of Manuscripts for 1831, p. 114.

" Another sort there be, that will
Be talking of the fairies still,
Nor never can they have their fill,
    As they were wedded to them :
No tales of them their thirst can slake,
So much delight therein they take,
And some strange thing they fain would make
    Knew they the way to do them."

So much for the Fairies.

CHAPTER V.

" Is there no play,
To ease the anguish of a torturing hour?"

WE agree with Mr. Heraud in his opinion, that the alleged unfitness of the Midsummer Night's Dream for representation on the stage is founded on incorrect data. In fact, the success that has attended its recent production at Covent Garden Theatre entirely controverts Mr. Knight's assertion, that " this play, with all its harmony of dramatic arrangement, is not for the stage—at least, for the modern stage."

It must, however, be admitted, that for a length of time the revivals of this drama have not been by any means eminently successful; but to attribute this to the play itself being too etherially poetic for the stage, is, we conceive, adopting too hasty a conclusion. " There is no drama," observes Mr. Heraud, " but what is so strictly considered;" and does not the poet himself say—" The best in this kind are but shadows ; and the worst are no worse if

our imagination amend them." It is most probable, that the extreme difficulty of personating
the characters of Oberon and the four lovers with
advantage, and of procuring, at the same time, actors
fitted by their peculiar talents for those parts, are the
principal causes of failure. Even in the present
unrivalled cast of the play as performed at Covent
Garden Theatre, where Oberon is very charmingly
represented by Mrs. Charles Mathews, one of the
most distinguished actresses of our time; yet it is
no disparagement to say of the four who personate
the lovers, and who are all in excellent repute, that
only one is really fitted for the complete realization
of Shakespeare's ideas.*

We have few early notices of the representation of
A Midsummer Night's Dream. Mr. Collier, in his
elaborate work on the stage, has given us, from a
manuscript at Lambeth Palace, a very singular account of a play represented at the Bishop of Lincoln's house on the night of Sunday, September
27th, 1631. The piece chosen for this occasion
was the Midsummer Night's Dream, and it was got
up as a private amusement. Laud, however, exerted
his influence to punish this breach of the due observ-

* We will here give the cast of A Midsummer Night's Dream,
as revived at Covent Garden Theatre on the 16th November,
1840, which has already had a run of nearly sixty nights, nor
do the public yet appear to be tired of it. Theseus=Cooper;
Egeus=Diddear; Lysander=Vining; Demetrius=Brindal; Phi-
lostrate=Hemming; Quince=Bartley; Bottom=Harley; Flute
=Keeley; Snout=Meadows; Snug=F. Matthews; Starveling
=Payne; Hippolyta=Mrs. Brougham; Hermia=Mrs. Nisbett;
Helena=Miss Cooper; Oberon=Madame Vestris; Titania=
Mrs. Walter Lacy; Puck=Miss Marshall; First Fairy=Miss
Rainforth; Second Fairy=Miss Grant.

ance of the Sabbath ; and the following extraordinary order is extracted from a decree made by a self-
constituted court among the Puritans, for the censure
and punishment of offences of this nature :—

"Likewise wee doe order, that Mr. Wilson, because hee was a speciall plotter and contriver of this
business, and did in such a brutishe manner acte the
same with an asses head, and therefore hee shall, uppon Tuisday next, from six of the clocke in the morning till six of the clocke at night, sitt in the Porter's
Lodge at my Lords Bishopps House, with his feete
in the stocks, and attyred with his asse head, and a
bottle of hay sett before him, and this subscription
on his breast :—

> "Good people I have played the beast,
> And brought ill things to passe :
> I was a man, but thus have made
> Myselfe a silly asse."

Bottom appears to have been then considered the
most prominent character in the play ; and " the
merry conceited humors of Bottom the Weaver" were
extracted from the Midsummer Night's Dream, and
made into a farce or droll,* which was very frequently
played " on the sly," after the suppression of the
theatres. " When the publique theatres were shut
up," observes Kirkman, " and the actors forbidden
to present us with any of their tragedies, because
we had enough of that in ernest; and comedies,
because the vices of the age were too lively and
smartly represented ; then all that we could divert

---

* " The merry conceited humors of Bottom the Weaver, as it
hath been often publikely acted by some of his Majesties come-
dians, and lately privately presented by several apprentices for
their harmless recreation, with great applause," 4to. Lond. 1661.

ourselves with were these humours and pieces of plays, which passing under the name of a merry conceited fellow called Bottom the Weaver, Simpleton the Smith, John Swabber, or some such title, were only allowed us, and that but by stealth too, and under pretence of rope dancing and the like."*

The information which Pepys has given us relative to the representation of this play, on September 29th, 1662, is anything but satisfactory, and does not reflect much credit on the acting drama of the time. Here is his extraordinary opinion :†—" To the King's Theatre, where we saw Midsummer Night's Dream, which I had never seen before, nor shall ever again, for it is the most insipid ridiculous play that ever I saw in my life." It was, perhaps, " too etherially poetic" for the gross mind of the eccentric secretary.

In the year 1692 the Midsummer Night's Dream was changed into an opera under the title of *The Fairy Queen*, and performed at Dorset Garden. This alteration was printed at London the same year, and was produced on a very splendid scale. " In ornament," says Downes, " it was superior, especially in cloaths, for all the singers and dancers, scenes, machines and decorations, all most profusely set off and excellently performed, chiefly the instrumental and vocal part composed by Mr. Purcel, and

---

* The Wits, 4to. Lond. 1673. A copy of this book is in the King's Library in the British Museum, and is an abridgement of Kirkman's *Wits, or Sport upon Sport*, 8vo. Lond. 1673. Both these contain *The humors of Bottom the Weaver*. It is said that Robert Cox, the player, was the person who adapted most of the pieces contained in *The Wits*.

† Diary, edited by Lord Braybrooke.

dances by Mr. Priest.   The court and town were
wonderfully satisfied with it; but the expenses in
setting it being so great, the company got very little
by it."

Richard Leveridge, in 1716, adapted from this
play *A Comick Masque of Pyramus and Thisbe,*
which was produced at the theatre in Lincoln's Inn
Fields.   It was printed at London the same year.

In 1755, Garrick produced, at Drury Lane, an
opera taken from the Midsummer Night's Dream,
under the title of *The Fairies.*   The parts of the
clowns were entirely omitted.   The following prologue, spoken by Garrick, may be interesting to
those who take delight in the history of our own
operatic performances :—

> " A moment stop your tuneful fingers, pray,
> While here, as usual, I my duty pay.
> Don't frown, my friends, (*to the band*) you soon shall
>   melt again ;
> But, if not there is felt each dying strain,
> Poor I shall speak and you will scrape in vain.
> To see me now you think the strangest thing !
> For, like friend Benedick, I cannot sing :
> Yet in this prologue, cry but you, Coraggio !
> I'll speak you both a jig, and an Adagio.
> A Persian king, as Persian Tales relate,
> Oft went disguised to hear the people prate ;
> So curious I sometimes steal forth, incog,
> To hear what critics croak of me—King Log.
> Three nights ago I heard a tête-a-tête
> Which fix'd, at once, our English opera's fate :
> One was a youth born here, but flush from Rome,
> The other born abroad, but here his home ;
> And first the English foreigner began,
> Who thus address'd the foreign Englishman :
> An English opera ! 'tis not to be borne ;
> I both my country and their music scorn,
> Oh, damn their Ally Croakers and their Early Horn.
> *Signor si—bat sons—wors recitativo :*
> *Il tutto, è bestiale e cativo,*

E

This said, I made my exit, full of terrors!
And now ask mercy for the following errors:
    Excuse us first, for foolishly supposing
Your countryman could please you in composing;
An op'ra too! play'd by an English band,
Wrote in a language which you understand;
I dare not say who wrote it; I could tell ye,
To soften matters, Signor Shakespearelli:
This awkward drama (I confess th' offence)
Is guilty too of poetry and sense:
And then the price we take—you'll all abuse it,
So low, so unlike op'ras—but excuse it,
We'll mend that fault whenever you shall choose it.
Our last mischance, and worse than all the rest,
Which turns the whole performance to a jest,
Our singers all are well, and all will do their best.
But why would this rash fool, this Englishman,
Attempt an op'ra?—'tis the strangest plan!
    Struck with the wonders of his master's art,
Whose sacred dramas shake and melt the heart,
Whose heaven-born strains the coldest breast inspire,
Whose chorus-thunder sets the soul on fire!
Inflamed, astonish'd! at those magic airs,
When Samson groans, and frantic Saul despairs.
The pupil wrote—his work is now before ye,
And waits your stamp of infamy or glory!
Yet, ere his errors and his faults are known,
He says, those faults, those errors, are his own;
If through the clouds appear some glimm'ring rays,
They're sparks he caught from his great Master's blaze!"

The music in this opera was composed by Smith, and contemporary journals speak of it in the highest terms.

Garrick again produced the Midsummer Night's Dream at Drury Lane on Wednesday, November 23rd, 1763. The interlude was restored; but it was very coldly received by a limited audience, and only acted once. The St. James's Chronicle, in a critique on this revival, describes it as " an odd romantic performance, more like a masque than a play, and presenting a lively picture of the ungoverned imagination of that great poet." It was then cut down to an afterpiece by Colman, under the title of *A Fairy Tale*, the supernatural characters being alone retained, and produced in that form on November 26th, when it met with rather better success.

Colman's alteration was again produced at the Haymarket Theatre on July 18th, 1777, with some songs added from Garrick's version. The Fairy Prince, also, acted at Covent Garden Theatre in 1771, contains a few lines taken from this play.

In 1816 another alteration of this play, in three acts, by Reynolds, was produced at Covent Garden Theatre on the 17th of January. In this revival, the part of Bottom was undertaken by Liston, Quince by Emery, Hermia by Miss Stephens, and Helena by Miss Foote. The music was by Bishop, and the journals agree that the piece was " got up" in a most magnificent style. It was played about twenty nights, but cannot be said to have been very successful.

But all these representations of the Midsummer Night's Dream must give place to its recent revival at Covent Garden Theatre. Every thing that fine taste, a most liberal management, and an excellent cast could accomplish, have been called into action ; and its success must have equalled the most sanguine expectations of the projectors. The alterations from the original version of the play are few, and made with that good judgment which characterizes every thing that Mr. Planché undertakes. We would, however, suggest that the omission which is made of a portion of Hermia's speech, when she loses Lysander, destroys the climax, and causes the whole to fall languidly on the ear ; it is better as it is in the original :—

" Lysander! what, remov'd? Lysander, lord!
What, out of hearing, gone? No sound, no word!
Alack, where are you? speak, and if you hear;
Speak, of all loves; I swoon almost with fear.
No? then I well perceive you are not nigh:
Either death or you I'll find immediately."

We would also ask how Theseus, unassisted by
the Prologue's description of the dumb show, which
Mr. Planché has omitted, can recognize the representation of moonshine? We are afraid that few of
us possess so penetrating a vision ; but perhaps the
heroes of old excelled the moderns in this as in other
attributes.

CHAPTER VI.

" Who first found out the man i' th' moon,
That to the ancients was unknown?"

ALTHOUGH the legend of the Man in the Moon
is perhaps one of the most singular and popular
superstitions known, yet we have been unable to discover early materials for a connected account of its
progress, nor have the researches of former writers
been extended to this curious subject.

It is very probable that the natural appearance of
the moon, and those delineations on its disc which
modern philosophers have considered to belong to
the geographical divisions of that body, may originally have suggested the similarity vulgarly supposed
to exist between these outlines and a man " pyc-
chynde stake." In fact, it is hardly possible to
account for the universality of the legend by any
other conjecture ; and it may perhaps be considered

a general rule, when a fable of this nature is found to be popular both at the same time and under similar forms, in countries widely separated from each other, that some natural phenomenon common to all places was the true origin of the myth. With regard to the legend now under consideration, we can do little more than furnish our readers with proofs of its existence at various periods, and beg them to form their own conclusions.

In a manuscript of the beginning of the fourteenth century, in the British Museum (MS. Harl. 2253) is preserved a very curious English poem on the Man in the Moon, probably of the thirteenth century. It has been printed by Ritson, but no apology is requisite for repeating so singular a document :—

> " Mon in the mone stond and strit,
>   On his bot forke is burthen he bereth,
> Hit is muche wonder that he na doun slyt,
>   For doute leste he valle he shoddreth ant shereth.
> When the forst freseth muche chele he byd,
>   The thornes beth kene is hattren to-tereth ;
> Nis no wytht in the world that wot wen he syt,
>   Ne, bote hit bue the hegge, whet wedes he wereth.
>
> " Whider trowe this mon ha the wey take,
>   He hath set is o fot is other to-foren,
> For non hithte that he hath ne sytht me hym ner shake,
>   He is the sloweste mon that ever wes y-boren.
> Wher he were o the feld pycchynde stake,
>   For hope of ys thornes to dutten is doren,
> He mot myd is twybyl other trous make,
>   Other al is dayes werk ther were y-loren.
>
> " This ilke mon upon heh when er he were,
>   Wher he were y the mone boren ant y-fed,
> He leneth on is forke ase a grey frere,
>   This crokede caynard sore he is adred.
> Hit is mony day go that he was here,
>   Ichot of is ernde he nath nout y-sped,
> He hath hewe sumwher a burthen of brere,
>   Therefore sum hayward hath taken ys wed.

> " ȝef thy wed ys y-take bring hom the trous,
>   Sete forth thyn other fot, stryd over sty,
> We shule preye the haywart hom to ur hous,
>   Ant maken hym at heyse for the maystry;
> Drynke to hym deorly of fol god bous,
>   Ant oure dame douse shal sitten hym by,
> When that he is dronke ase a dreynt mous,
>   Thenne we shule borewe the wed ate bayly.
>
> " This mon hereth me nout, thah ich to hym crye,
>   Ichot the cherl is def, the del hym to-drawe,
> Thah ich ȝeȝe upon heth nulle nout hye,
>   The lostlase ladde con nout o lawe.
> Hupe forth, Hubert, hosede pye,
>   Ichot thart a-marstled into the mawe;
> Thah me teone with hym that myn teh mye,
>   The cherld nul nout adoun er the day dawe."

Grimm (Deutsche Mythologie, p. 412,) informs us that there are three legends connected with the Man in the Moon; the first, that this personage was Isaac carrying a bundle of sticks for his own sacrifice; the second, that he was Cain; and the other, which is taken from the history of the sabbath-breaker, as related in the Book of Numbers. In the poem, entitled *The Testament of Creseide*, printed in Chaucer's works, there is an allusion to the same legend :—

> " Next after him come lady Cynthia,
>   The laste of al, and swiftest in her sphere,
> Of colour blake, buskid with hornis twa,
>   And in the night she listith best t' apere,
>   Hawe as the leed, of colour nothing clere,
>   For al the light she borowed at her brother
>   Titan, for of herselfe she hath non other.
>
> " Her gite was gray and ful of spottis blake,
>   And on her brest a chorle painted ful even,
> Bering a bushe of thornis on his bake,
>   Whiche for his theft might clime no ner the heven."

We have been favoured by a friend with the following copy of the first stanza of a traditional Somersetshire song, which curiously illustrates the

popularity of the Man in the Moon, but unfortunately he cannot recollect any more of it :—

> " The man in the moon drinks claret,
> But he is a dull Jack-a-Dandy,
> Would he know a sheep's head from a carrot,
> He should learn to drink cyder and brandy."

Another old ballad commences in the same manner :

> " The man in the moon drinks claret,
> With powder-beef, turnip, and carrot."

And Ashmole (MS. Ashm. 36, 37,) has even had
the audacity to make a pun upon this mighty individual :—

> " Tis strange! yet true : He's but a month-old man,
> And yet hath liv'd ere since the world began."

From this it would appear that the legend itself
had been lost sight of before Ashmole's time.

Gryph, in his *Absurda Comica*, entitled *Herr
Peter Squentz*,* has copied Shakespeare's idea of in-
troducing a person to represent Moonshine. Other
characters in the same play are also taken from
Shakespeare. Bully Bottom is transformed to
" Meister Bulla Butäin," and he plays " die wand."
Peter Squentz, or Peter Quince, refers at once to
Ovid's Metamorphoses :—

> " *Kr.* Was wollen wir aber vor eine tröstliche *Comædi* tragiren?
> *Sq.* Von Piramus und Thisbe.
> *Kl.* Das- ist übermassen trefflich, man Kan allerhand schöne
> Lehre Trost und Vermahnung draus nehmen, aber das ärgeste
> ist, ich weisz die Historie noch nicht, geliebt es nicht E. Herrlig-
> keit dieselbte zu erzehlen.

---

* Teutsche Gedichte, 8vo. Bres. und Leip. 1698, p. 718-752.

Sq. Gar gerne. Der heil. alte Kirchen-Lehrer *Ovidius* schreibet in seinem schönen Buch *Memorium phosis*, das Piramus die Thisbe zu einem Brunnen bestellet habe, inmittelst sey ein abscheulicher häszlicher Löwe Kommen, vor welchem sie aus Furcht entlauffen, und ihren Mantel hinterlassen, darauf der Löwe Jungen ausgehecket; als er aber weggegangen, findet Piramus die blutige Schaube, und meinet der Löwe habe Thisben gefressen, darum ersticht er sich aus Verzweiffelung, Thisbe Kommet wieder und findet Piramum todt, derowegen ersticht sie sich ihm zu Trotz.

Pick. Und stirbet?

Sq. Und stirbet.

Pick. Das ist tröstlich, es wird ubermassen schön zu sehen seyn : aber saget Herr Peter Squentz? Hat der Löwe auch viel zu reden?

Sq. Nein, der Löwe musz nur brüllen.

Pick. Ey so wil ich der Löwe seyn, denn ich lerne nicht gerne viel auswendig.

Sq. Ey nein! Monsieur Pickelhäring musz ein Hauptperson *agiren.*

Pick. Habe ich denn Kopffs genug zu einer Hauptperson.

Sq. Ja freylich. Weil aber vornehmlich ein tapfferer ernsthaffter nud ansehnlicher Mann erfordert wird zum *Prologo* und *Epilogo*, so will ich dieselbe auff mich nehmen, und der Vorreder und Nachreder des Spieles, das ist, Anfang und das Ende seyn."

It will be remembered that Quince remarks that Pyramus and Thisbe, " as the story goes, did meet by moonlight." Gryph puts the same into the mouth of Herr Peter Squentz, with another allusion to Ovid's *Metamorphoses,* or, as Squenk miscalls it, *Memorium phosis.* A calendar is then referred to, and the same ingenious methods of solving the difficulty proposed, as in Shakespeare's Midsummer Night's Dream. In fact Gryph's *Herr Peter Squentz* is a paraphrastical translation of the comic portions of Shakespeare's drama. But to return to our subject.

Throughout Germany the legend agrees with that given above, and our version of it was probably derived from that quarter. Hebel gives us, in his Alemannic Poems, a metrical account of the " Mann in Mond," in form of dialogue between a mother and her child.

The Italians of the thirteenth century imagined the Man in Moon to be Cain, who is going to sacrifice to the Lord, thorns—the most wretched production of the ground. Dante refers to this in the twentieth canto of the Inferno :—

> " chè già tiene 'l confine
> D'amenduo gli emisperi, e tocca l'onda
> Sotto Sibilia, Caino e le spine."

One of our English nursery rhymes is pertinent to this subject, and is, we believe, the only authority to be found for an actual journey having been undertaken by this eccentric and solitary inhabitant of a lunatic asylum, to visit the beings of this sublunary world :—

> " The man in the moon
> Came tumbling down,
> And asked his way to Norwich.
> He went by the south,
> And burnt his mouth,
> With supping hot pease porridge."

From Manningham's Diary* we learn that among the " devises" at Whitehall, in 1601, was " the man in the ꝑmoone with thornes on his backe, looking downeward." Middleton also refers to this mythological personage,—" as soon as he comes down, and the bush left at his back, Ralph is the dog behind him." Shakespeare mentions the dog; and in the interlude, the person who represents Moonshine is actually accompanied by a bush of thornes, a lantern, and a dog. It is possible that the hare, which animal is in the east considered to be the emblem of the

---

* MS. Harl. 5353.   See Hunter on the Tempest, p. 69.

moon's divinity, may have been in the middle ages
intermingled with the European legend. The *Hee-*
topades * contains the following allusion to this belief:—" Then I will declare what are the commands
of the God Chandra. He bade me say, that in
driving away and destroying the hares who are appointed to guard the fountain which is consecrated
to that deity, you have done ill; for, said he, they
are my guards, and it is notorious that a figure of a
hare is my emblem."

Daniel O'Rourke, a famous Irish tippler, chroni-
cled in Croker's Fairy Legends, is said to have had
a brief but very unsatisfactory interview with this
same inhabitant of the moon. " Out there walks—
who do you think but the man in the moon himself?
I knew him by his bush." It is to be regretted that
Daniel has not furnished us with a more accurate
account of his habiliments.

---

* Wilkins, in his translation of this book, interprets the animal
mentioned to be a rabbit.   We think that the original word more
properly signifies *a hare.*

CHAPTER VII.

" Give it an understanding."

IN the 5th Act, Philostrate produces a list of the various amusements which had been proffered by the people of Athens, for Theseus to wear away the " long age of three hours, between his after-supper and bed-time." The exact meaning of one of these has never been satisfactorily explained :—

> " The thrice three Muses mourning for the death
> Of learning, late deceased in beggary."

Theseus rejects this, and adds—

> " That is some satire, keen and critical,
> Not sorting with the nuptial ceremony."

Now, it will be remembered that out of the four " sports which are rife," three of them certainly refer to a period and action consistent with the nature of the plot. We have

> " The battle with the Centaurs, to be sung,
> By an Athenian eunuch, to the harp."

Next in order,

> " The riot of the tipsy bacchanals,
> Tearing the Thracian singer in their rage."

And lastly,

> " A tedious brief scene of young Pyramus,
> And his love Thisbe : very tragical mirth."

It is probable that the two lines we have given
above were either inserted after the play itself was
written, or that the poet merely makes a general
allusion to the low state of literature at the time;
and this supposition accords sufficiently with Shakespeare's usual practice. For instance, as we have
before mentioned, he evidently alludes, nearly at the
beginning of the play, to the state of the weather in
the year 1594; but this description is not at all
incompatible with the circumstances of his drama.
Now we think that a particular allusion to some real
person and some real death has this difficulty. Theseus rejects one " sport,"

> " In glory of my kinsman Hercules."

and another, because it was

> " an old device; and it was play'd
> When I from Thebes came last a conqueror."

Is it reasonable to suppose that at the same time
Shakespeare wrote the above lines, he would have
considered it at all consistent to introduce a personal
allusion to any of his own contemporaries? For, it
must be remembered, such an allusion evidently
could not apply also to the period of Theseus. If
any allusion be intended, we think it must be general; and Daniel, in the *Cleopatra*, printed in 1594,
complains sadly of the " barbarism" of the time.
Perhaps, however, the plague of 1593 may have
simultaneously destroyed learning and some of its
professors.

Some have considered the lines in question to relate to the death of Spenser. If so, they must have
been inserted immediately before the first publication

of the play, in 1600, for Spenser died sometime in
the year 1599. Although we do not think that this
conjecture is supported by much probability, yet we
are glad of the opportunity to insert another extract
from Lane's *Triton's Trumpet*, because it not only
contains an interesting allusion to Spenser's death,
but also mentions other English poets :—

" Madam, quoth hee, I chaunced this Aprill springe
Survaienge manie coasts on wanderinge winge,
To see a sight, did please mee to the hart,
In which I deeme yourselfe ought beare a part :
The sight was somptuous, buildings, ample hie,
Vauncinge magnificence, and maiestie,
Trophies also, which hope fullie maie breede,
As well good mindes, as greate mindes of suche seede :
Intendinge bewteous schooles for sacred learninge,
To everie one ingenious of dicerninge :
Onlie there wants to fullfill speculation,
Vnto the muses duteous conservation,
Woold but your Ladieshipp in lovinge gree !
Leave this hott zone, and com along with mee !
   Whither quoth shee? to England Danus said.
To England ! quoth shee, no : that place me traidd,
Sithe none theare loves mee ; which I knowe by proofe,
Yon they from my deere Spencer stood alooff,
When verbale drones of virtuous merit scant
Suffred that gentile poet die of want :
One onlie knowinge generositie,
And findinge he woold crave for modestie,
Him sent in greatest sicknes, crownes good store,
So Robert Essex did (honors decore)
Nathles of pininge griefe, and wantes decaie,
Hee much thoncke that slowt Earle, that thus gann saie,
The medcine comes too late to the pacient,
Tho died.   And so shoold I, yf thither went !
   Alas ! was that his ende ? quoth Danus tho,
I pittie him, yet theareof this I kno,
Hee had on him bestowd a funeral,
After the rites of Laureat coronal.
   At that Vipoda laughd, naie swore these strive
To dandle poets dead, yet leave alive.
Ne had that cost vppon him binn imploid,
But for my lovinge frend Lodovick Lloyd.

Yet lett that passe! sithe I do love force none,
Ne crave of right annothers, but mine own:
Ha, yet they saie, that folke binn chaunged quite
Fro mental thewes to Mammons appetite.
Avaunt! for wheare I see one that waie bend,
Of him I never meane to make my frend.
  O but, quoth Danus, Madam, yet are theare
Some able, active, valient, stowt, austeare:
Besides, amongst them, theare bee some good witts,
So farr as drincking, wenchinge, eake permitts!
Yet graunt I touchinge them, that they of late,
Have lost theire Father's footestepps in their gate.
Natheless I hope well of theire generous,
They wil bee to us like th' old gratious,
And by November's mirror elevate,
Correct own faultes, which they in others hate.
  On that condicion, quoth shee, I will wend,
To chalke how they which after come may mend.
  Full glad was Danus when hee heard her yeild,
Tho proffred him hert, beare ore sea, and feild.
Just as herselfe, her owne course vp shoold steare,
And safelie woold her ferrie anie wheare:
Nowe, as shee shoold be pleasd to name the place,
His winges shoeld fetch yt vp in litle space.
  Tho uppon Danus back Vipoio sitts,
Bowt whome with golden girdle a knott he knitts,
And shee fast holding his forelock up they flewe,
So for a while, bidds Amara adiewe.
But Danus, quoth shee, rowz up all your might!
For wee from hence, must take a weerie flight.
Now when the wind had opened Danus winges,
And all his plumage spred, aloft hee flinges,
Wheare fruishinge foorth his aierie pineond quills,
Delightfullie, through Auraes bosom thrills.
But in the midle region soringe, viewd,
What of each innovation greene ensewd.
The peacefull plaines shee sawe with sweete delight,
The troublous seas eake under came her sight,
Th' ambitious projects mountinge up to skye,
The stench of everie pollute misterie,
All which shee lawghd, in that herselfe was heere,
And bought not of theire wares at handes so deere.
Danus, quoth shee, the queene of love they saie,
Borne on a wave, at Venice first did swaie,
Thence must I fetch a retort glasse full bright,
Th' engredientes ceremonial to indight.
Tho soone they crossd the Medeterranean,

Next th' Adriatick : then the Gulf did span,
Wheare Danus, like a sodaine stoopinge kite,
Up snaught a Venice glasse in surging flight.
Thence, steerd to Rochel for some savorie salt,
Thence crossd to Greece, which did fore criple halt,
Hence to the promontorie Helicon,
From whose greene ribbes cleere Hippocrane rann :
The silver veines whereaof in glasse shee putt,
The which for England, prisoned close gann shutt,
Thence to England wheare snaught water of the rose,
Muske, civet, amber, also did inclose;
That donn, shee Danus higher bidds convaie her,
Into the fierie region, bove all aier,
Wheare flame invisible aie dwells simplie pure,
Discreete, swifte, meeke, of incorrupted powr :
With purest flame, Vipoiaes lillie hand,
Thrice three times fill'd, enshrind in cristal band,
For hott Balneo Mariæ made to ascent,
In which old Helicon's new font shee pent.
    Now when Vipoiaes cominge well was known,
And ore all Englandes easterne sea coast flown,
The Ladie Cantabrigia speedelie,
And all her learn'd with greate solemnitie,
Went gravelie dight to entertaine the Dame,
They muchlie lov'd, and honor'd in her name :
To grace whome, Titan flunge his night-gown off,
Havinge his candel burnt untill a snoff,
Now donn'd more glorious robes of maiestie,
And thenn ore spredd with golden canopie.
    Vipoio cladd in white, as winter's sno,
Sweete as sweete blossoms on mayes flourish groe,
Was of Dame Cantabrigia deerelie mett,
And greater honor'd, as b' her best witts fett,
Whose Laureate poesies fro' Apollo brought,
And in Minervaes finest samplers wrought,
Orestrewd the grownd, yea hunge each peopled streete :
But that each stranger mote both heere ! and seete !
The milke white swannes then strain'd in stile sublime,
Of ornate verse, rich prose, and nervous rime.
In short, to tellen all, doth not behove,
Wheare wellcome, sat weare powr'd in cuppe of love.
    Tho after complements wear overpast,
And everie colleage visited in haste,
Vipoio by that licence (call'd her own)
Of ancient privileage, as well is known,
And in the schooles archivis faire enrold,
Which hitherto by no man was controld,

Thus boldlie to Dame Cantabrigea sedd,
Her pupills her shooed waite alive and dead
In those schooles bredd : so sommond them to her !
To doe theire duties to theire visiter.
Don Lidgate ! noble Sidney ! Spencer diepe !
By her up call'd arose fro deadlie sleepe.
And Hugo Holland, whoe my lines did chide,
For hee ann ill-made verse could near abide.
Whoe comd, shee to Dame Cantabrigia thus,
Sister ! my sonnes and yee, shall wend with us,
Our sister deere Oxonia to behold,
Once in our lives before wee waxen old.
    Content with all myne hart, Cambrigia said,
And so what likd is, neare is longe delayd.
    Danus the pursevaunt first beare the newes,
Which made th' Oxoniens whett theire golden muse,
And quicklie done theire learn'd formalities :
The bringing reverence in theire steddfast eies,
Mustred poesies feilds of endlesse store,
Which soone declard theire treasures never poore.
Tho backe againe swift Danus to them flewe,
To ussher to the schooles this learned crewe.
But Oxon sheene with all her scholy gent,
Beyond th' east gate in goodlie order went.
Wheare when they sawe Vipoio bewteous,
They lowlie lowted her obsequious,
And sweetlie gann embrace (as well became
Theire quicke conceipts) before so rare a dame,
Whoe them accepts of ladie-like deport,
They takinge her swete favr in kindest sort.
The first thinge that shee did which long was wisht,
Shee caus'd that both those learned sisters kisse :
Whome linckinge arme in arme, and hand in hand,
Shee peremptorelie gave this command,
That neither of presum'd antiquitie,
Shoold hencefoorth challenge for prioritie !
But thus demonstrates in a three fold walke,
As they three in one front the walkes end stalke,
Shee, whoe the right hand had (as uppermost)
At theire next turne shoold chaunge for th' neathermoste.
But at next turne, each changd to eithers place,
Much like to th'ay dawnce, by which interlace,
Wittelie spedd, theire mutuall consent,
Inferior yielded saunce disparagement.
By which device, the sisters kinder twind,
And thereto trothe for aye, each other mind.
For which loves knott, Vipoto they invite

Of their magnific Macoasines take a sight!
Danus them ussheringe, so in they went,
Conducted by the bownteous President :
Whoe shewinge th' ample buildinges firme, faire hie,
Gave to demaund applause in everie eie.
  Vipoio tho, went to the faire quadrangle,
To reade what embleams kervers arts theare handle !
But first did Samforde call ! and Daniel fett !
Twoe sweetlie singinge swannes of Somerset !
Of all which embleames, that shee gann behold,
Wheare a younge man doth wrastel with an old.
Demaunds he Poetes what theareof befel !
But they had all forgott, or could not tell.
Wherefore shee th' poets idelnes did blame,
For not recordinge th' art so full of fame,
Which bears the prototype of soveraigntie
Of England over France in misterie :
Which thinge they feare, as thinges of prophecie,
Catch theire designe unwares yet certainelie.
  This English Burrel hight, a Cornish man,
To the late Henry th'eight a gardian,
Beinge in daringe yoath esteem'd so stronge
As that great Kinge, to trie his force did longe.
Whome Burrel spar'd because hee was the Kinge,
Ne (wrestlinge with him) woold not cast, or wringe ;
Which caus'd the Kinge thus saie, Burrel, I heard
That thow the strongest weart of all my gard ;
I doe not find yt so ; whereat some said,
Hee knowes it is the Kinge with whome hee plaid :
Ells mote yoe quicklie feele him verefie,
That this is Cornish Burrel certainlie.
So, at the next concert Kinge Henry feeles,
Burrel had strength, but not so many weeles.
Long after this, (Kinge Henry dead and gone)
And his brown daughter Marie in his throne,
And Burrel strooken old, yet of her gard,
And Philip weddinge her, becom her ward,
Hither hee brought a Frenchman, goodlie, younge,
Whoe in the feates of wrastlinge, prov'd so stronge
As foil'd, or cast downe all, or most her gard,
And no man fownd (as yet) coold him discard.
In so much that King Philip joid as much,
As Marie at her gards reproch did grutch.
Which urg'd old Burrel make a suite to her,
That he mote trie Kinge Philipes wrasteler.
   Ha, quod the Queene, thine age hath thee dispoild,
Ells I presume hee shoold not scape unfoild.

F

But when before the princes in they came,
In manner naked (as in thold embleame)
With baggs calld collers on theire showlders plact,
And to the concert either graplinge fast,
Old Burrel aged neere three score yeeres and tenn,
Rowzd his stiff jointes, and Cornish stratagem :
Wheare thus befell, that Burrel at the last,
Tore out the Frenches showlder blead, and cast,
So as the man was carried from the place,
Quite vanquish'd, whereof died in litle space.
Lo ! heere theire embleam in this monument,
The rest depends on future contingent.
  This storie by Vipoio thus reviv'd,
Which ells had by olivion binn depriv'd ;
Shee Danus willd to lead waie to Saint Maries,
Wheare oft thus chiden tu prævaricaris,
From thence hee ledd to the greate librarie,
Thence ore the schooles to the large gallerie.;
Which place at first invites her to content,
As solitarines in it was pent :
But soone that turn'd to this consideration,
That manie witts mote breed braines inundation,
Sith manie heads as manie senses breede,
As manie purposes as sowen seede,
Wheareof some good, some badd (lock'd in one cell)
Witts modells through theire visnomies to spell.
  The search shee made through the Vatican rowt,
For Lidgate ! Spencer ! Daniel ! quite left out,
Though so ringe on that high ideal spirit,
Which none of them send Germanists inherit :
Which urg'd her sweare, and confidentlie frett,
Never was Germaniste sownd poet yett,
Though Camden takes one plaienge Furæfar,
Prints twice as own, a poet of Exeter ;
Whence, shee the painters pensills did accuse,
Sith knewe not good to chouse, ne badd refuse :
Wherefore down flunge them (meere Pieridistes)
Void of ideal light, dull skulld Lanists,
But Chaucer shee bidds com down off his spheare !
And 'mongst the Laureat poets waite on her !"

Mr. Knight conjectures that Shakespeare alludes
to the death of Robert Greene, who deceased in
1592, in a condition that might truly be called beggary. There is much reason in this, although the

Midsummer Night's Dream was not written till two years afterwards; for in the year 1594 was published *Greene's Funeralls*, from which Mr. Collier quotes the following passage :—

" For judgement Jove, for *learning* deepe he still Apollo seemde;
For floent tongue, for eloquence, men Mercury him deemde ;
For curtesie suppose him Guy, or Guyons somewhat lesse.
His life and manners, though I would, I cannot halfe express :
  Nor mouth, nor minde, nor Muse can halfe declare,
  His life, his love, his laude, so excellent they were."

In the year 1594 was also published Greene's last work, written in conjunction with Thomas Lodge, entitled *The Looking Glass for London and England.* Chalmers has dwelt upon an animosity which is said to have existed between Lodge and Shakespeare : and, if this were the case, we may perhaps be justified in conjecturing that the " thrice three Muses" mourned, or rather were intended to mourn, on the last production of a famous writer which was wholly unworthy of his pen. The above-mentioned work is, indeed, very poor ; and, as far as Greene was concerned, the productions of his learning might then be truly said to be " late deceased in beggary." This conjecture will also bear out the apprehension of Theseus :—

" That is some satire, keen and critical,
Not sorting with the nuptial ceremony."

It is scarcely necessary to observe, that the term *critical* is here used in the sense of *censuring*.

CHAPTER VIII.

"Have me excused if I speak amiss;
My will is good."

" I CANNOT forbear," says Mr. Hunter, " to make
one or two remarks on editorial duties in general,
and particularly on such duties as applied to Shakespeare.   We see the value of the old copies, and the
wisdom of reading them, rather than the sophisticated
text which the modern editors have given us, if we
desire to know what Shakespeare really left to us.
They have, to be sure, some very strange corruptions ; but then the very strangeness and the gross-
ness work their own correction.   We see, at once,
that Shakespeare did not write what is set down for
him ; and we can often see at once what he did
write, through the same disguise; while the modern
editors, by the application of their principles, too
frequently lay suspicion asleep, giving us a text
which, without being very bad, is not so good as that
which this fine spirit had itself bequeathed to us.
It is quite manifest, therefore, that in any modern
edition, the old copies should form the basis of any
new text, to the entire exclusion, in the first instance,
of the text of Rowe, and I am sorry to add, of every
other editor who has yet followed him."

To these just remarks we have little to add.
Every one who has critically studied the text of
Shakespeare must be convinced of the truth of Mr.
Hunter's statement, and we are glad to fortify an

opinion, which we could wish were more generally adopted, by the authority of so distinguished a writer.   But we might with propriety proceed further, and say that no alteration from the original text of Shakespeare's plays is justifiable, unless it can be clearly proved that the typographical error which such an alteration must or ought necessarily to imply, could have been committed by the compositor of the time.   We are convinced that this is really the only safe method to be adopted, and we most strongly deprecate the wholesale system of conjectural emendation employed by Theobald and a few other editors.

We will now venture to offer our readers a few observations on some passages of the Midsummer Night's Dream.

Act I. Sc. 1.

" Ah me ! for aught that ever I could read,
Could ever hear by tale or history,
The course of true love never did run smooth."

A similar passage occurs in Shakespeare's poem of *Venus and Adonis*, where he represents Venus, after the loss of her lover, denouncing her vengeance on the unlucky passion : —

" Since thou art dead, lo ! here I prophesy,
Sorrow on love hereafter shall attend ;
It shall be waited on with jealousy,
Find sweet beginning but unsavoury end ;
Ne'er settled equally to high or low ;
That all love's pleasures shall not match his woe.
It shall be fickle, false, and full of fraud,
And shall be blasted in a breathing while,
The bottom poison and the top o'erstrew'd
With sweets, that shall the sharpest sight beguile:
The strongest body shall it make most weak,
Strike the wise dumb, and teach the fool to speak."

The fifth line satisfactorily shows that the alteration which has been made from *love* to *low* in another
line is perfectly correct :—

> " O cross! too high to be enthrall'd to low !"

It cannot, however, be denied, that Lysander's
speech would be improved by the omission of the
interpositions of Hermia.   It has been so printed by
Dodd and Planché.

In the second folio we have *Hermia* in the place
of the words *Ah me*, which the first folio omits altogether.   The remainder of this line has been used
by Butler, in *Hudibras*, Part I. Canto 3. l. 1026.

An old proverb which we find in MS. Sloane,
No. 1825, is to the same effect :—

> " Y shal you say, and well y can,
> The tide of love abidith no man."

Act I. Sc. 1.

> " If thou lov'st me, then
> Steal forth thy father's house to-morrow night ;
> And in the wood, a league without the town,
> Where I did meet thee once with Helena,
> To do observance to a morn of May,
> There will I stay for thee."

At the present day the celebration of the first of
May is chiefly confined to those of our fellow creatures who employ themselves the remainder of the
year in sweeping chimneys, and on that day recreate
themselves with parading through all places with
rude music, and a "jack in a green" habitation made
expressly for the purpose.   Formerly, the case was
very different ; and princes even " performed their
observation."   Churchyarde published one of his
works on the first of May ; to ensure its success, we

suppose, as the subject of the volume was political.
The reign of puritanical doctrines contributed, perhaps, in a great measure to the neglect of observing
this custom; and in MS. Harl. 1221, is a curious
poem against it, entitled, " A maypooles speech to
a traveller," from which we extract the following :—

" Men, women, children, one a heap,
Do sing and dance, and frisk and leap,
Yea, drums and drunkards one a rout,
Before me make a hideous shout,
Whose loud alarum and blowing cries
Do fright the earth and pierce the skies.

" Hath holy Pope his holy guard,
So have I to it watch and ward,
For where it's noysed that I am come,
My followers summoned are with drum,
I have a mighty rank anew,
The scum of all the rascall crew.

" Of fidlers, pedlers, fayle scape slaves,
Of tinkers, turncoats, tospot knaves,
Of theives and scapethrifts many a one,
With bouncing Bess and jolly Joan,
Of idle boys and journeymen,
And vagrants that the country run.

" The hobby horse doth hither prance,
Maid Marrian and the Morris dance,
My summons fetcheth far and near
All that can swagger, swil, and swear,
All that can dance, and drab, and drink,
They run to me as to a sink."

Act I. Sc. 1.

" Call you me fair ! that fair again unsay.
Demetrius loves you, fair : O, happy fair !
Your eyes are lode-stars ; and your tongue's sweet air,
More tuneable than lark to shepherd's ear,
When wheat is green, when hawthorn buds appear !
Sickness is catching ; O, were favour so,
Your words I catch, fair Hermia, ere I go ;

> My ear should catch your voice, my eye your eye,
> My tongue should catch your tongue's sweet melody."

We print this as it stands in the first quarto, without preserving the orthography of the time. Some discussion has arisen on the meaning of the seventh line, and Hanmer has altered it to

> " Your's would I catch, fair Hermia, ere I go."

The second folio, however, gives another reading, which is doubtlessly the genuine one—

> " Your words I'd catch, fair Hermia, ere I go."

For *favour* is not here used, as all editors and commentators have supposed, in the sense of *countenance*, but evidently in the common acceptation of the term—" O, were favour so," i. e., favour in the eyes of Demetrius; a particular application of a wish expressed in general terms. The reading of the second folio renders the whole passage perfectly intelligible.

Something similar to a portion of the above may be found in Grange's Garden, 1577 :—

> " Eache leafe upon the tree, the grasse upon the grounde,
> The Hathorne buddes new sprung, on earth what may be found,
> Doth yeelde as pleasant scentes, as nature can devise :
> All things in lusty greene, appeares displaying wise.
> And every bird that lives, then strayneth forth his voyce :
> So that of each delight, each man may take his choyce."

Act. I. Sc. 1.

> " And in the wood, where often you and I
> Upon faint primrose-beds were wont to lie,
> Emptying our bosoms of their counsel *sweet*,
> There my Lysander and myself shall meet :
> And thence from Athens turn away our eyes,
> To seek new friends and *stranger companies*."

Here again an unnecessary alteration has been made from the original.   In all the early editions we have this passage as follows:—

> " And in the wood, where often you and I
> Upon faint primrose beds were wont to lie,
> Emptying our bosoms of their counsel *swell'd*,
> There my Lysander and myself shall meet :
> And thence from Athens turn away our eyes,
> To seek new friends and *strange companions.*"

We owe the alteration to Theobald; but it is very evident that the author could not have written it so, for it would be impossible in that case to account for the corruption.   If Shakespeare had written *sweet* and *stranger companies*, it is very improbable that these words could have been so changed either by the actors or printers.   Moreover, the antithesis in the first of these instances is a strong argument in favour of the old reading—

> " *Emptying* our bosoms of their counsel *swell'd.*"

Our ears have perhaps become familiarized with Theobald's version ; but it is safer to receive Shakespeare's own words, even if, at first hearing, they do not seem quite so harmonious as the others.

Act I. Sc. 2.

> " *Quin.* Francis Flute, the bellows-mender.
> *Flu.* Here, Peter Quince.
> *Quin.* You must take Thisby on you.
> *Flu.* What is Thisby ? a wandering knight ?
> *Quin.* It is the lady that Pyramus must love.
> *Flu.* Nay, faith, let me not play a woman ; I have a beard coming.
> *Quin.* That's all one; you shall play it in a mask, and you may speak as small as you will."

Flute is proud of his approaching signs of manhood, which he calls a beard.   Cf. Lily's *Endimion*, 1591 :

" *Top.* I pray thee feel on my chin, something pricketh me.
What dost thou feel or see?
Epi. There are three or four little hairs.
Top. I pray thee call it my beard. How shall I be troubled
when this young spring shall grow to a great wood."

It is scarcely necessary to observe that the female
characters were at this period performed by boys.

ACT I. Sc. 2.

" *Bot.* Well, I will undertake it. What beard were I best to
play it in ?
Quin. Why, what you will.
Bot. I will discharge it in either your straw-coloured beard,
your orange-tawny beard, your purple-in-grain beard, or your
French-crown-coloured beard, your perfect yellow.
Quin. Some of your French crowns have no hair at all, and
then you will play barefaced."

Sanderson, in his Diary, complains of the sad ex-
travagance of his apprentice in the way of barbers :
in a letter to a friend, he informs him that " the very
cuttinge of his sharpe chinne hath cost me to the
barber more then I spent in myselfe in seven years."
Mr. Repton has printed a tract expressly on the subject of the different forms in which beards were worn,
some of which are exceedingly fantastic. A pun is
concealed in the term of *French-crown;* in MS. Harl.
280, fol. 81, mention is made of " French-crowne
gould." A curious song on beards may be found in
MS. Harl. 6931, but allusions to the different colours
of them are not very numerous. See, however, Middleton's Works by the Rev. A. Dyce, vol. i. p. 259.

ACT I. Sc. 2.

" *Bot.* We will meet ; and there we may rehearse most *ob-
scenely* and courageously. Take pains ; be perfect ; adieu.
Quin. At the duke's oak we meet.
Bot. Enough ; hold or cut bowstrings."

Bottom the weaver, like Mrs. Malaprop in a later production, is continually using his " select words, so ingeniously misapplied, without being mispronounced;" at the same time, seeming to think that " if he reprehends anything in this world, it is the use of his oracular tongue, and a nice derangement of epitaphs." He here uses the word *obscenely* for *obscurely*. Shakespeare is fond of making his clowns miscall their words.

Act II. Sc. 1.

> " Either I mistake your shape and making quite,
> Or else you are that shrewd and knavish spirite,
> Call'd Robin Goodfellow: are you not he
> That fright the maidens of the villagre;
> *Skim milk;* and sometimes labour in the quern,
> And bootless make the breathless housewife churn;
> And sometime make the drink to bear no barm;
> Mislead night-wanderers, laughing at their harm?
> *Those that Hobgoblin call you,* and sweet Puck,
> You do their work, and they shall have good luck:
> Are not you he?"

In Randolph's *Amyntas* there is an allusion to the fairies skimming milk :—

> " I know no haunts I have but to the dairy,
> To skim the milk-bowls like a liquorish fairy."

Robin's name of Hobgoblin is mentioned in MS. Harl. 6482. The whole passage is worth transcription :—

> " *Of spirits called Hobgoblins, or Robin Goodfellowes.*
>
> " These kinde of spirits are more familiar and domestical then the others, and for some causes to us unknown, abode in one place more then in another, so that some never almost depart from some particular houses, as though they were their proper mansions, making in them sundry noises, rumours, mockeries, gawds and jests, without doing any harme at all, and some have heard them play at gitterns and Jews' harps, and ring bells and make answer to those that call them, and speake with certain signes,

laughters and merry gestures, so that those of the house come at
last to be so familiar and well acquainted with them that they
fear them not at all.   But in truth, if they had free power to put
in execution their mallicious desire, we should finde these pranks
of theirs not to be jests, but earnest indeed, tending to the destruction both of our body and soul, but their power is so re-
strained and tyed that they can passe no further then to jests
and gawds, and if they do any harm at all, it is certainly very
little, as by experience hath been founde."

Act II. Sc. 2.

" And never, since the *middle-summer's spring.*"

The " middle-summer's spring" means probably
the beginning of midsummer.   In Churchyard's
Charitie, 1595, we have a similar expression :—

" A warmer time in better tune may bring
This hard cold age, when comes a summer spring."

Spring is here used for *beginning*.

Act II. Sc. 2.

" And, in the *spiced* Indian air, by night,
Full often hath she gossip'd by my side;
And sat with me on Neptune's yellow sands,
Marking th' embarked traders on the flood."

Cf. *Bartholomæus de Glanvilla*, 1582, fol. 252:—
" As the rivers there are very many, so are they very
great, through whose watery overflowing it commeth
to passe that in the moyst grounde, the force of the
sunne approaching, ingendreth or bringeth forth all
things in great quantitie and seemeth almost to fill
the whole world *with spice* and precious stones, of
which it aboundeth more than all other countries of
the world."

Act II. Sc. 2.

" Yet mark'd I where the bolt of Cupid fell :
It fell upon a little western flower,

> Before milk-white, now purple with love's wound,
> And maidens call it Love-in-Idleness."

" Viola tricolor, hart's ease ; herba Trinitatis, herba clavellata, paunsies, love-in-idlenes."— MS. Sloan. 797, fol. 61.

Act II. Sc. 2.

> " You draw me, you hardhearted adamant,
> But yet you draw not iron, for my heart
> Is true as steel. Leave you your power to draw,
> And I shall have no power to follow you."

" The Adamant is a stone of Inde, small and rare, in colour like to iron, but in clear reflection and representation of image more christal like. It yeeldeth or giveth place to nothing. Diascorides saith that it is called the stone of reconsiliation and of love,"— *A Grene Forest, by John Maplet*, 1567. Again, in the same book we read that " The lodestone draweth iron to it, even as one lover coveteth and desireth another." Lord Bacon says,—" I read that in nature there be two kinds of motions or appetites in sympathy ; the one of iron to the adamant for perfection ; the other of the vine to the stake for sustentation."

Act II. Sc. 2.

> " And even for that do I love you the more.
> I am your spaniel ; and, Demetrius,
> The more you beat me, I will fawn on you.
> Use me but as your spaniel, spurn me, strike me,
> Neglect me, lose me ; only give me leave,
> Unworthy as I am, to follow you,
> What worser place can I beg in your love
> (And yet a place of high respect with me),
> Than to be used as you use your dog ? "

We suppose Shakespeare here alludes to the old proverb :—

" A spaniel, a woman, and a wallnut tree,
The more they're beaten, the better still they be."

Act. III. Sc. 1.

" *Bot.* Why do they run away? this is a knavery of them, to
make me afeard.

Re-enter Snout.

Snout. O Bottom, thou art changed! what do I see on thee?
Bot. What do you see? *you see an ass's head of your own ;*
do you?"

" It is plain by Bottom's answer," says Johnson,
" that Snout mentioned an ass's head."   No such
thing; the phrase is a common one of the time.
Mrs. Quickly, in the Merry Wives of Windsor, says,
" You shall have a fool's head of your own."

Act III. Sc. 1.

" The ousel-cock, so black of hue,
    With orange-tawny bill;
The throstle with his note so true ;—
    The wren with little quill;

" The finch, the sparrow, and the lark ;
    The plain-song cuckoo gray,
Whose note full many a man doth mark,
    And *dares* not answer, nay ;—

for, indeed, who would set his wit to so foolish a bird? who
would give a bird the lie, though he cry ' cuckoo' never so?"

Why Bottom should here enumerate these birds is
not very evident, except we believe, as Aristotle has
assured us, that all small birds hate the ass.   It is
unnecessary to remind the reader of a belief that
Shakespeare very frequently refers to, and which was
prevalent in his day, viz. the identity of the cuckoo's
note, and a certain term of great disgrace.   The meaning of the last line of Bottom's song has not been satisfactorily explained.   It refers to an opinion then

common, that the unfaithfulness of a woman to her husband was always guided by a destiny which no human power could avert. In *Grange's Garden*, 1577, we have an allusion to this :—

> " And playing thus with wanton toyes, the cuckow bad good
> morow,
> Alas, thought I, a token 'tis for me to live in sorrow ;
> Cuckow sang he, Cuckow sayd I, what destiny is this?
> Who so it heares, he well may thinke it is no sacred blisse.
> Alas, quoth she, what caun have you, as yet thus for to say,
> In Cuckow time few have a charme, to cause his tongue to stay;
> Wherefore,
> Content yourselfe as well as I, let reason rule your minde,
> As cuckolds come by destiny, so cuckowes sing by kinde."

Compare also Nicolls' poem on the cuckoo, 1607, p. 12 :—

> " Meanetime Dan Cuckow, knowing that his voice
> Had no varietie, no change, no choice :
> But through the wesand pipe of his harsh throate,
> Cri'd only Cuckow, that prodigious note !"

Again, in *Wit's Recreations*, 12mo. Lond. 1641 :—

> " Thy stars gave thee the cuckold's diadem :
> If thou wert born to be a wittol, can
> Thy wife prevent thy fortune ? foolish man !"

And in a note in the English translation of Ariosto's Satires, 1608, we have a singular tale on the same subject: " Many hold of opinion that to be a cuckold is destiny and not their wives dishonesties, as a good fellow in the world said to a friend of his, who telling him he was sorry that so honest a man as he should be abused as he was, seeing the fault was his wives and not his. I thanke you, neighbour, replied he, for your good conceit of me, but I assure you I think it was not her own fault, but rather

mine own fortune that made me a cuckold ; for I
verily believe whosoere I had married, would have
bin naught as well as she.   Nay then, quoth his
neighbour, if you think so, God forbid I should dis-
suade you from an opinion you hold so confidently,
and so left him."

Act III. Sc. 2.

" And the country proverb known,
That every man should take his own,
In your waking shall be shown :
    Jack shall have Jill ;
    Nought shall go ill ;
The man shall have his mare again, and all shall be well."

Well is so bad a rhyme to *ill*, that Steevens pro-
poses to read *still*.   In Heywood's *Epigrammes upon
Proverbes*, 1567, we have,—

" All shal be wel, Jacke shal have Gil;
Nay, nay; Gill is wedded to Wil."

This shows that the common reading is quite correct.

Act IV. Sc. 1.

Tita. " Or, say, sweet love, what thou desir'st to eat.
Bot. Truly, a peck of provender; I could munch your good
dry oats.   Methinks, I have a great desire to *a bottle of hay :*
good hay, sweet hay, hath no fellow."

A *bottle* of hay was not merely a *bundle*, but some
measure of that " provender."   So in the *Choyce
Poems*, 12mo. Lond. 1661, p. 43,—

" Do you at livery stand, or by the bottle
Get you your hay, your oats by peck or pottle ?"

Act IV. Sc. I.

" I have had a most rare vision.   I have had a dream,—past
the wit of man to say what dream it was :—man is but an ass, if

he go about to expound this dream. Methought I was,—there
is no man can tell what. Methought I was, and methought I
had,—but man is but a patched fool, if he will offer to say what
methought I had. The eye of man hath not heard, the ear of
man hath not seen; man's hand is not able to taste, his tongue
to conceive, nor his heart to report, what my dream was."

Warner, in his manuscript annotations on Shakespeare, says, that " this seems to be a humorous
allusion to the Scripture account of the happiness
of a future state." We should not think that any
such allusion is intended, and there is no necessity
for the conjecture. We may mention here that
Warner's collections on Shakespeare have recently
been added to the library of the British Museum.
He appears to have been very liberal in communicating these collections to his friends, and we have
lately seen a letter from Steevens to Garrick, dated
July 28th, 1771, in which he applies for the loan
of Warner's MS. annotations on the Midsummer
Night's Dream, then in Garrick's possession, lent to
him by the author himself.

ACT V. Sc. 1.

" A tedious brief scene of young Pyramus
And his love Thisbe: very tragical mirth."

Dunston Gale, in 1596, wrote a poem called
Pyramus and Thisbe, the earliest known printed
edition of which appeared in 1617. There is no
allusion whatever to A Midsummer Night's Dream.
A copy of a later edition (viz. 1626, sometimes found
with Greene's *Arbasto*) is in Malone's Collection,
No. 295. It is very rare, and the poetry is exe-
crable. Mr. Collier has given some extracts in his
Catalogue of the Bridgewater Library.

G

We shall perhaps offer an acceptable service to those who have no opportunity of referring to the early editions of Shakespeare's plays, by here reprinting the first part of A Midsummer Night's Dream *verbatim* from the earliest quarto, which appeared in the year 1600, under the following title,— *A Midsommer Nights Dreame, as it hath beene sundry times publickely acted by the Right Honourable the Lord Chamberlain his servants. Written by William Shakespeare. Imprinted at London for Thomas Fisher, and are to be soulde at his shoppe at the signe of the White Hart, in Fleete Streete.*

" Now faire *Hippolita*, our nuptiall hower
Draws on apase : fower happy daies bring in
An other Moone : but oh, me thinks, how slow
This old Moone wanes ! She lingers my desires,
Like to a Stepdame, or a dowager,
Long withering out a yong mans reuenewe.
   Hip. Fower daies will quickly sleepe themselues in night :
Fower nights will quickly dreame away the time :
And then the Moone, like to a siluer bowe,
Now bent in heauen, shall beholde the night
Of our solemnities.
   The. Goe *Philostrate*,
Stirre vp the *Athenian* youth to merriments,
Awake the peart and nimble spirit of mirth,
Turne melancholy foorth to funerals :
The pale companion is not for our pomp.
Hyppolita, I woo'd thee with my sword,
And wonne thy loue, doing thee iniuries :
But I will wed thee in another key,
With pompe, with triumph, and with reueling.

Enter Egeus *and his daughter* Hermia, *and* Lysander, *and* Helena, *and* Demetrius.

   Ege. Happy be *Theseus*, our renowned duke.
   The. Thankes good *Egeus*. Whats the newes with thee ?
   Ege. Full of vexation, come I, with complaint
Against my childe, my daughter *Hermia*.

Stand forth Demetrius.

My noble Lord,
This man hath my consent to marry her.

Stand forth Lisander.

And my gratious Duke,
This man hath bewitcht the bosome of my childe,
Thou, thou *Lysander*, thou hast giuen her rimes,
And interchang'd loue tokens with my childe:
Thou hast, by moone-light, at her windowe sung,
With faining voice, verses of faining loue,
And stolne the impression of her phantasie:
With bracelets of thy haire, rings, gawdes, conceites,
Knackes, trifles, nosegaies, sweete meates (messengers
Of strong preuailement in vnhardened youth)
With cunning hast thou filcht my daughters heart,
Turnd her obedience (which is due to mee)
To stubborne harshnesse. And, my gratious Duke,
Be it so, she will not here, before your Grace,
Consent to marry with *Demetrius*,
I beg the auncient priuiledge of *Athens*:
As she is mine, I may dispose of her:
Which shall be, either to this gentleman,
Or to her death; according to our lawe,
Immediatly prouided, in that case.

The. What say you, *Hermia?* Be aduis'd, faire maid.
To you, your father should be as a God:
One that compos'd your beauties: yea and one,
To whome you are but as a forme in wax,
By him imprinted, and within his power,
To leaue the figure, or disfigure it:
Demetrius is a worthy gentleman.

Her. So is *Lisander*. *The.* In himselfe he is:
But in this kinde, wanting your fathers voice,
The other must be held the worthier.

Her. I would my father lookt but with my eyes.

The. Rather your eyes must, with his iudgement, looke.

Her. I doe intreat your grace, to pardon mee.
I know not by what power, I am made bould;
Nor how it may concerne my modesty,
In such a presence, here to plead my thoughts:
But I beseech your Grace, that I may knowe
The worst that may befall mee in this case,
If I refuse to wed *Demetrius*.

The. Either to dy the death, or to abiure,
For euer, the society of men.
Therefore, faire *Hermia*, question your desires,

Knowe of your youth, examine well your blood,
Whether (if you yeelde not to your fathers choyce)
You can endure the liuery of a Nunne,
For aye to be in shady cloyster, mew'd
To liue a barraine sister all your life,
Chaunting faint hymnes, to the colde fruitlesse Moone.
Thrise blessed they, that master so there bloode,
To vndergoe such maiden pilgrimage:
But earthlyer happy is the rose distild,
Then that, which, withering on the virgin thorne,
Growes, liues, and dies, in single blessednesse.

Her. So will I growe, so liue, so die my Lord,
Ere I will yield my virgin Patent, vp
Vnto his Lordshippe, whose vnwished yoake
My soule consents not to giue souerainty.

The. Take time to pawse, and by the next newe moone,
The sealing day, betwixt my loue and mee,
For euerlasting bond of fellowshippe,
Vpon that day either prepare to dye;
For disobedience to your fathers will,
Or else to wed *Demetrius,* as he would,
Or on *Dianaes* altar to protest,
For aye, austeritie and single life.

Deme. Relent, sweete *Hermia,* and, *Lysander,* yeeld
Thy crazed title to my certaine right.

Lys. You haue her fathers loue, *Demetrius:*
Let me haue *Hermias:* doe you marry him.

Egeus. Scornefull *Lysander,* true, he hath my loue:
And what is mine, my loue shall render him.
And she is mine, and all my right of her
I doe estate vnto Demetrius.

Lysand. I am my Lord, as well deriv'd as hee,
As well possest: my loue is more than his:
My fortunes euery way as fairely rankt
(If not with vantage) as *Demetrius:*
And (which is more then all these boastes can be)
I am belou'd of beautious Hermia.
Why should not I then prosecute my right?
Demetrius, Ile auouch it to his heade,
Made loue to *Nedars* daughter, *Helena,*
And won her soule: and she (sweete Ladie) dotes,
Deuoutly dotes, dotes in Idolatry,
Vpon this spotted and inconstant man.

The. I must confesse, that I haue heard so much;
And, with *Demetrius,* thought to haue spoke thereof:
But, being ouer full of selfe affaires,

My minde did loose it, But *Demetrius* come,
And come *Egeus*, you shall goe with mee :
I haue some priuate schooling for you both.
For you, faire *Hermia*, looke you arme your selfe,
To fit your fancies, to your fathers will ;
Or else, the Law of *Athens* yeelds you vp
(Which by no meanes we may extenuate)
To death, or to a vowe of single life.
Come my *Hyppolita* : what cheare my loue ?
Demetrius and *Egeus* goe along :
I must employ you in some businesse,
Against our nuptiall, and conferre with you
Of some thing, nerely that concernes your selues.
  Ege. With duety and desire, we follow you. *Exeunt.*
  Lysand. How now my loue ? Why is your cheeke so pale?
How chance the roses there doe fade so fast?
  Her. Belike, for want of raine : which I could well
Beteeme them, from the tempest of my eyes.
  Lis. Eigh me : for aught that I could euer reade,
Could euer here by tale or history,
The course of true loue neuer did runne smoothe :
But either it was different in bloud ;
  Her. O crosse ! too high to be inthrald to loue.
  Lis. Or else misgraffed, in respect of yeares ;
  Her. O spight ! too olde to be ingag'd to young.
  Lis. Or else, it stoode vpon the choyce of friends;
  Her. O hell, to choose loue by anothers eyes !
  Lys. Or, if there were a sympathy in choyce,
Warre, death or sicknesse, did lay siege to it ;
Making it momentany, as a sound ;
Swift, as a shadowe ; short, as any dreame ;
Briefe, as the lightning in the collied night,
That (in a spleene) vnfolds both heauen and earth ;
And, ere a man hath power to say, beholde,
The iawes of darkenesse do deuoure it vp :
So quicke bright things come to confusion.
  Her. If then true louers haue bin euer crost,
It stands as an edict, in destiny :
Then let vs teach our triall patience :
Because it is a customary crosse,
As dewe to loue, as thoughts, and dreames, and sighes,
Wishes, and teares ; poore Fancies followers.
  Lys. A good perswasion : therefore heare mee, *Hermia* :
I haue a widowe aunt, a dowager,
Of great reuenew, and she hath no childe :
From *Athens* is her house remote, seauen leagues :
And she respects mee, as her only sonne :

There, gentle *Hermia*, may I marry thee :
And to that place, the sharpe *Athenian* law
Can not pursue vs. If thou louest mee, then
Steale forth thy fathers house, to morrow night :
And in the wood, a league without the towne
(Where I did meete thee once with *Helena*
To do obseruance to a morne of May)
There will I stay for thee.
   Her. My good *Lysander,*
I sweare to thee, by *Cupid's* strongest bowe,
By his best arrowe, with the golden heade,
By the simplicitie of *Venus* doues,
By that which knitteth soules, and prospers loues,
And by that fire, which burnd the *Carthage* queene,
When the false *Troian* vnder saile was seene,
By all the vowes that euer men haue broke,
(In number more then euer women spoke)
In that same place thou hast appointed mee,
To morrow truely will I meete with thee.
   Lys. Keepe promise loue : looke, here comes *Helena.*

Enter HELENA.

   Her. God speede faire *Helena :* whither away ?
   Hel. Call you mee faire ?   That faire againe vnsay.
Demetrius loues you faire : ô happy faire !
Your eyes are loadstarres, and your tongues sweete aire
More tunable than larke, to sheepeheards eare,
When wheat is greene, when hauthorne buddes appeare.
Sicknesse is catching : O, were fauour so,
Your words I catch, faire *Hermia,* ere I goe,
My eare should catch your voice, my eye, your eye,
My tongue should catch your tongues sweete melody.
Were the world mine, *Demetrius* being bated,
The rest ile giue to be to you translated.
O, teach mee how you looke, and with what Art,
You sway the motion of *Demetrius* heart.
   Her. I frowne vpon him ; yet hee loues mee still.
   Hel. O that your frowns would teach my smiles such skil.
   Her. I giue him curses ; yet he giues mee loue.
   Hel. O that my prayers could such affection mooue.
   Her. The more I hate, the more he followes mee.
   Hel. The more I loue, the more he hateth mee.
   Her. His folly, *Helena,* is no fault of mine.
   Hel. None but your beauty ; would that fault were mine.
   Her. Take comfort ; he no more shall see my face :
Lysander and my selfe will fly this place.
Before the time I did *Lisander* see,
Seem'd *Athens* as a Paradise to mee

O then, what graces in my loue dooe dwell,
That hee hath turnd a heaven vnto a hell!
  Lys. Helen, to you our mindes wee will vnfould:
To morrow night, when *Phœbe* doth beholde
Her siluer visage, in the watry glasse,
Decking, with liquid pearle, the bladed grasse
(A time, that louers flights doth still conceale)
Through *Athens* gates, haue wee deuis'd to steale.
  Her. And in the wood, where often you and I,
Vpon faint Primrose beddes, were wont to lye,
Emptying our bosomes, of their counsell sweld,
There my *Lysander*, and my selfe shall meete,
And thence, from *Athens*, turne away our eyes,
To seeke new friends and strange companions.
Farewell, sweete playfellow; pray thou for vs:
And good lucke graunt thee thy *Demetrius*.
Keepe word *Lysander*: we must starue our sight,
From louers foode, till morrow deepe midnight.

         Exit HERMIA.
  Lys. I will my *Hermia*, *Helena* adieu:
As you on him, *Demetrius* dote on you.   *Exit* LYSANDER.
  Hele. How happie some, ore othersome, can be!
Through *Athens*, I am thought as faire as shee.
But what of that? *Demetrius* thinkes not so:
He will not knowe, what all, but hee doe know.
And as hee erres, doting on *Hermia's* eyes:
So I, admiring of his qualities.
Things base and vile, holding no quantitie,
Loue can transpose to forme and dignitie.
Loue lookes not with the eyes, but with the minde:
And therefore is winged *Cupid* painted blinde.
Nor hath loues minde of any iudgement taste:
Wings, and no eyes, figure, vnheedy haste,
And therefore is loue said to bee a childe:
Because, in choyce, he is so oft beguil'd,
As waggish boyes, in game, themselues forsweare:
So, the boy, Loue, is periur'd euery where.
For, ere *Demetrius* lookt on *Hermias* eyen,
Hee hayld dovne othes, that he was onely mine.
And when this haile some heate, from *Hermia*, felt,
So he dissolued, and shours of oathes did melt.
I will goe tell him of faire *Hermias* flight:
Then, to the wodde, will he, to morrow night,
Pursue her: and for this intelligence,
If I haue thankes, it is a deare expense:
But herein meane I to enrich my paine,
To haue his sight thither, and back againe."

CHAPTER IX.

" Let us make us a name, lest we be scattered abroad upon the face of the whole earth."

'Ως αγαθον εστ' επωνυμιας πολλας εχειν.

IF the authority of any living writer could be considered decisive on a disputed point of minute criticism, where there are neither established rules to lead to a right conclusion, nor sufficient evidence to decide positively on either side, then the opinion of the author of the " Curiosities of Literature " would deserve to be placed very high in the rank of such a recognition, and carry conviction to the minds of those who had not previously adopted another theory.

The dispute on the orthography of the name of our national bard is in this position. Mr. D'Israeli's opinion on the subject will therefore be considered by some an argument in itself. " While a drop of ink circulates in my pen," exclaims the patriarch of English literature, " I shall ever loyally write the name of SHAKESPEARE." Mr. D'Israeli is supported in this opinion by Messrs. Collier, Dyce, and Hunter ; and every one will admit that these are good authorities in any question connected with Shakespearian literature.

The authority of opinion will not, however, in the present enquiring age, be considered adequate to establish the truth of any πορισμα of this nature.

The authority of tradition and of custom is of even inferior value, and it is perhaps better to leave their influence almost out of the scale, if we would judge correctly of the point at issue; and yet this constitutes the only evidence in support of one belief. We prefer confining ourselves to materials that are more easily determined by the usual criteria of error and truth.

Within the last two centuries the confidence which was formerly placed in the evidence of tradition has materially diminished, and in proportion as the necessity of having recourse to that method of communicating facts from age to age has decreased, so the accuracy with which that knowledge is preserved has declined. Numerous examples might be adduced in confirmation of this statement, and none would afford a more efficacious proof than the few traditional anecdotes which have been handed down to us respecting our great dramatic bard. For instance, there are very many who take for granted the alleged authenticity of Shakespeare's epitaph on Combe, the usurer; and yet a more palpable fabrication could scarcely have been committed, for the epitaph itself appeared in various collections, both before and after the time they were said to have been composed. There is every reason to believe that the epitaph in a more general form belongs to a much earlier period : —

> " Here lies ten in the hundred,
>   In the ground fast ramm'd ;
> 'Tis an hundred to ten,
>   But his soule is damm'd."

The epitaph said to have been written by Shakespeare is differently constructed : —

" Ten in the hundred lies here engrav'd,
'Tis an hundred to ten his soul is not sav'd ;
If any man ask who lies in this tombe?
Oh! Ho! quoth the devil, 'tis my John-a-Combe."

The sharpness of the satire is said to have stung
the usurer so that he never forgave it. But Combe's
will is fortunately preserved in the Prerogative Office
at Doctors' Commons, and affords most satisfactory
proof to the contrary ; for among the numerous lega-
cies which he leaves is one " to Mr. William Shackspere, five poundes." The following version of the
tale differs from the common one, and may be partly
correct ; it is taken from MS. No. 38, in the Ashmolean Museum at Oxford :—

> " *On John Combe a covetous rich man, Mr. Wm.*
> *Shakspear wright this att his request while hee was*
> *yett liveing for his epitaph,*
>
> Who lies in this tomb,
> Hough, quoth the Devill, 'tis my son John a Combe.
>
> *But being dead and making the poore his heiers, hee*
> *after wright this for his epitaph,*
>
> Howere he lived, judge not.
> John Combe shall never be forgott,
> While poor hath memorye, for hee did gather
> To make the poore his issue : hee their father
> As record of his title and seede,
> Did crowne him in his latter seede.
>
> *Finis W. Shak.*"

The manuscript which contains this was not
written long after the death of Shakespeare, and
includes another anecdote respecting him, which we
take the opportunity of inserting in this place :—

> " *Mr. Ben. Johnson and Mr. Wm. Shakespeare be-*
> *ing merrye att a tavern, Mr. Jonson haveing begane*
> *this for his epitaph*

Here lies Ben Johnson that was once one.

He gives it to Mr. Shakspear to make upp, who presently wrights

> Who while hee lived was a sloe thinge,
> And now being dead is nothinge."

We here see that Shakespeare's name is spelt in two different ways in the very same paragraph. No proof, indeed, is needed of the extreme licentiousness that was then admitted in the orthography, or rather cacography, of proper names. When Alexander Hume addressed his Treatise on Orthography (MS. Bib. Reg. 17 A. xi.) to King James, he saw " sik uncertentie in our men's wryting, as if a man wald indyte one letter to tuentie of our best wryteres, nae tuae of the tuentie without conference wald agree." When spelling was in such a state of misrule, can the written documents of the period be fairly referred to as authorities by which we can regulate orthography at the present day?

In the literary metropolis the name of our dramatic bard was pronounced SHAKE-SPEARE. There are many evidences of this, and in many of the early editions of the plays, the name is printed with a hyphen between the two syllables. Bancroft thus alludes to him :—

> " Thou hast so used thy pen, *or shook thy speare;*
> That poets startle ———"

And we do not see that this example, which Mr. D'Israeli has given, is to be rejected, because it proceeds from a punster. One critic, indeed, says, that " we might with as much reason contend, on the authority of a certain pictorial pun, that the new translator of *Demosthenes de Corona* was once my

Lord *Broom;*" and we really think that, although a
picture is of much inferior evidence in a question of
this nature than even a pun, that this fact would
afford some proof that his lordship's name was *pronounced* Broom. And this is what we wish to be
admitted respecting the name of Shakespeare :—that
by his educated contemporaries it was *pronounced*
Shake-speare.

"The same surname," says Fuller, "hath been
variously altered in writing, because time teacheth
new orthography;" and we are so far from sup-
porting the common method of spelling Shakespeare's
name on account of the sanction which antiquity
may give to it, that we should be quite willing to
adopt the new system of writing it, provided it were
not liable to cause a change in the pronunciation.
The new* method of spelling it, viz. *Shakspere,* has
this objection ; for although the alteration in the
orthoepy will not necessarily produce a corresponding change in the pronunciation with those who have
been accustomed to the old system ; yet we cannot
help thinking that there are many who receive their
pronunciation from the orthography alone, and such
persons will, undoubtedly, be liable to adopt the
short and sharp pronunciation, if they depended
upon the "barbaric curt shock" of *Shakspere.* In
the family documents at Stratford, the name is most
frequently written *Shackspere,* and *Shackspere's close*

---

* We say "new," because *Shakspere* is generally considered
to be an innovation only recently suggested. Such, however, is
not the case, for the critics of the last century nearly exhausted
the subject in question, and ultimately decided on the correctness
of the old orthography. In Bell's edition of the works of Shakespeare, 1788, the odious cacography is adopted.

formed part of the property of Combe the usurer, as
appears by his will. The pronunciation suggested
by this mode of spelling is merely, as Mr. D'Israeli
expresses himself, " the twang of a provincial corruption."   Shall we pronounce the sacred name of
Shakespeare as " rare Ben" and all his literary
friends pronounced it, or be guided by the practice
of the Stratford clowns? Shall we spoil half the
allusions to our poet by adopting a provincial barbarism ? When any contemporary poet speaks of the
bard, the orthography is invariably *Shakespeare,* and
the metre always shows that the first syllable must
be pronounced long. Remember the following lines,

> " What need my Shakespeare, for his honour'd bones,
> The labour of an age in piled stones? "

Then think of *Shakspere,* and shudder at the transformation.

Sir Frederick Madden asks whether the simple
Saxon *spere* is not " entitled to as much respect as
the *speare* of the fourteenth century?" We suppose
it is ; but we really do not see how this admission
can bear upon the present question. If we are permitted to separate the syllables, we shall find many
evidences in favour of the old orthography.   In the
early editions of Shakespeare's plays, we read of
a certain weapon designated by the word *speare,*
which we now term *spear,* and our Saxon ancestors
spere. But if we turn to the Saxon language for
the other part of the surname, and combine it with
spere, we should effect a very strange metamorphosis. It is, indeed, about as difficult to correct
the cacography of a surname by appealing to the
elements of the language,

" As to o're-walke a current roaring loud,
On the unstedfast footing of a *speare*."*

These are some of the considerations which have
led us to the conclusion that there is not a sufficient
reason for the proposed elimination of the letter *e* in
the first syllable of Shakespeare's name.† With
regard to the orthography of the second syllable, it
is perfectly immaterial, as far as we can see, whether
we adopt *spere*, *spear*, or *speare*; and because it is
so, we are opposed to a deviation being made from
the accustomed method of writing it, *speare*. "Do
not deviate," observes a very eminent writer, "into
quirks and affectations, but spell the name as it was
invariably spelt by his contemporaries." Affectation
of singularity curtailed the name of the reformer of
Lutterworth to *Wiclif* on no authority whatever, and
that same affectation has probably been the cause of
the partial adoption of the new method of spelling
the name of our great dramatic bard.

And now, perhaps, the reader of the preceding
pages will permit their author to say a few words
for himself in extenuation of his presumption in entering a field of research already trodden by so many
writers of established reputation, some of whom have
devoted their lives to the sole study of this department of criticism.

---

* First Part of Henry IV. Act i. Sc. 3, old edition.
† The family name was originally so spelt. At least we find
the name of *Shakespare* in MS. Burney, 360, in a handwriting
of the time of Henry the Eighth.

This field is open to any one acquainted with the stores of Elizabethan literature; and it may be safely said, that there is scarcely a book belonging to that period that does not, more or less, afford illustration of some part of Shakespeare's works. A length of time must therefore necessarily elapse ere the immense extent for research which this literature offers can be completely exhausted, to the entire exclusion of the discovery of new illustrative matter. Hence have arisen the numerous commentaries on the plays of our great dramatist, few of which are without their use; and I, for one, cannot persuade myself to reject any illustrations whatever of his works, however minute and comparatively trifling they may appear; for when they contribute to enable us to understand more fully those wonderful productions. do they not raise themselves on a level tantamount with individual value? If there be any of my readers who agree with me in this, they may perhaps consider the materials here brought together worthy their consideration, and it will depend upon their verdict given on the present occasion whether I shall be induced to offer to their notice similar annotations on some of the other plays.

This, however, I may be allowed to say, without fear of being accused of egotism, that, whatever may be the opinion of the public respecting the merits of my little volume, I have always endeavoured to present the reader with new facts rather than adaptations of old ones, and have carefully avoided a system, now, I am sorry to say, much in practice, of appropriating the best and attacking the weaker points of the older commentators, who have, despite of the outcries of some modern critics against their errors, done so much towards the right understanding of their author. "It would be well," observes Mr. Hunter, "if we who follow them, and profit so much by their labours, would imitate the research and industry of some of them, or could possess ourselves of the sagacity and genius of others." A capability, indeed, for research and minute criticism, and a power to philosophize the information so obtained, seldom occur united in the same mind.

Shakespeare was, of all modern authors, my first, and has ever been my greatest favourite. No encomium of his writings is now needed from any of his followers, for never perhaps was there an author whose memory is so generally idolized.* It has always been my wish to be able to read his works with an ample knowledge of the language and manners of the times in which they were written; and fortified with this knowledge, to enter as far as possible into the spirit of those sublime compositions, undisturbed by the disputes of verbal critics. This, I am convinced, must be accomplished by full and judicious illustrations from contemporary writers; and continual reference to the early editions of the text itself. It may be said that no one person is sufficient for this, but surely the old adage of "What is every body's business, is no one's business," will not be considered applicable in the present case. Shakespeare's works are not yet in the position, as far as regards explanatory criticism, of those of the ancient

---

* He was not so general a favourite while he was living, but as early as the year 1662, Sir Thomas Browne, in one of his journeys, considered "Shakspear tombe in Stretford" an object worthy of an especial visit. See MS. Sloane, 1900, fol. 15.

classic writers of Greece and Italy, and we fortunately possess more ample materials for the regulation of his text than mere philological canons can afford. It is, then, a task due to the readers of Shakespeare from those who have it in their power, to assist as far as possible in placing these materials within their reach; and a belief that the few notes here collected together would contribute, in some degree, however trifling, towards this desirable end, was the motive that induced me to hazard an ordeal before the judgment of those who are much better able than myself to decide upon their relative utility. I have perhaps ventured too far, and may be destined to receive the punishment due to presumption in the discovery of my error. If I am doomed to this, at least I may hope that in after years, my unhappy attempt may escape the affliction of being converted into a testimony in favour of universal censure. Then, after a while, if it be permitted me, when the host of reviewers inimical to this class of learning shall have exhausted their criticisms,

> " I'll break my staff,
> Bury it certain fathoms in the earth,
> And deeper than did ever plummet sound,
> I'll drown my book."

APPENDIX.

[THE following curious tract, which is reprinted from a copy preserved in the British Museum, is of a political nature, but, at the same time, affords some illustration of the popular character of Robin Goodfellow, and is in many respects curious and interesting. The tract itself is printed on four leaves, in very small quarto.]

" *The Midnight's Watch, or Robin Goodfellow his serious observation; Wherein is discovered the true state and strength of the kingdome as at this day it stands, without either Faction or Affaction. London, printed for George Lindsey*, 1643.

" The harmlesse spirit and the merry, commonly knowne to the world by the name of Robin Goodfellow, having told his Fairy mistresse of fleering upon strangers Elves, and the tickling of her nose with her petulant finger, and receaving but frownes for his favours and checks for his counsailes, he grew weary of her service, and being as light of love as he was of care he resolved to visit her no more. The troubles and commotions in the upper world had wrought his thoughts another way, and in a serious humour one night he resolved to goe abroad, to observe the new courses and alterations of the world.

" The first place he came at was Windsor, where he found a good part of the Army newly come from Redding, he heard them talke as confident of victory as if they had killed the Cavaliers already, he much admired the understanding and resolution of their Generall, and daring not to stay there any longer for feare he should be taken for a Malignant and be whipt, he made a swift dispatch for Oxford ; yet not farre from Windsor he met at the townes end many sentinells and incountered some Courts of Guard,

every wench as he passed by a blue and secret nip on the arm without awakening her. He heard among the sentinells, as he was departing from Oxford, of a great victory obtained by one Sir Ralph Hopton against a part of the Parliaments forces, wherein the Earle of Stamfords regiments were said to be quite routed, many of his Souldiers slaine, many taken prisoners and great store of Armes, and Ammunition with them, amongst which a great brasse piece on which the Crown and the Rose were stampt, was most remarkable. Robbin had a great desire to go thither himself, and to justifie the truth of so absolute a Victory. He had not gone as far as Ensham, but he espied the nine Muses in a Vinteners Porch crouching close together, and defending themselves as well as they could from the cold visitation of the winters night. They were extream poore, and (which is most strange) in so short an absence and distance from Oxford they were grown extreamly ignorant, for they took him for their Apollo, and craved his Power and Protection to support them. Robbin told them they were much mistaken in him, for though he was not mortal he was but of middle birth no more than they, they being the daughters of Memorie, and he the son of Mirth, but he bade them take comfort for that now in Oxford there was sure news of Peace and a speedy hope of their return to their discontinued habitations: at this they seemed with much joy to rouse up themselves, and did assure him that if what he reported did prove true, they would sing his praises throughout all generations. The Elf proud of such a favour in the name of Oberon did thank them, and did conjure them to perform it, and in the twinkling of an eye he conveyed himself to Salt-ash in Cornwall, where Sir R. Hopton's forces were quartered. He found the defeat given to the Earl of Stamford nothing so great as Fame in Oxford confirmed it to be. Collonell Ruthens regiment indeed was sorely shaken, and some of his men slain, and many taken prisoners. With a curious eye he observed what Arms and Ammunition were taken, and above all he had a labouring desire to see the brasse piece with the Crowne and the Rose on it, which so much dignified his conquest: he searched up and down the Army, and in and about the Magazine, but he could not find it. At length despairing of what he looked for, the venterous Elf came into Sir Ralphs chamber, and finding him asleepe, and safe as Wine and Innocence, he dived into his pocket, and the first thing he took out, hee found to beare the impression of the Rose and Crowne, and it was a brave piece indeed, for it was a farthing token which was all peradventure that was in it. Robbin ashamed to see himself so deluded could not at the first but smile at the conceit, and putting it into its Magazine repenting himself of his journey, he did sweare that he would never trust fame, nor Pamphlet more, though printed in a thousand universities.

" From thence with much indignation, and more speed he flung away, and in a moment placed himselfe at Bristoll, where he found the face of things just like the aire of an April morning, it smiled and it rained both at once, some were greedy of peace, and some againe were as eager of war; here some stood for the King, there others for the Parliament, the greater number was for the one side, but the better for the other. The husband was divided against the wife, the sister against the brother, and the son lifting forbidden hands against the father. Robin beholding so strange a division amongst people so neer in blood, wished himselfe againe in Fairy Land; for, said he, we have no such dinne, no such tumults, nor unnaturall quarrels, but all silence and oblivion and a perpetuall peace. And quickly abandoning the place, he in an instant came into Glocestershire, to a Towne called Tedbury, where the more to increase his misery he met with the spirit of faction and distempered zeale. This was the spirit that was accustomed to make a great hubbub in the churches to teare off the Surplice from the Ministers shoulders, and when the children were to be signed with the signe of the Crosse (like a Divell dispossessed) to teare himself for fury, and with great noyse and foaming to runne out of the Temple. This spirit would faine have persuaded Robin to turne Roundhead, and told him that they were the best sort of Christians: I, replyed Robin, that is even as true as God is in Glocestershire. As he was proceeding in his discourse, he was intercepted by a great noyse and tumult of people, who cried out flye, flye, flye. Amazed at the suddennesse of the cry, and the multitudes of the people that came thronging by; he looked about him to understand what the businesse was, he found it a company of people, whom flying from Cirencester, the ignorant fury of the sword had spared. Prince Rupert had newly entred the Towne, and having thrice summoned it, and they refusing to yeeld it into his hands, he seized on it by violence, and on his first entrance he burned a great part of the Towne, the shot from the windowes by the muskets of the Towne did wonderfully among his men, and he found no better meanes to prevent that mischiefe but by setting fire on the houses, there was a great overthrow, and Colonell Carre, and Colonell Massey, two Chiefe Commanders for the Parliament, were either slaine, or desperately wounded. Robin found this Prince to be a Gentleman of himselfe of a Civill and serious disposition, a man few in words, and very little beholding to Fame for the many strange reports he had delivered of him; affrighted at the thunder of his Armes, Robin dispatched himselfe from him with as much speed as the bullets flew from the mouth of his angry Canons, and on the first summons of the cocke he came to New-arke, where either through feare of some new designe upon them, or through some great cold they had taken, he found every man of the Earl of Newcastles garrison Souldiers to be sicke of a Palsey: loath to continue amongst those crasie people, with an invitive dispatch hee came to Pontefract, where he found the Earle of Newcastle, with the greatest part of his Armie gone towards Yorke, not so much through feare as it was suggested, but for complement rather, and to entertaine the Queene of England, who was expected to be either at Newcastle or at Yorke. He found the Army of the Recusants, though in many combats shaken and scattered, yet not to receive so great an overthrow as many tongues too credulously have voiced it.

" Neither did he find in York masse to be said in every

Church, it being crosse to the method of the close and
subtill generation of the Papists to make a publick profes-
sion of their religion before they had fully perfected their
intentions and by the' strength of Authority made both
the ends of their designes to meet together. Howsoever
it being discovered that the warre which was pretended,
for the maintaining of the King's Prerogative tended now
indeed to the innovation of Religion, and to make the
Papists appeare the Kings best Subjects, it hath. turned
many hearts and armed many hands against them. The
newes of the Queens landing made Robbin so brisk, and
so overcharged him with newes, that being as unable to contain it, as he was greedy to receive it, he could not take a
full survay of Yorke, nor had the leisure to go unto Newcastle to discover what good service those foure Ships have
done to hinder any malignant Vessells that come either
from Holland or from Denmark, from landing at Newcastle; a mad vagary tooke him to come up to London,
which the vagabond elfe performed with such a suddennesse that could he be discovered in his way, he would
have proved rather the object of the memory then of the
eye. The first place hee came into, it was a Conventicle
of the Family of Love, it was then much about two of the
Clock in the morning, and the Candles being put out, they
were going from one exercise unto another. Robbin presented himself before them all, and seemed lusty as the
spirit of youth when it it is newly awakened from the
mornings sleep: the women were well contented to stay,
but the men cryed out a Satyre, a Satyre, a Satyre, and
thrusting them before them all tumbling headlong, down
the staires together, they left him laughing to himself
alone."

ON

THE CHARACTER

OF

SIR JOHN FALSTAFF,

AS ORIGINALLY EXHIBITED BY

SHAKESPEARE

IN THE

TWO PARTS OF KING HENRY IV.

BY

JAMES ORCHARD HALLIWELL, Esq., F.R.S.,

HON. M.R.I.A., F.S.A., F.R.A.S., ETC. ETC. ETC.

" In spite of faction this would favour get ;
But Falstaff stands inimitable yet."

LONDON :
WILLIAM PICKERING, CHANCERY LANE.
1841.

TO

JOHN PAYNE COLLIER, ESQ.,

THIS LITTLE VOLUME

IS INSCRIBED,

AS A SLIGHT TESTIMONY

OF

RESPECT AND ESTEEM.

ADVERTISEMENT.

THE object of the following pages is to endeavour to place in a clearer light a question which has been frequently discussed, but still left in considerable obscurity.

In the earlier ages of Shakespearian criticism, it appears to have been taken for granted that the character of Falstaff was intended to represent a person equally historical with the other *dramatis personæ ;* and the absurd notion that its prototype was Sir John Fastolf appears to be hardly yet exploded. In the present tract I have endeavoured to establish what appears to me an important fact connected with this subject, and I have fortunately been enabled to illustrate it with several documents and passages from rare books, which have escaped the researches of former critics.

I have taken the opportunity of publishing a few notes relating to Shakespeare, but not immediately connected with the subject of this essay.

35, Alfred-place, London,
Eve of St. Michael, 1841.

AN ESSAY

ON THE

CHARACTER OF FALSTAFF.

THE two parts of Henry IV. are unquestionably the most original of Shakespeare's
historical dramas; or, in other words, to avoid
ambiguity, he was not so deeply indebted in
those two plays to the labours of previous
dramatists. We recognize in them the forms
only of the old compositions; and they have
undergone so complete a transformation, in
passing through his hands, that little else than
the title and general character can be traced.
These still remain in an old play entitled " The
Famous Victories of King Henry the Fifth,"
which has been satisfactorily proved to have
been written before the year 1588. The
connexion which exists between a character in

that production, Sir John Oldcastle, and Shakespeare's ever famous fat knight, is a subject to which I wish to draw the attention of critical readers of our great dramatist, in the following pages. I propose to discuss, and I hope I shall be able satisfactorily to set at rest, a question which has arisen, grounded hitherto on a tradition of no earlier date than the commencement of the eighteenth century,* whether Shakespeare in the first instance borrowed the name as well as amplified the character of the above-mentioned nobleman, who is so highly distinguished in the history of the reformed religion.

This question does not in any way affect the fame of Shakespeare. It may be good

---

* I allude, of course, to the well-known tradition handed down to us by Rowe, in his " Life of Shakespeare :"—" It may not be improper to observe that this part of Falstaff is said to have been written originally under the name of Oldcastle ; some of that family being then remaining, the Queen was pleased to command him to alter it ; upon which he made use of Falstaff."

policy to premise this, for I observe with regret
that there are many readers of our immortal
poet's works, who, without a knowledge of the
subject, despise the literature and criticism
which have set the emanations of his genius in
their true historical light, and who are also
greatly averse to the idea of accusing Shakespeare of being indebted to previous writers
for any portion of the material on which he
has founded his dramas.   I am now alluding
to the πολλοι, and not to those who, with a
competent knowledge of contemporary literature, have made it a matter of study.   Among
the numerous readers of Shakespeare, with
whom I have had the fortune to converse, I
have never yet found one who did not consider
him, in the words of an author who ought to
have known better, as " the great poet whom
nature framed to disregard the wretched
models that were set before him, and to create
a drama from his own native and original
stores."   The real fact is, that no dramatist
ever made a freer use of those " wretched
models" than Shakespeare.   It may safely be

said that not a single plot of any of his dramas is entirely his own.   It is true that the sources of some of his plays have not yet been discovered, but they are those that we know he would not have invented, leaving the capability of doing so out of the question.   There can, at any rate, be no doubt that all the historical plays which are ascribed to Shakespeare were on the stage before his time, and that he was employed by the managers to remodel and repair them, taking due care to retain the names of the characters, and preserve the most popular incidents.   In the two parts of Henry IV., as I have observed above, he has so completely repaired the old model, that they may almost be considered in the light of original dramas.

I can scarcely imagine a more interesting subject for literary enquiry than the tracing out the originals of these plays, and the examination of the particular *loci* where the master hand of Shakespeare has commenced his own labours; yet it is a study so inadequately encouraged, and so little valued, that few have

the courage to enlist in its cause. The public
appear to consider it an obstacle, rather than
otherwise, to the free reading of his works, and
wonder more especially what possible connexion
there can be between literary history and romantic dramas. It was but recently that one of our
most learned and acute critics in this way was
pronounced a perfect barbarian — a savage
without a poetical soul, because he fixed by
historic wand the scene of Prospero's enchant-
ments. The master stroke of the photogenic
art was thought unfavourable to the interests
of true poetry, and a " local habitation and a
name " incompatible with the nature of the
theme. Surely, in common fairness, the "still-
vex'd Bermoothes " ought to be expunged,
and all the earthly concomitants deposited,
like Lampedusa, in ethereal uncertainty.

But do we, as Mr. Hunter asks, by researches
such as these, lose any particle of the admira-
tion in which we hold Shakespeare? If the
positive be maintained, there is at least a satisfaction in knowing what is the real fact; and
there is a love of truth, as well as a love of

Shakespeare, and a homage due to both.   A
careful historian would pause, no matter how
strong the evidence was, before he would
attribute to any genius, however vast, the
mighty revolutions in poetry or science which
are vulgarly ascribed to Shakespeare.   The
labours of successive, or more rarely, com-
bined minds, alone are able to accomplish
such things.   When Pope said—

" Nature and Nature's laws lay hid in night :
God said, ' Let Newton be,' and all was light !"

he expressed himself very eloquently; and the
opinion implied in the couplet has become a
popular dogma.   But Newton owed as much to
Kepler as Shakespeare did to Marlowe; and
Coleridge could not have been far wrong when
he extended the weight of those obligations
even beyond the boundary usually adopted by
professed critics.   In plain words, Shakespeare
did not invent—he perfected a drama already
ennobled by the labours of others; and the
history of that drama forms a very curious and
important epoch in our vernacular literature.

Plays were ascribed to Plautus, if we may believe Aulus Gellius, which he only retouched and polished.   They were, to use his own expression, *retractatæ et expolitæ.*   It was so also with Shakespeare ; but few now would be guilty of ascribing that " drum and trumpet " thing, called the " First Part of Henry VI.," to his pen, written doubtlessly before he entered the arena of dramatic competition, though it may have been afterwards slightly revised by him.   I can see little evidence or reason for including it in his works, but as it is often inserted as a genuine play, I will take it as a document in the history of his historical dramas, rather than consider it to have any necessary connexion with them.   To tax Shakespeare with the character of *Fastolf,* as exhibited in that play, is an absolute libel on his genius.   Who, indeed, can reasonably accuse him of introducing the same character in Henry VI., whose death he had described in Henry V. in a manner so remarkable ?   There is not, in fact, any ground for believing that the charac-

ters of *Fastolf* and *Falstaff* have any connexion
whatever with each other.   I much doubt
whether Shakespeare even had the former in
his memory, when he changed the name, as I
shall afterwards show, of Oldcastle to Falstaff;
and I think it extremely probable that the latter name might have been inserted merely for
the purpose of marking one of the principal
traits in his character.

Yet we find historians and journalists con-
stantly giving countenance to this vulgar error,
and Fastolf is mentioned as the prototype of
Falstaff with as much positiveness as though he
were an actual original of a genuine historical
character.   Mr. Beltz, in his recent work on
the Order of the Garter, and a reviewer of that
book in a literary journal of high pretensions,
have fallen into the same error.   The point is
of importance, because it affects a good deal of
our reasoning on the sources of Shakespeare's
most celebrated historical plays; and we are
surprised to find so many writers of reputation
giving their authority to the common mistake.

This leads us to old Fuller,* who was one of the earliest delinquents.   In speaking of Sir John Fastolf, he says :—

" To avouch him by many arguments valiant, is to maintain that the sun is bright, though since the stage hath been overbold with his memory, making him a *thrasonical puff*, and emblem of mock valour.

" True it is, Sir John Oldcastle did first bear the brunt of the one, being made the make-sport in all plays for a coward.   It is easily known out of what purse this black peny came; the Papists railing on him for a heretick, and therefore he must also be a coward, though indeed he was a man of arms, every inch of him, and as valiant as any in his age.

" Now as I am glad that Sir John Oldcastle is put out, so I am sorry that Sir John Fastolfe is put in, to relieve his memory in this base ser-

* "Worthies of England," Edit. 1811, vol. ii., p. 131-2.   Fuller died in 1661, and this work was published for the first time soon afterwards.   This enables us to fix a limit to the date of the passage about to be quoted.

vice, to be the anvil for every dull wit to strike upon. Nor is our comedian excusable by some alteration of his name, writing him Sir John Falstafe, and making him the property of pleasure for King Henry the Fifth to abuse, seeing the vicinity of sounds intrench on the memory of that worthy knight—and few do heed the inconsiderable difference in spelling of their name."

This extract from Fuller, a very credible writer, will of itself go a considerable way towards establishing the truth of Rowe's tradition; but I have other and more important documents to introduce to the notice of my readers, by means of which I hope to be enabled to prove—

1. That the stage was in the possession of a rude outline of Falstaff before Shakespeare wrote either part of Henry IV., under the name of Sir John Oldcastle.

2. That the name of Oldcastle was retained for a time in Shakespeare's Henry IV., but changed to Falstaff before the play was printed.

3. That, in all probability, some of the

theatres, in acting Henry IV., retained the name of Oldcastle after the author had made the alteration.

4. That Shakespeare probably made the change before the year 1593.

I must leave the consideration of the first of these propositions until I have examined the second, because in this case the similarity consists rather in the adoption of the same *dramatis personæ* and subject by Shakespeare and his predecessors, than in the manner in which they are treated.   My first witness for the truth of the second problem, which, with the others, I hope to transform into theorems, is one whose veracity is unimpeachable, because he could have had no possible object in publishing an untruth—I mean Dr. Richard James, librarian to Sir Robert Cotton, a contemporary of Shakespeare, and an intimate friend of " rare " Ben Jonson.   He may thus, through the latter dramatist, have had access to the very best sources of information for the account which he gives in the following dedicatory epistle prefixed to his work entitled

B

" The Legend and Defence of the Noble
Knight and Martyr, Sir John Oldcastel," never
published, but preserved with his other manuscripts in the Bodleian Library,* and which
undoubtedly is a most valuable independent
testimony in favour of the truth of Rowe's
tradition :—

" *To my noble friend Sir Henrye Bourchier.*¦

" Sir Harrie Bourchier, you are descended of
Noble Auncestrie, and in the dutie of a good
man loue to heare and see faire reputatioń pre-
serued from slander and oblivion.   Wherefore
to you I dedicate this edition of Ocleve, where
Sir Jhon Oldcastell apeeres to haue binne a
man of valour and vertue, and onely lost in

* MS. James, 34.   See Bernard's "Catalogus
Librorum Manuscriptorum Angliæ et Hiberniæ,"
fol. Oxon. 1697, par. 1, p. 263.   I am indebted for
my knowledge of this very important document to
the Rev. Dr. Bliss, whose liberality in communicating the results of his extensive reading, when he
can aid the researches of others, has benefited so
many.   I beg leave to return my grateful and
respectful acknowledgments.

his owne times because he would not bowe
vnder the foule superstition of Papistrie, from
whence in so great light of Gosple and learning that there is not yet a more vniversall
departure is to me the greatest scorne of men.
But of this more in another place, and in preface will you please to heare me that which
followes. A young Gentle Ladie of your acquaintance, having read the works of Shakespeare, made me this question: How Sir
John Falstaffe, or Fastolf as it is written in the
statute book of Maudlin Colledge in Oxford,
where everye daye that societie were bound
to make memorie of his soule, could be dead in
Harrie the Fifts time and againe liue in the
time of Harrie the Sixt to be banisht for
cowardize? Whereto I made answeare that
this was one of those humours and mistakes
for which Plato banisht all Poets out of his
commonwealth, that Sir Jhon Falstaffe was in
those times a noble valiant souldier as apeeres
by a book in the Herald's office dedicated vnto
him by a herald whoe had binne with him if I
well remember for the space of 25 yeeres in
the French wars; that he seemes allso to haue

binne a man of learning because in a librarie
of Oxford I finde a book of dedicating
churches sent from him for a present vnto
Bishop Wainflete and inscribed with his owne
hand. That in Shakespeare's first shewe of
Harrie the Fifth, the person with which he
undertook to playe a buffone was not Falstaffe,
but Sir Jhon Oldcastle, and that offence beinge
worthily taken by personages descended from
his title, as peradventure by manie others allso
whoe ought to haue him in honourable memorie, the poet was putt to make an ignorant
shifte of abusing Sir John Falstophe, a man
not inferior of virtue though not so famous in
pietie as the other, who gaue witnesse vnto the
trust of our reformation with a constant and
resolute martyrdom, vnto which he was pursued
by the Priests, Bishops, Moncks, and Friers of
those dayes.   Noble sir, this is all my preface.
God keepe you, and me, and all Christian people from the bloodie designes of that cruell
religion.

    " Yours in all observance,

      " RICH: JAMES."

With respect to this important letter, it will be observed that, by the " first shewe of Harrie the Fifth," James unquestionably means Shakespeare's Henry IV. He could not have confused Shakespeare's play with " The Famous Victories," for in the latter drama the *nomen* of the character of Oldcastle had not been altered. The " young gentle ladie" had read the *works* of Shakespeare, most probably the folio edition, and it is not at all likely she would have alluded to a play which had then been entirely superseded. James and his lady friend also confuse the characters of Fastolf and Falstaff, another example of the unfortunate circumstance of the poet choosing a name so similar to that of the real hero.

Dr. James died at the close of the year 1638, and consequently the work, from which I have quoted the letter given above, must have been composed either in Shakespeare's life-time, or shortly after his death. On a careful comparison of the handwriting with other of his papers which are dated, I came to the conclusion that 1625 was the year in which the

manuscript was written. This, however, must
not by any means be considered conclusive; but
a few years either way are not of great con-
sequence. I have not succeeded in discover-
ing the date of Bourchier's death, the person
to whom the dedicatory epistle is addressed, or
I might perhaps have been enabled to com-
press the uncertain date within even narrower
limits.

I have said that Dr. James, whom Wood
calls "a humorous person," was intimate with
Ben Jonson. I derive my knowledge of this
fact from the papers of the former in the Bodleian Library, but I was disappointed in my
expectation of finding notices of other dramatists. Jonson is frequently spoken of in high
terms, and in one letter particularly he receives
the greatest compliment from James that one
scholar could pay to another:—"Jam patres
illi libenter spectarent ingenium fœcundissimi
Benjamini Jonsoni, quem, ut Thuanus de
Petro Ronsardo, censeo cum omni antiquitate
comparandum, si compta et plena sensibus
poemata ejus et scenica spectemus." When

Jonson's "Staple of News" was produced in 1625, the Doctor addressed him poetically in the following lines, which are here given from the same collection of manuscripts:—

" *To Mr. Benj. Jhonson, on his Staple of Niews*
first presented.

" Sir, if my robe and garbe were richly worth
The daringe of a statute comming forth,
Were I or man of law or law maker,
Or man of Courte to be an vndertaker,
For judgment would I then comme in and say
The manye honours of your *staple* play :
But being nothing so, I dare not haile
The mightie floates of ignorance, who saile
With winde and tide—their Sires, as stories tell,
In our eighth Harrie's time crownd Skelton's Nell,
And the foule Boss of Whittington with greene
Bayes, which on living tronkes are rarelye seene,
Soone sprung, soone fading, but deserving verse,
Must take more lasting glorie from the herse ;
When vulgars loose their sight, and sacred peeres
Of poetrie conspire to make your yeeres
Of memorie eternall, then you shal be read
By all our race of Thespians, board and bed,

And bancke and boure, vallie and mountaine will
Rejoice to knowe somme pieces of your skill !
Your rich Mosaique workes, inled by arte
And curious industrie with everie parte
And choice of all the Auncients, so I write,
Though for your sake I dare not say and fighte."

This brief digression from our immediate
argument is not without its use, because it
satisfactorily shows that Dr. James was acquainted with one of the leading men in the
drama of the time, and of course renders his
testimony on such a subject of more than ordinary value. I will now proceed to give other,
though less important, authorities for the truth
of my second proposition ; and joined with those
already placed before the reader's notice, they
will be found, I think, sufficient to place that
conclusion beyond a doubt

My first extract is from a tract entitled
" The Meeting of Gallants at an Ordinarie, or
the Walkes in Powles," 4to. Lond. 1604. The
only known copy of this work is in Malone's
collection in the Bodleian Library, but it will
shortly be reprinted by the Percy Society, with

the addition of notes and introduction. Some
gallants are " entering into the ordinarie,"
when the following dialogue takes place between one of them and the " fatte hoste":—

" *Host.*   What, Gallants, are you come?
are you come? welcome, Gentlemen; I haue
newes enough for ye all; welcome againe, and
againe: I am so fatte and pursie, I cannot
speake loude inough, but I am sure you heare
mee, or you shall heare me: Welcome, welcome, Gentlemen! I haue Tales, and Quailes
for you; seate yourselues, Gallantes; enter,
Boyes and Beardes, with dishes and Platters; I
will be with you againe in a trice ere you looke
for me.

" *Sig. Shuttlecocke.*   Now, Signiors, how
like you mine Host? did I not tell you he was
a madde round knaue, and a merrie one too:
and if you chaunce to talke of fatte Sir Iohn
Old-castle, he wil tell you he was his great
Grandfather, and not much vnlike him in
Paunch, if you marke him well by all descriptions; and see where hee appeares againe.
Hee told you he would not be longe from you;

let this humor haue scope enough, I pray, and
there is no doubt but his Tales will make vs
laugh ere we be out of our Porridge."

This merely shows that Sir John Oldcastle
had been represented somewhere or other as a
fat man, but I know of no existing account of
any such representation, unless the supposition of the identity between Falstaff and Oldcastle be correct. My next extract is to the
same effect, and is taken from a pamphlet entitled "The Wandering Jew telling Fortunes to
Englishmen," 4to. Lond. 1640, p. 38, which
was certainly written before the year 1630.*
The character Glutton is speaking:—

"A chaire, a chaire, sweet master Jew, a
chaire. All that I say is this,—I'me a fat
man. It has been a West-Indian voyage for
me to come reeking hither. A kitchin-stuffe
wench might pick up a living by following me

* This appears from internal evidence. The plan
and the names of the characters in this work appear
to have been borrowed from a well-known tract
called "The Man in the Moone telling Strange Fortunes, or the English Fortune-teller," 4to. Lond. 1609.

for the fat which I loose in stradling. I doe
not live by the sweat of my brows, but am
almost dead with sweating. I eate much, but
can talke little. Sir John Oldcastle was my
great-grandfather's father's uncle,—I come of
a huge kindred! And of you desire to learne
whether my fortune be to die a yeere or two
hence, or to grow bigger, if I continue as I
doe in feeding, for my victuals I cannot leave.
Say, say, mercifull Jew, what shall become of
me?"

Again I have recourse to Fuller, who, in
another work,* repeats what he said before,
but asserting more distinctly that the character
of Falstaff was *substituted* for that of Oldcastle:

"Stage poets have themselves been very
bold with, and others very merry at, the memory of Sir John Oldcastle, whom they have

---

* "Church History of Britain," edit. 1655, p.
168. Oldys, in his MS. notes to Langbaine, says, in
a marginal note, "If Falstaff appears in this first
part, then he could not be substituted for Oldcastle."
He afterwards thought better of it, and has added, in
a later hand, " Yes, he might."

fancied a boon companion, a jovial royster, and yet a coward to boot, contrary to the credit of all chronicles, owning him a martial man of merit. The best is Sir John Falstaffe hath relieved the memory of Sir John Oldcastle, and of late is substituted buffoone in his place, but it matters as little what petulant poets as what malicious Papists have written against him."

In "Amends for Ladies," 4to. Lond. 1639, a play by Nathaniel Field, which, according to Mr. Collier, could not have been written before 1611, Falstaff's description of honour is mentioned by a citizen of London as if it had been delivered by Sir John Oldcastle :—

———" I doe heare
Your Lordship this faire morning is to fight,
And for your honor. Did you never see
The play wheere the fat knight, hight Oldcastle,
Did tell you truely what this honor was ?"

This single passage will alone render my third proposition highly probable, viz., that some of the theatres, in acting Henry IV.,

retained the name of Oldcastle after the author
had altered it to that of Falstaff.

Early in the year 1600* appeared " The
first part of the true and honorable history of
the life of Sir John Oldcastle, the good Lord
Cobham, as it hath bene lately acted by the
Right Honorable the Earle of Notingham,
Lord High Admiral of England, his servants.
Written by William Shakespeare," 4to. Lond.
The name of the author is supposititious, and
now it is a matter of wonder how so glaring an
imposition could have been suffered to pass
unpunished, and even unnoticed.   Such works
were then of much less moment than they are
now.   Bodley, who was then forming his collection, classes plays under the head of " riffe
raffes," and declares " they shall never come
into mie librarie."   It is possible, however, that
Shakespeare may have edited this play, but,

---

* On Thursday, March 6th, 1599-1600, the Lord
Chamberlain's players acted the play of Sir John
Oldcastle before Vereiken, the Austrian ambassador,
" to his great contentment."   See the "Sidney State
Letters," by Collins, vol. ii. p. 175.

if he allowed his name to be put on the title-page, it shows a carelessness for his own reputation, of which there are but too many instances. The speech of Lord Cobham (Sir John Oldcastle) to the King, at p. 27, may confirm my conjecture:—

" My gracious Lord, unto your Majesty,
Next unto my God, I owe my life ;
And what is mine, either by nature's gift,
Or fortune's bounty, all is at your service.
But for obedience to the Pope of Rome,
I owe him none ; nor shall his shaveling priests
That are in England, alter my belief.
If out of Holy Scripture they can prove
That I am in an error, I will yield,
And gladly take instruction at their hands :
But otherwise, I do beseech your Grace
My conscience may not be encroach'd upon."

These, I think, are the only lines in the whole play which could with any probability be ascribed to Shakespeare, and even they possess but slender claims. The prologue contains an argument for two of the propositions I have

been endeavouring to establish.   It is as follows :—

" The doubtfull title (Gentlemen) prefixt
Vpon the Argument we haue in hand,
May breed suspence, and wrongfully disturbe
The peacefull quiet of your setled thoughts :
To stop which scruple, let this breefe suffice.
It is no pamper'd Glutton we present,
Nor aged Councellour to youthfull sinne :
But one, whose vertue shone aboue the rest,
A valiant Martyr, and a vertuous Peere,
In whose true faith and loyalty exprest
Vnto his Soueraigne, and his Countries weale :
We striue to pay that tribute of our loue
Your fauours merit: Let faire Truth be grac'd,
Since forg'd inuention former time defac'd."

If we now turn to the following scene in the
same play, we shall find that the change in the
name of Shakespeare's knight must have been
made about the same time.   The King in
disguise has just met with Sir John, the thieving
parson of Wrotham, when this dialogue takes
place :—

"*Priest.*   Stand, true man, says a thief.

King. Stand, thief, says a true man. How, if a thief ?

Priest. Stand, thief, too.

King. Then, thief or true man, I must stand, I see. Howsoever the world wags, the trade of thieving yet will never down. What art thou ?

Priest. A good fellow.

King. So am I too ; I see thou dost know me.

Priest. If thou be a good fellow, play the good fellow's part. Deliver thy purse without more ado.

King. I have no money.

Priest. I must make you find some before we part. If you have no money, you shall have ware, as many sound blows as your skin can carry.

King. Is that the plain truth ?

Priest. Sirrah, no more ado. Come, come, give me the money you have. Dispatch, I cannot stand all day.

King. Well, if thou wilt needs have it, there it is. Just the proverb, one thief robs another.   Where the devil are all my old thieves?   Falstaffe, that villaine is so fat, he cannot get on's horse; but methinks Poins and Peto should be stirring hereabouts.

Priest.   How much is there on't, of thy word?

King.   A hundred pound in angels, on my word.   The time has been I would have done as much for thee, if thou hadst past this way, as I have now.

Priest.   Sirrah, what art thou?   Thou seemst a gentleman.

King.   I am no less; yet a poor one now, for thou hast all my money.

Priest.   From whence camst thou?

King.   From the court at Eltham.

Priest.   Art thou one of the King's servants?

King.   Yes, that I am, and one of his chamber.

Priest.   I am glad thou'rt no worse.   Thou may'st the better spare thy money; and think thou mightst get a poor thief his pardon, if he should have need?

King.   Yes, that I can.

Priest.   Wilt thou do so much for me, when I shall have occasion?

c

King.   Yes, faith, will I, so it be for no murder.

Priest.   Nay, I am a pitiful thief.   All the hurt I do a man, I take but his purse.   I'll kill no man.

King.   Then of my word I'll do it.

Priest.   Give me thy hand of the same.

King.   There 'tis.

Priest.   Methinks the King should be good to thieves, because he has been a thief himself, although I think now he be turn'd a true man.

King.   Faith, I have heard he has had an ill name that way in's youth; but how canst thou tell that he has been a thief?

Priest.   How?   Because he once robb'd me before I fell to the trade myself, when that villanous guts that led him to all that roguery was in's company there, that Falstaff."

I next consider the internal evidence in Shakespeare's plays themselves that Oldcastle once supplied the place of Falstaff. Every one will remember the rout of Falstaff and his companions by the Prince and Poins, near Gadshill, when Henry triumphantly exclaims—

" Got with much ease.   Now merrily to horse :
The thieves are scatter'd, and possess'd with fear
So strongly, that they dare not meet each other ;
Each takes his fellow for an officer.
Away, good Ned ; Falstaff sweats to death,
And lards the lean earth as he walks along :
Wer't not for laughing, I should pity him."

It will be seen that in the fifth line a foot is
actually deficient, and *Oldcastle,* instead of
Falstaff, would perfectly complete the metre.
It is true that some other explanation might be
offered, perhaps equally plausible ; but it is at
any rate a singular coincidence that in the very
first place where the name Falstaff occurs in
the text, an additional syllable should be
required.

In the second scene of the first act, Falstaff
asks the Prince, "Is not my hostess of the tavern
a most sweet wench ?"   Prince Henry answers,
" As the honey of Hybla, my *old* lad of the
castle."   I consider this to be a pun, in the
original play as first written, on the name of *Sir
John Oldcastle.*   The commentators say this
passage was transferred from the old play ; but,

c 2

as Master Ford observes, " I cannot put off
my opinion so easily." I am confirmed in my
conjecture by a passage in the play of Sir John
Oldcastle, where there is a similar play upon
words :—

" There's one, they call him Sir John Oldcastle.
He has not his name for nought ; for like a castle
Doth he encompass them within his walls.
But till that castle be subverted quite,
We ne'er shall be at quiet in the realm."

I now beg to call the reader's particular
attention to a passage in Part 2, Act iii., Sc. 2,
which affords undeniable proof that the name
of Oldcastle once occupied the place which
Falstaff now holds. Shallow is recalling remi-
niscences of his younger days, and he brings
Falstaff in among other wild companions :—
" Then was Jack Falstaff, now Sir John, a boy,
and *page to Thomas Mowbray, Duke of Norfolk.*" It was Sir John Oldcastle, and not
Falstaff, who was page to that nobleman.
Shakespeare could not have fallen into an error
by following the older play, because the cir-

cumstance is not there mentioned; and it
would be arming oneself against the force of
evidence, which already is so overpowering
on the opposite side, to class this among
Shakespeare's historical blunders. I do not
consider it necessary in this place to multiply
references to the old chroniclers, in support
of my assertion, that the historical fact, to
which Shakespeare alludes in this passage,
applies to Oldcastle, and not to Falstaff. One
will be sufficient, and I have selected the following extract from Weever's poetical Life
of Oldcastle, 12mo. Lond. 1601, where he
is introduced speaking in his own person :—

> " Within the spring-tide of my flowring youth,
>   He [his father] stept into the winter of his age ;
>   Made meanes (Mercurius thus begins the truth)
>   That I was made Sir Thomas Mowbrais page."

Perhaps, however, the conclusion of the
epilogue to the two plays furnishes us with the
most decisive evidence that Shakespeare had
delineated a character under the name of Oldcastle which had given offence, confirming the

tradition handed down to us by Rowe, and the relation which Dr. James gives :—

" One word more, I beseech you. If you be not too much cloyed with fat meat, our humble author will continue the story with Sir John in it, and make you merry with fair Katharine of France : where, for anything I know, Falstaff shall die of a sweat, unless already he be killed with your hard opinions; for Oldcastle died a martyr, and this is not the man."

It is unnecessary to pursue this subject further. The other notices I have collected are mere repetitions of what are given above,* and add little weight to the general evidence. I have now only my fourth position to defend, for I shall pass over my first proposition, as a point already decided, with a reference to Mr. Collier's work on the English stage, who gives it as his opinion that Shakespeare was indebted for the " bare hint" of the delightful creation of

* Heylen, as quoted by Farmer, says, " This Sir John Fastolfe was, without doubt, a valiant and wise captain, notwithstanding the stage hath made merry with him."—See *Boswell's Malone,* vol. xviii., p. 16.

Falstaff to the old play of " The Famous Victories," and nothing more.

There must of course be great uncertainty
in fixing the precise date when Shakespeare
made the alteration in the name of the character of his fat knight; and my conjecture on this
point depends entirely upon an opinion which
I have formed, and shall hereafter publish,
on the date of the composition of another
play—the " Merry Wives of Windsor." It
would be unfair, then, of course, to place my
view of the subject in any other light than that
of conjecture formed upon premises, the probability of which must at present be taken upon
my own authority. I believe the first sketch
of the " Merry Wives" to have been written
in the year 1593, and the name of Oldcastle
must have been changed to Falstaff before
that sketch was written. Everything tends to
prove this. For instance, the first metrical
piece which occurs in it could not have been
written with the former name :—

" And I to Ford will likewise tell
How Falstaff, varlet vile,

Would have her love, his dove would prove,
And eke his bed defile."

It may be objected that, as the "Merry
Wives" has little or no necessary connexion
with the historical plays—as we have no certain evidence to show whether it was written
before or after the two parts of Henry IV.,
the settlement of the question of names, if I
may so express myself, in the former, is no
guide whatever to the period at which the
change was made in the other plays.   In
reply, I must confess this position is hypotheti-
cal, unless my readers agree with me in believing the "Merry Wives" to have been
written after the Second Part of Henry IV.,
and before Henry V., a subject which it would
be irrelevant to discuss in this place.

The First Part of Henry IV. was entered
at Stationers' Hall, on Feb. 25th, 1597-8,
under the title of, "A booke intitled the His-
torye of Henry the iiij.th, with his battaile at
Shrewsburye against Henry Hottspure of the
Northe, with the conceipted Mirth of Sir John

Falstaffe." Falstaff was the name, then, at least
as early as the year 1597.   After this period
we have frequent allusions to the character.
Ben. Jonson, in the epilogue to " Every Man
out of his Humour," acted in 1599, thus
alludes to the " thrasonical puff :"—

" Marry, I will not do as Plautus in his
Amphytrio, for all this, ' Summi Jovis causa,
plaudite,' beg a plaudite, for God's sake ; but
if you, out of the bounty of your good-liking,
will bestow it, why you may in time make lean
Macilente as fat as *Sir John Falstaff.*"—
Gifford's Jonson, vol. ii., p. 210.

I will give one more example of the Knight's
popularity from Roger Sharpe's " More Fooles
Yet," 4to. Lond. 1610 :—

" In Virosum.

" How Falstaffe like doth sweld Virosus looke,
As though his paunch did foster every sinne ;
And sweares he is injured by this booke,—
His worth is taxt, he hath abused byn :
Swell still, Virosus, burst with emulation,
I neither taxe thy vice nor reputation."

It would not be difficult to multiply similar extracts. Mr. Collier has printed a document which shows how Falstaff was probably attired for the stage at this early period, which is attested by the creditable name of Inigo Jones. A character is to be dressed "*like* a Sir John Falstaff, in a roabe of russet, quite low, with a great belley, like a swolen man, long moustacheos, the sheows shorte, and out of them great toes, like naked feete : buskins to sheaw a great swolen leg." Thus it would seem that size has always been the prevailing characteristic of Falstaff's theatrical appearance.

This consideration leads me to remark that the character of Oldcastle, as exhibited in "The Famous Victories," could not by itself have developed so popular and general a notion of "hugeness," as that suggested in the extracts I have given relative to him or Falstaff. On the whole, then, independently of the entire evidence being in its favour, I think the account given by Dr. James would be the most plausible conjecture we could form, were we without the aid of that evidence.

The only objection, as far as I can see, which can be raised against the veracity of Dr. James's account, is the slight discrepancy I have previously mentioned. My own faith is not at all shaken by this circumstance, because he was repeating from memory the doubts of another, as he had heard them in conversation, and was probably more solicitous of placing the question in a position to enable him to defend his hero Oldcastle, than of giving a correct version of what he considered an error in Shakespeare. I cannot think that he would have introduced Shakespeare in the manner in which he has, if he had not been pretty certain of the truth of the anecdote. Fastolf, too, was an Oxford man, and he resents his supposed degradation under the title of Falstaff. His successors were apparently impressed with the same notion. Warton tells us that "the magnificent Knight, Sir John Fastolf, bequeathed estates to Magdalen College, part of which were appropriated to buy liveries for some of the senior scholars; but the benefactions in time yielding no more than a penny a week to the scholars who received the liveries, they were called, by way of contempt, *Falstaff's buckram-men.*"

An anonymous and inedited poet of the early part of the seventeenth century, whose MS. works were formerly in the possession of Oldys, complains sadly of Shakespeare, for a similar reason :—

" Here to evince that scandal has been thrown
    Upon a name of honour, charactred
From a wrong person, coward and buffoon ;
    Call in your easy faiths, from what you've read
To laugh at Falstaffe ; as a humour fram'd
To grace the stage, to please the age, misnam'd.

" No longer please yourselves to injure names
    Who lived to honour : if, as who dare breathe
A syllable from Harry's choice, the fames,
    Conferr'd by princes, may redeem from death ?
Live Fastolffe then ; whose trust and courage once
Merited the first government in France."

The " De sacramentis dedicationis sermo," which Dr. James mentions, is still preserved in the archives of Magdalen College, Oxford,

with the following curious original memo-
randum :—

" Suo domino colendissimo magistro Wil-
lelmo Waynflete, sedis ecclesiæ Sancti Swy-
thini Wyntoniensis episcopo, quæ olim ante
tempus consecrationis dictæ ecclesiæ templum
Dagon vocabatur tempore Paganorum gen-
tium, et præsentatur domino præscripto episcopo de beneficio domini Johannis Fastolf
militis, ob memoriam sui, quamvis modicum
fuerit quantitatis, die sextodecimo mensis
Decembris, Anno Christi 1473, per Willel-
mum Wyrcestre."*

But I have said enough respecting Sir John
Fastolf, who, brave as he probably was, has
acquired only an adventitious importance, by
being confused with our poet's "coward and
buffoon." The two were confused because

* William Wyrcestre was Fastolf's physician.
In his commonplace-book, in MS. Sloan. 4, p. 78,
Wyrcestre informs us that Fastolf, " obiit ex dictis
passionibus [*i. e.* asmatis] infra 158 diebus a prima
die inceptionis dictæ febris ethicæ, ut bene per expe-
rientiam numeram."

few, as Fuller says in a passage I have quoted,
"do heed the inconsiderable difference in
spelling of their names." What reason have
we for thinking that Shakespeare took more
"heed" of this matter than his contemporaries, when he chose the name of Falstaff? If
writers on the absurd dispute concerning the
orthography of the poet's name would but remember this, how much trouble might be saved
in refuting the affected innovation.

With these observations I conclude my collection of facts and arguments, all of which
tend more or less to confirm the literal truth of
the tradition handed down to us by Rowe.
Mr. D'Israeli, in his recently published work,
justly remarks, that, "though the propagators
of gossip are sad blunderers, they rarely aspire
to be original inventors;" and, in this instance,
the course of a century has not accumulated
any posthumous additions to the original fact
as it really happened.

Rowe's life of our poet is valuable, inasmuch
as he occasionally gives us information not to
be found elsewhere, though evidently not

always in a very accurate manner.   As an
editor, he was below par; but it must be remembered that, after the four folios, he was the first
to collect the works of Shakespeare together.
" This Rowe," says the Earl of Oxford,* " a
special editor, though he pretended to be a
poet, yet he knew little of what he was about,
for there never was a worse edition ; he not
only left the errors that had been in other
editions, but added many more of his own, with
most vile prints."

Unwearied industry has exerted itself for
biographical particulars relative to Shakespeare.   How little has hitherto been discovered !   Yet I am not wholly without
hopes, even now, of something more turning
up, for many private collections still remain
unsearched—and there is no telling what the
archives of our ancient nobility contain.   At
all events, let us hope, that whoever can in any
manner aid this important enquiry, will not
hesitate in sending any new information forth
to the world at once, for documentary evidence

* MS. Harl. 7544 ; a book containing some curious biographical information.

on this subject is of so high a value, that it
ought not to be suffered to remain in manuscript.
Under this impression, I will here contribute
two ανεκδοτα, albeit fragments, which have
hitherto escaped the researches of all the
biographers of our great dramatist.

My readers will perhaps be surprised to
learn that the fragments I allude to were discovered in Aubrey's manuscript collections, in
the Ashmolean Museum at Oxford, which have
been so repeatedly referred to by the biographers and critics.   It will be recollected, that
Aubrey, in his life of D'Avenant, in that collection, gives us two anecdotes regarding
Shakespeare.   These have been frequently
printed; but, during a recent visit to Oxford,
I had the curiosity to inspect the original
manuscript, and found that two paragraphs,
*scratched through, but not with a contempo-
rary pen,* had escaped notice.   By the aid
of a strong light, and a powerful magnify-
ing glass, I was enabled to read them entirely,
with the exception of a few letters.   I here
present them to the reader :—

    1. "I have heard parson R—b— say, that

Mr. W. Shakespeare here gave him a hundred kisses."

The passage immediately preceding this, and which is not erased, is as follows:—" Mr. William Shakespeare was wont to goe into Warwickshire once a yeare, and did commonly in his journey lye at this house in Oxon, where he was exceedingly respected." The word "here," of course, in the above paragraph, refers to Oxford.

Aubrey again speaks of Shakespeare, and in the other erased passage I found the following:

2. " His mother had a very light report."

The first is a striking, but, considering the period, not at all an improbable, anecdote of the friendship which existed between Shakespeare and D'Avenant.   On the second I shall make no comment.   I may, however, add, that Mr. Kirtland, assistant keeper of the Ashmolean Museum, who is deeply skilled in palæography, agreed with me in my reading of the blotted passages.

On any other person but Shakespeare,

D

minute enquiries of this nature would be considered trifling; but so little do we know of the
personal character of our national bard, that
every early notice of him is worthy of pre-
servation. His pre-eminence was not acknowledged by his contemporaries; his works fell
into neglect while written memorials of him
remained; and when he emerged into universal
celebrity, we find nought but a few accidental
notices of him preserved, and five autograph
signatures!

But although, as I have just said, his pre-
eminence was not acknowledged by his contemporaries, his reputation must have been
very considerable, even in those days; perhaps,
however, eclipsed by the fame of other dramatists. Yet it is seldom that we find so just a
tribute paid to his genius, while he was yet in
the land of the living, as Samuel Sheppard
gives in a poem* entitled "The Fairy King,"

* MS. Rawl. Poet. 28, in the Bodleian Library;
a folio volume on paper. I have never seen this MS.
mentioned in print.

written in imitation of Spenser, soon after the
year 1610.　The author, in this poem, not
only mentions Shakespeare, but marshalls the
other English poets in chronological order,
commencing with Chaucer and Skelton.　I am
tempted to give rather a long extract from
this part of the work :—

" Spencer the next, whom I doe thinke't no shame
　　To imitate, if now his worke affords
So vast a glory !　O how faire a fame,
　　Had hee not doated on exploded words,
Had waited on him !　Let his honour'd name
　　Find veneration 'bove the Earth's great lords !
Great Prince of Poets, thou canst never die,
Lodg'd in thy rare immortall history !

" Immortall Mirrour of all poesie,
　　Sprit of Orpheus, bring your pretious balms !
God of Invention, to thy memory
　　Wee'l offer incense, singing hymns and psalms !
Joy of our laurell, Jove's deare Mercury,
　　Ingyrt his grave with myrtle and with palms,
Whose rare desert first kindled my desire,
And gave mee confidence thi s to aspire.
　　D 2

" Then Harrington, whose sweet conversion vies
    With Ariosto's fam'd originall ;
O what a passion will his soule surprize,
    Whose mind's not clog'd with lumpish earth,
        who shall
Peruse thy Annotations and applies
    Their severall heights as they in order fall :
Nor, this omitted, hadst thou miss'd of fame ;
Thy Epigrams shall canonize thy name !

" Chapman the next, who makes great Homer's
        song,
    Th' eternall boast of the Pernassides,
To vaile its bonnet to our English tongue ;
    What can the power of wit or art expresse,
That, without offering all that's holy wrong,
    Wee lodg'd in his large brest, must not confesse ?
Nor can wee match his most admired play,
Either in Sophocles or Seneca.

" Wooton the next, whose fragments have farre
        more
    Of worth then mighty volumes full compleat ;
The richest wit may borrow from his store ;
    A generall scholler, flowing pithie neat ;
An able minister of state, therefore
    Quallifide by his prince for actions great ;

'Tis a measuring cast which of them were
The wiser king or wiser councellour.

" Daniell the next, grave and sententious,
   In all high knowledge excellent hee sung
The brawles 'twixt Yorke and Lancaster 'mongst
     us,
   With an angel-like and a golden tongue;
Nothing in him vaine or ridiculous,
   His lines like to his fancie, hie and strong ;
More haughty tragedies no age hath seene
Then his ' Philotas,' or ' Ægyptian Queene.'

" King James the next, a prince without compare,
   During whose reigne the heavens were pleas'd
     to smile ;
Hee hated swords and loath'd the name of warre,
   And yet all nations feard this Borean ile :
His works, his learning, and great parts declare,
   Hee wrot a most succinct elaborate stile ;
His converse with the Nine, let that rare worke
Declare, where Don John once more beats the
     Turke.

" Bacon the next. Cease, Greece, to boast the parts
   Of Plato or great Aristotle!   Wee,

In this rare man, have all their radyant arts,
   Who was a walking, living librarie ;
Wonder of men, thy high, thy vast deserts
   Deserve a Plutarch's pen !   By thee wee vie
And vanquish all the auncients; thou alone
Hast rais'd our tongue to full perfection.

" Shakespeare the next; who wrot so much, so
      well,
   That, when I view his bulke, I stand amaz'd ;
A genius so inexhaustible,
   That hath such tall and numerous trophies
      rais'd,
Let him bee thought a block, an infidell,
   Shall dare to skreene the lustre of his praise :
Whose works shall find their due, a deathlesse
      date,
Scorning the teeth of time or force of fate !"

   Now " my charms are all o'erthrown."   I
have brought together what I have been able
to collect on a few points in Shakespeare's
literary history—points undoubtedly of interest and curiosity; and if I have succeeded in
setting at rest any disputed question, or made
an approach to it on either side, I shall not

consider my labour entirely thrown away.   A time may come when the very names of all our Shakespearian editors and commentators shall be forgotten; but will the " Apalachian mountains, the banks of the Ohio, and the plains of Sciota," ever resound with the accents of our great dramatist?   The beneficial effects of their researches may then remain, perhaps when the memory of that language which styled the genius of England a " barbarian," shall have perished.   But I will not dive further into futurity.

THE END.

CURIOSITIES OF MODERN

SHAKSPERIAN CRITICISM.

BY

J. O. HALLIWELL, ESQ. F.R.S. &c.

LONDON:

JOHN RUSSELL SMITH, 36, SOHO SQUARE.

MDCCCLIII.

CURIOSITIES, ETC.

THE judgment of contemporary criticism, with respect to the merits of works of learning and research, has scarcely a perceptible influence on the opinions of those for whom they are chiefly designed; and its effect even on the general reader is of a very ephemeral character, for whenever a work possesses valuable information peculiar to itself, there is a certainty that it will be appreciated in time, in opposition to all adverse testimonies. To be convinced of the truth of this, it is sufficient to refer to the older reviews, to their angry denunciations of books which have outlived even the names of the critics, or lavish praises of others long since forgotten, and to the well-established fact that scarcely ever, even by accident, does a contemporaneous critic assign to a work the exact place that it occupies in the estimation of posterity. It is hardly requisite to refer to examples, which will occur to almost every reader; yet there may be selected one as peculiarly bearing on the subject of the present pamphlet—Douce's *Illustrations*—a work which now holds so distinguished and standard a place in Shaksperian literature, but which was so unfairly attacked on its first publication, its too sensitive author never subjected himself to a similar assault, and the other results of his vast reading are unfortunately reserved for the benefit of a future age—one of the many lamented consequences arising from the license conventionally permitted to the periodical critics.

Deeply impressed with the slight importance, in regard to the work itself, to be attached to the angry denunciations of the weekly reviewers, I was fully prepared for the opinion of my friends that any reply to a rancorous attack on my folio edition of the Works of Shakespeare, which appeared in the *Athenæum*, would be unnecessary for the sake of any readers of the work itself, and would, in fact, be giving the assault a character of greater importance than could reasonably be attached to it. And such an opinion would, under ordinary circumstances, have been most sound. Had the reviewers, for example, merely ridiculed the design of the work, expressed their contempt for its archæological commentaries, disagreed with all its criticisms, and exercised their severity in any other way that might by possibility have been conscientious,—not a word would have been extracted from me in reply. I should have been well contented to have allowed the work to have awaited the opinion of the student. But the *Athenæum* reviewers have gone further than this, although they have not given expression to so sweeping a condemnation : they have done worse, though the effects of their criticism will certainly be ultimately more innocuous. In despair of injuring the work by fair means, they have descended *to misrepresent facts* for the sake of establishing a censure against its editor. It is for the public to decide whether they will accept this mode of criticism—whether, in short, they will in future give credence to reviewers, who, rather than forego an attack on a work against which they are prejudiced, will assert circumstances not at all warranted by facts.

It is not my intention to bandy words with the reviewers—I shall confine myself most exclusively to bare matters of fact, that are capable of proof. I entreat the reader to look into the subject for himself, and decide *on facts alone*, not allowing his judgment to be influenced by subtle reasoning, which convinces only by words;—and I shall not be afraid of the result. The reviewers, having the command of circulation, and addressing chiefly those who will not take the trouble to examine for themselves, may persuade the indifferent to adopt almost any view they may please to support; but there will still be a few, who will eventually exercise an important influence on the opinions of the many, and will give an impartial judgment derived from the real facts. I will now, without further preface, give the reviewers' own words, and conclusively demonstrate to every unbiassed reader that I have been subjected to the unfairest kind of criticism.

1. The reviewers, after observing the work "contains a multitude of pretty little illustrations by Fairholt and facsimiles by Netherclift, all which have been worked most carefully, and show to great advantage on stout paper manufactured by Dickinson," proceed to say,—"*The illustrations of Stratford scenery and objects have all been borrowed from other works of Mr. Halliwell and Mr. Fairholt; but they tell well in their present places, and enable Mr. Halliwell to make a great display in his first volume. Certainly, if Mr. Halliwell is able to borrow as many illustrations for his subsequent volumes,*

and shall carry out his scheme with anything like the spirit of this beginning, the subscribers will have good reason to congratulate themselves on possessing a handsome-looking set of books which can be in the hands of only very few people." This statement is not correct, there being no fewer than thirty-eight new engravings and facsimiles relating to Stratford, and to the Shakespeares in connection with Stratford; Mr. Fairholt having accompanied me again over the localities which connect themselves with the history of the poet and his family, and examined anew the entire series of church books and corporation papers that in any way relate thereto, for the purpose of completing facsimiles of the entire series. Even in the account of the birth-place in Henley Street, in respect to which I have necessarily used for the most part previous engravings, and where one would have thought new artistic material impossible of access, there are two interesting objects never previously engraved in any work on the subject, viz. the garret over the room in which Shakespeare was born, and the lower room in John Shakespeare's house, both of which are important as conveying a clear idea of the original state of the house. The reviewers may have been misled in some respect by several of the new woodcuts being necessarily very similar to other engravings of the same objects, but they should have examined them more minutely before they inferred that they had all been borrowed. I can truly say I have not spared, on account of the expense, a single engraving I thought might be interesting or valuable.

2. "*The first part is a reprint, with some few alterations,*

of Mr. Halliwell's 'Life of Shakespeare,' published in one volume, octavo, 1848.* *This occupies half of the volume, running from p.* 1 *to p.* 263." So far from this being the case, the biography has been almost entirely re-written, *and nearly one half is additional matter,* not to be found in the octavo edition. There are several newly-discovered papers respecting John Shakespeare, and no fewer than six new documents respecting Shakespeare himself, besides the three very curious notices of the poet at p. 223, which contain the last mention of him previous to his death. The whole biography has been corrected, added to, and materially altered in every respect, as might be ascertained by any one making even a cursory examination of the two works; and it is altogether unfair to call it a " reprint, with some few alterations." Throughout this portion of my work, I did not rely even on what I had previously published, but again examined every document, wherever it was located, and devoted a month at Stratford to the most minute collation of the important papers there. I can conscientiously say, that I spared neither labour nor expense in my examinations; and all matters which I had previously taken on

---

* A very curious instance of the reviewers' accuracy occurs in their notice of this work, in which they accuse me of omitting an " important portion " of the passage in Dugdale's 'Diary' respecting the monumental bust at Stratford. Having quoted the whole of the passage with literal accuracy, it was very long before I discovered the probable cause of such a singular mis-statement; but I have since found the account in Dugdale quoted altogether incorrectly, *with the interpolation of several words from another document,* in Mr. Cunningham's *Hand-book of London.* Because, therefore, I did not repeat this oversight, I am accused of omitting a passage in Dugdale which no one but Mr. Cunningham has been fortunate enough to find.

trust, I took great pains to examine for myself: I was rewarded by saving myself from the error of again quoting the Bridgewater papers as genuine.

3. "*There are now published two or three facsimiles of formal legal documents relating to the Henley Street house.*" This merely shows how carelessly the reviewers have examined the work, there being only one facsimile of the kind —and a very important one it is, being the only early document of the slightest value in showing the probability that Shakespeare was born in the house now shown as the birth-place. It exhibits the slight attention paid by reviewers to these subjects, to find that with one exception—which occurred in an able Shaksperian article in the *Times* —not a single critic has observed the real importance of this deed. One would have thought that the leading members of a Committee that gave so large a sum for the house, would have adopted with avidity the only evidence yet discovered that will justify their zeal. The copy of it was procured by me at the cost of great trouble and expense.

4. "*A gentleman, who is very sharp on the blunders of other people, should be a little more accurate himself. Mistakes which Mr. Halliwell sets down as evidences of the ignorance of the scrivener, are shown by these facsimiles to be mere mis-readings by himself.*" This is a curious specimen of the haphazard sort of criticism indulged in by the reviewers. In the first place, I am not aware that there is a single instance in my work in which I have been "very sharp" —to use the reviewers' phraseology—on the blunders of

other people. In the second, it is a positive fact, that the only mistake pointed out by me as an error of the scrivener, *cum pertinentiis jacentium,* in the documentary evidence alluded to, viz., that respecting the house in Henley Street, *is* to be found in the facsimile! What can one say to criticism of this kind?

5. *" The Essay on the formation of the text is perhaps the best of Mr. Halliwell's additions to Shakespeare criticism. It has, however, but slender claims to originality. It is an enlargement of a paper printed in the first volume of the old Variorum, entitled ' Essay on the Phraseology and Metre of Shakespeare and his Contemporaries.'"* This is an excessive exaggeration, and can only, I fear, be considered as a wilful mis-statement. The Essay alluded to will be found in vol. i, pp. 507-585, of Malone's Shakespeare, ed. Boswell, 8vo, 1821, and I do not think any one will openly say that mine is a mere enlargement of it :—there is scarcely indeed, any similarity to be traced between the two. The Essay in Boswell is chiefly on the metre, and the observations on the phraseology are restricted to a few peculiarities of diction; while the Essay in my work—I do not see why I should affect reserve in such a matter—chiefly consists of an elaborate inquiry into Elizabethan idiom, which, with the exception of a very small proportion of the examples, is entirely original.

6. The reviewer, after giving a slight note of the principal features of my introduction to the *Tempest,* and absolutely mentioning the history of the Dead Indian, observes, —*" In all this—and these subjects comprise everything of*

importance in the Introduction—there is nothing new."
Now it is difficult to imagine a greater mis-statement than
this. The account of the Dead Indian is almost entirely
new—I may mention especially the curious notices now
for the first time collected from records of the time, furnish-
ing a connected history of the Indian, and the exceedingly
curious drawing from a MS. in Canterbury Cathedral, the
examination of which entailed the trouble of a journey to
Mr. Fairholt and myself, that we thought was amply repaid
by the acquisition of one of the most interesting pictorial
illustrations of Shakespeare ever discovered. In addition
to these, I may mention the account of the exhibition of a
' strange fish,' from the singular broadside in Mr. Daniel's
collection, as quite new ; and the notice of Ayrer's play is
given at greater length than in any other publication. In
fact, the Introduction to this play is full of new information
and original reasoning ; and, as the impression of the work
is so limited, it may not be amiss to draw attention to an
important supplementary notice at pp. 504-6, which shows
clearly who was the historical prototype of Prospero. The
conclusion of the Italian extract indicates, for the first time,
the real foundation of one of the chief incidents of the
Tempest.

7. *" What Mr. Halliwell has written about Ayrer's play,
although he undervalues its importance when excusing himself for not saying more, is really of sufficient interest to
stimulate fresh inquiry on the subject. But where is this
play to be seen? Whence did Mr. Halliwell derive his
knowledge of it? If from an account by Mr. Thoms, where
is that to be found? Information of this kind ought never*

to be omitted.   Editors should remember that they do not write for those who know, but for those who do not,—and that their judgments are valueless unless they give the most distinct opportunity of going to their authorities." But for their own confession, I should have thought it incredible that the reviewers have so little knowledge of the commonest works of dramatic criticism, as not to know that Ayrer's play is to be found in one of Tieck's best known publications ; but the reviewers again misrepresent me, *as I have distinctly stated that the play alluded to was reprinted by Tieck*, observing that the similarities to be traced between that production and the *Tempest* are of so insignificant a character, that its repetition in my work was altogether unnecessary.   It may well be asked, as the reviewers have never seen Ayrer's play, how is it possible for them to know that I have undervalued its importance ?   Is not this an evidence of the reviewers' mere guess-work in their opinions on such subjects ?   I have given as full an account of those parts of Ayrer's play which are analogous to incidents in the *Tempest*, as they at all deserve ; an account derived from a perusal of the play itself.

8. *" He (Mr. Halliwell) describes how it was customary to dress ancient magicians on the stage ; and he gives Inigo Jones's representation of an ' aery spirit ;' but without any hint of where he got it from."* The reviewers must have examined the work very hastily, because I distinctly state, in the text, that the representation is taken from Inigo's sketches for his masques ; and in the List of Illustrations, the most conspicuous part of the book, I describe it as, " the figure of an ' aery spirit ' from the illustrations

to Inigo Jones's Masques, published by the Shakespeare Society." Surely these are sufficient references to a work so exceedingly well known.

9. "*Mr. Halliwell's text of 'the Tempest' differs but little from that of the old Variorum.*" So far from this being the case, it differs in nearly every page, and, in some respects, very materially. It is, indeed, scarcely credible that the reviewers, having made this sweeping statement, should confess, only a few lines afterwards,—" *We do not pretend to have gone through the play*; *but we have dipped into it here and there.*" If so, how could the reviewers honestly state that my text differs but little from that of the old Variorum? It would be difficult to imagine a more striking example than this affords of the reviewers' own confession of their absolute unfairness.

10. "*All the difficulties in the text remain entirely untouched by Mr. Halliwell; not one of them—so far as we have noticed—is got rid of, or even lightened.*" The " difficulties" in the text of this play are not numerous, but there is scarcely one on which I have not thrown some new light. The reader will remember that an absolute explanation of the few words in Shakespeare not *at all* understood, can only be recovered by vast labour and reading : nevertheless, even in this well-known play, the peculiar use of the term *Amen*—perhaps the greatest stumbling-block to the critics —is unravelled for the first time by two extracts quoted in my edition. On the other difficulties—such as *scamels, trash, Butt, deck'd, busy-least, twilled, the hair line,* and *rack* —there is always some novelty to be found in my notes;

and, with respect to the last, I find I have arrived, by a different line of reading, to the opinion given by Mr. Dyce in his excellent *Few Notes*, which was published after (though written before) the appearance of my edition of the play. In fact, with one trifling exception, Mr. Dyce has adopted the same views as myself in his notes on the readings of this drama.

11. *Mr. Halliwell gives*, p. 474, " *three extracts to prove that vanity was used for the physical or mental affection designated by light-headedness,—that, however, being admitted not to be the sense in which Shakespeare uses the word.*" This conveys a misrepresentation of my note, which runs thus,—" *Vanity*, delusion, illusion. A person, who was light-headed, was formerly said to have the *vanity in his head*," where the word *vanity* of course stands for *delusion* or *illusion*. The three extracts show clearly that such was the meaning of the term, *not that the word vanity, by itself, was ever used for light-headedness.*

12. Perhaps the reviewers have reached the climax of misrepresentation, when they boldly state that, " *much of it* (*the annotation on the play*) *is derived from the old Variorum.*" Any reader, who will take the trouble to compare the two editions, will find how small a portion is derived from the latter work; and how much is original. Such an accusation is so obviously contrary to fact, that it scarcely deserves contradiction ; were it not that there are always persons to be found who will not be at the pains to examine for themselves. For the sake of these, it may be well to observe that out of *one hundred and eight* folio pages of notes, only *sixteen*

pages are derived from the Variorum, and even those few chiefly consist of extracts re-collated at the cost of great labour and trouble.

It is unnecessary to pursue the subject further. If, in a short notice of little more than two pages, the *Athenæum* reviewers can condescend to misrepresentations of so obvious and unfair a nature, their animus towards the Editor of the work they are criticising is too apparent to require further exposure. I am perfectly contented to leave the matter to the judgment of the public, begging them again and again to derive that judgment from "facts," and not from "opinions."

It may, however, be worth while to ascertain, how far the *Athenæum* reviewers, who venture to pronounce so arrogant a judgment on my edition of the *Tempest*, minutely understand the text of Shakespeare ; and again I will adhere to subjects that are undoubted matters of fact, not mentioning those that depend for their determination on critical opinions, in respect to which there is naturally so much room for disagreement. In the second scene of the third act, where Ariel creates confusion between Caliban, Stephano, and Trinculo,—

Ste. Didst thou not say he lied ?
Ari. Thou liest !
Ste. Do I so ? take thou that [*strikes him*]. As you like this, give me the lie another time.
Trin. I did not give thee the lie;

the reviewers, observing that the introduction of *thee* in the last line is " entirely unnecessary and wrong"—an opinion at all events open to question—say, " *what can be said in defence of this, we cannot conjecture.*" But this reading, ignored by the reviewers, is positively to be found in one of the folios, being one of the best of the few emendations made by the editor of 1685! How is it possible to argue on these subjects with those who are unprovided with the simple knowledge absolutely necessary to render any discussion profitable?

In the preparation of the text I have, for reasons given in my essay on Elizabethan phraseology, considered the singulars and plurals, in certain cases, to be interchangeable; and the variations hence introduced are alone very numerous, but they are generally too simple and obvious to require in all cases separate notification. Thus, in Ferdinand's speech, at the commencement of the third act,—

> —— I forget:
> But these sweet thoughts do even refresh my *labours*,
> Most busy-less when I do *it*.

According to the principles on which I have worked, we must either alter *labours* to *labour*, or *it* to *them;* and I have adopted the former alteration as the most simple and obvious. The amiable reviewers, however, attribute the alteration to "*mere carelessness*," not observing the necessity of any change—a question I shall be well contented to leave to be determined by any reader's common sense. The reviewers misquote me when they make me say that the passage, as above, is "unquestionably corrupt." I regard in that light the reading of the first folio, *most busy least*, but consider that Theobald has restored the author's true language by his admirable suggestion of *busy-less*.

In the reading last mentioned, as in all instances of the kind where the old text is corrupt, I have selected the best conjectural emendation that has been suggested. The *Athenæum* reviewers recommend me to " strive to amend obvious corruptions by entering into the author's spirit," a recommendation in itself sufficiently obvious ; but it is easy to see, from their late criticisms, that the taste of these reviewers evidently inclines to violent alterations in the text, in passages that mostly require only a little attention to be perfectly intelligible as they stand in the original. If it were fair to select examples from their criticisms on the whole of the plays, I could indeed produce a singular testimony as to their want of knowledge and judgment ; but I will adhere to the single play of the *Tempest*, and, even from their few notices of that play alone, I shall be enabled to exhibit instances of the incompetency of the reviewers to comprehend some of the simplest passages in the text. I will take, for example, the speech of CERES, in the fourth act,—

> Earth's increase, foison plenty,
> Barns and garners never empty ;
> Vines, with clust'ring bunches growing ;
> Plants, with goodly burden bowing :
> *Spring come to you, at the farthest,*
> *In the very end of harvest !*
> Scarcity and want shall shun you ;
> Ceres' blessing so is on you.

Where the meaning of the two lines printed in Italics is so exceedingly obvious—Let Spring come to you, at latest, at the end of harvest, so that no Winter shall intervene—that not even one of the much abused commentators thought they needed any explanation.* It is, indeed, scarcely credible that any men, professing to understand the spirit of Shakespeare's language, should now propose to read,—

> *Rain* come to you, at the farthest,
> In the very end of harvest !

or that the *Athenæum* reviewers should select this strange corruption as one of the alterations which "recommend themselves to adoption by that surest of all criticisms, the judgment of common sense !" Surely, if the judgment of common sense is to decide these questions, they should be referred to the common sense of those who understand something more of the author's meanings.

The reviewers have scarcely committed a less error in recommending the new reading which is based on the incorrect supposition that the term *flote* was not a genuine English word ; but I will pass to another instance, appreciable by every reader, in which the reviewers again are wanting in a knowledge of Shakespeare's common mode of expression. It occurs in the fifth act, in Prospero's speech, where he says, addressing the fairies—

> —— you demy-puppets, that
> By moonshine do the *green-sour* ringlets make,
> Whereof the ewe not bites ;

---

* The note on the passage in my folio edition was in print before the appearance of the comments of Mr. Knight and Mr. Smibert on the same lines. Both these critics adopt in effect the same interpretation, and, indeed, it is impossible two opinions can be entertained on the subject. "But for the evidence of eyesight," observes Mr. Smibert, "I should scarcely have believed it possible for any one to have proposed the reading of *rain* for *spring*. The mere agricultural absurdity is huge, inasmuch as Ceres would be thus absolutely desiring the destruction of all husbandry, and assigning the blessing of rains only when the fields were bared, and showers unneeded."

where the reviewers, not aware that compound adjectives abound in Shakespeare, and losing sight of the second epithet being required by the sense of the following line, approve of the substitution *green-sward*. The meaning of the original is obvious, the fairy-rings being dark green in colour, and the grass of which they are composed, rank. It may be well to add a few examples of similar compounds for the reviewers' information :—

> The *white-cold* virgin snow upon my heart
> Abates the ardour of my liver.
> *The Tempest*, act iv.

> Turns into yellow gold his *salt-green* streams.
> *A Midsummer Night's Dream*, act iii.

> If thou didst put this *sour-cold* habit on,
> To castigate thy pride, 'twere well.
> *Timon of Athens*, act iv.

The above examples   the reviewers' criticisms are selected from their brief notice of one play alone, and I would confidently ask any impartial reader whether critics, who are thus proved to understand so little of Shakespeare's meaning and language, are competent to pass a censure on the labours of others? I have shown indisputably that they reject readings as worthless and unauthorised, without taking the trouble to refer even to the first four folios; and that they do not comprehend some of the simplest passages in the poet's works. The public will hardly surrender their judgment to men thus convicted of incompetency, though the latter may be concealed for a time from the unreflecting by the extreme arrogance with which their opinions are promulgated.

It is still more extraordinary that the reviewers should

inconsiderately accuse me of being severe on the errors of others, because there is not a single passage in the work that can be produced in which I have used any language that can by possibility be contorted into a semblance of discourtesy ; and it is unjust on their part in the extreme that they should lead the public to infer I have acted differently. With respect to the new annotations, instead of dismissing them " very contemptuously," as the reviewers assert, I have calmly discussed in the notes every one of the slightest importance ; and on examining my remarks upon them, I cannot find any that are expressed in other than the fairest language. The nearest approach made to censure is calling the new reading—" most busy, blest"— *a very unhappy conjecture*, my sincere opinion still, and most certainly given without any intention of being uncourteous. If, indeed, this be language too severe, what must be said of Mr. Dyce's, who, coming after me, styles the emendation "forced and awkward in the very extreme," and a " scarcely intelligible alteration ?" So far from treating any critic " contemptuously," I am one of those who firmly believe that such and so vast is the compass of knowledge comprehended in the works of Shakespeare, there is scarcely an individual to be found who could not, in one way or other, add to our knowledge of his meanings; and, in this spirit, I have despised no sources of information, but have dispassionately examined all that were accessible, with the sole object of the determination of accuracy and truth. The new folio edition of Shakespeare is, I venture to assert, the first comprehensive edition yet published which aims at the accumulation of useful information, entirely free from the squabbles and controversies of opposing critics; and when the reviewers assert my "commentator-like propensity to pick holes in the labours of other men," they have committed themselves to a serious misrepresentation, which I am perfectly satisfied will impair their character for fairness in the estimation of every impartial reader of the work itself.

I now pass to one of the most important subjects animadverted upon by the reviewers—the spuriousness of the celebrated Bridgewater MSS.—and here, as it seems to me, the reviewers of the *Athenæum* may well be considered to have revealed one reason of their animosity towards the work. If I am correct in thinking that the whole of the Shakesperian MSS. in the possession of the Earl of Ellesmere are modern forgeries,—that an important letter, discovered at Dulwich College, has been misinterpreted,—or, that some remarkable ballads are compositions of comparatively recent date —it is unnecessary to say that the chief of the far-famed Shakesperian discoveries of Mr. Collier are of small value indeed; and Mr. Collier is generally understood to be one of the *Athenæum* reviewers! On the subject of these MSS. I shall again request the reader's attention to facts, reprinting in the first place the following observations on the subject from the first volume of my folio edition :—

"It is much to be regretted that it now seems necessary to pass, for a time, from the consideration of the authentic records on which the account of Shakespeare's personal history is founded. They have not, it is true, furnished as much as could be wished of that description of information which is chiefly of use to the moralist or philosopher; but what little has been laboriously collected from the ancient manuscripts of Stratford, London, and Worcester, is certainly not to be despised. It has, at least, the merit of perfect authenticity; for, aware of the lamentable attempts that have been made to deceive the world in all that relates to the great dramatist, I was determined, at the risk of encountering a vast labour which can only find its reward in the future appreciation of the authority of the work, to make a personal inspection and examination of every document of the slightest importance respecting the history of Shakespeare and his family. It appeared to be more advisable to hazard the possibility of rejecting a genuine paper by an excess of caution, than to impair the value of the biography by the insertion of any that were subject to the expression of the slightest doubt; and in the prosecution of these enquiries, I have been aided by the judgment of Mr. W. H. Black, an assistant-keeper of Her Majesty's records, and well known as one of the most accomplished palæographists of the day, whose advice has been always most kindly and generously afforded. The reader may, therefore, be assured that every care has heen taken to avoid the possibility of deception ; and that all the evidences here printed have been submitted to the minutest examination, and the most anxious scrutiny.

"Having adopted these severe regulations for the guidance of my researches, it was inevitably essential that the remarkable papers which were discovered by Mr. Collier in the archives of the Earl of Ellesmere, and published by him in the year 1835, should be carefully examined. There was, in fact, a special necessity for these documents, beyond all others, being critically scrutinized, for they were the only records that of late years have found a place in the biographies of Shakespeare, the genuineness of which has been questioned. There is nothing in the account of their discovery to suggest a doubt. 'They were derived,' observes Mr. Collier, 'from the manuscripts of Lord Ellesmere, whose name is of course well known to every reader of our history, as Keeper of the Great Seal to Queen Elizabeth, and Lord Chancellor to James I. They are preserved at Bridgewater House ; and Lord Francis Egerton gave me instant and unrestrained access to them, with permission to make use of any literary or historical information I could discover. The Rev. H. J. Todd had been there before me, and had classed some of the documents and correspondence ; *but large bundles of papers, ranging in point of date between* 1581, *when Lord Ellesmere was made Solicitor-General, and* 1616, *when he retired from the office of Lord Chancellor, remained unexplored, and it was evident that many of them had never been opened from the time when, perhaps, his own hands tied them together.*' It was amongst these latter that the Shakespeare manuscripts were discovered; and if, as is possible, a fabricator had inserted them in those bundles, a more recent enquirer, investigating the collection under the impression it had not been examined for upwards of two centuries, would be inclined to receive every paper as genuine, and as not requiring any minute investigation for the establishment of its authority. Suspicion would be disarmed, and it is possible that in this way Mr. Collier has been deceived.

" When I came to make a personal inspection of these interesting papers, facilities for which were kindly granted by their noble owner, grave doubts were at once created as to their authenticity. The most important of all, the certificate from the players of the Blackfriars' Theatre to the Privy Council in 1589, instead of being either the original or a contemporary copy, is evidently at best merely a late transcript, if it be not altogether a recent fabrication.

" The question naturally arises, for what purpose could a document of this description have been copied in the seventeenth century, presuming it to belong to so early a period? It is comparatively of recent times that the slightest literary interest has been taken in the history of our early theatres, or even in the biography of Shakespeare; and, unless it was apparent that papers of this kind were transcribed for some legal or other special purpose, there should be great hesitation in accepting the evidence on any other but contemporary authority. The suspicious appearance of this certificate is of itself sufficient to justify great diffi- culties in its reception; but the doubt thus induced as to the integrity of the collection was considerably increased by an examination of a paper in the same volume, purporting to be a warrant appointing Daborne, Shakespeare, Field, and Kirkham, instructors of the Children of the Queen's Revels, which unquestionably appears to be a modern forgery. This docu- ment is styled by Mr. Collier ' a draft either for a Patent or a Privy Seal.' It is not a draft, for the lines are written book-wise, and it is also dated; neither is it a copy of a patent, as appears from the direction, ' Right trustie and welbeloved;' but, if genuine, it must be considered an abridged transcript of a warrant, under the sign-manual and signet, for a patent to be issued. Now if it be shown that the letters patent to ' Daborne and others ' were granted on the same day on which Lord Ellesmere's paper is dated; and if it be further proved that the contents of the latter are altogether inconsistent with the circumstances detailed in the real patent, it will, I think, be conceded that no genuine draft or transcript, of the nature of that printed by Mr. Collier, can possibly exist.

"It appears that the following note occurs in an entry-book of patents that passed the Great Seal while it was in the hands of Lord Ellesmere in 7 James I. :—'A Warrant for Robert Daborne and others, the Queenes Servants, to bring up and practise Children in Plaies by the name of the Children of the Queen's Revells, for the pleasure of her Majestie, 4° Januarii, anno septimo Jacobi." This entry may have suggested the fabrication, the date of the questionable MS. corresponding with that here given ; though it is capable of proof that, if it were authentic, it must have been dated previously, for the books of the Signet Office show that the authority for Daborne's warrant was obtained by the influence of Sir Thomas Munson in the previous December, and they also inform us that it was granted 'to Robert Daborne, and other Servauntes to the Queene, from time to time to provide and bring up a convenient nomber of Children to practize in the quality of playing, by the name of the Children of the Revells to the Queene, *in the White Fryers, London,* or any other convenient place where he shall thinke fit.' The enrolment of the instrument, which was issued in the form of letters patent under the Great Seal, recites, 'Whereas the Quene, our deerest wyfe, hathe for hir pleasure and recreacion, when shee shall thinke it fitt to have any playes or shewes, appoynted hir servantes Robert Daborne, Phillippe Rosseter, John Tarbock, Richard Jones, and Robert Browne, to provide and bring upp a convenient nomber of children, whoe shalbe called Children of hir Revelles, Know ye that wee have appoynted and authorised, and by theis presentes do authorize and appoynte the said Robert Daborne, &c., from tyme to tyme, to provide, keepe, and bring upp a convenient nomber of children, and them to practice and exercise in the quality of playing, by the name of Children of the Revells to the Queene, within the White Fryers in the suburbs of our Citty of London, or in any other convenyent place where they shall thinke fitt for that purpose.' This patent is dated January 4th, 7 Jac. I., 1609-10, so that any draft, or projected warrant, exhibiting other names than the above, could not possibly have had this exact date. It will be observed that the names, with the exception of that of Daborne, are entirely different in the two documents, and this company of children was to play at the Whitefriars, not at the Blackfriars. The fabricator seems to have relied on the supposition that the entry relative to "Daborne and others" referred to the latter theatre; and consequently inserted the name of Edward Kirkham, who is known to have been one of the instructors to the Children of the Revels at the Blackfriars in the year 1604. There is, in fact, no reasonable supposition on which the Ellesmere paper can be regarded as authentic. Had no date been attached to it, it might have been said that the whole related merely to some contemplated arrangement which was afterwards altered; although, even in that case, the form of the copy would alone have been a serious reason against its reception. In its present state, it is clearly impossible to reconcile it with the contents of the enrolment just quoted. Fortunately for the interests of truth, indications of forgery are detected in trifling circumstances that are almost invariably neglected by the inventor, however ingeniously the deception be contrived. Were it not for this, the search for historical truth would yield results sufficiently uncertain to deter the most enthusiastic enquirer from pursuing the investigation.

The remaining Shakesperian MSS. in the possession of the Earl of Ellesmere, consist of a letter of Daniel the poet mentioning the great dramatist as a candidate for the Mastership of the Queen's Revels; accounts in which a performance of *Othello* is stated to have taken place in the year 1602; a remarkable paper detailing the values of the shares held by Shakespeare and others in the Blackfriars' Theatre; and a presumed early copy of a letter signed "H. S.," supposed to have been written by Lord Southampton, and containing singular notices of Burbage and Shakespeare. The first two of these I have not seen, the volume including only a recent transcript of Daniel's letter; but the other two, which have been carefully inspected, present an appearance by no means satisfactory. Although the caligraphy is of a highly skilful character, and judging solely from a facsimile of the letter, I should certainly have accepted it as genuine, yet an examination of the original leads to a different judgment, the paper and ink not appearing to belong to so early a date. It is a suspicious circumstance that both these documents are written in an unusually large character on folio leaves of paper, *by the same hand*, and are evidently not contemporaneous copies. Again may the question be asked, why should transcripts of such papers have been made after the period to which the originals are supposed to refer? It is also curious that copies only of these important records should be preserved; and, on the whole, without offering a decisive opinion as to the spuriousness of the two last mentioned, there is sufficient doubt respecting the whole collection to justify a reasonable hesitation for the present in admitting any of them as genuine. The interests of literature demand that these documents should be submitted to a careful and minute examination by the best record-readers of the day, by those who are continually engaged in the study of ancient manuscripts; such, for example, as are the Deputy and various Assistant-keepers of the Public Records, and the Keeper of the MSS. in the British Museum. Should such an investigation take place, the water-marks in the paper should be observed, and no minutiæ omitted that are deserving of notice in such an enquiry."

In the above observations, I have endeavoured to put the matter in the clearest possible light, with the utmost fairness to Mr. Collier. I firmly believed in the genuineness of the papers till the day on which I examined the originals— and that my own convictions on the subject are sincere may be gathered from the fact that, on the evening of that day, I cancelled at the printer's that portion of the biography in which I had previously inserted copies of the documents, and I also omitted the fac-simile of the Southampton letter, the expense of lithographing which had already been incurred. *I am convinced that one paper, at least—the Daborne warrant—is a modern forgery, and so badly executed, that it will not even pass muster in a facsimile.* But fac-similes will not be sufficient to prove the authenticity of suspected papers. The documents themselves must be submitted to the scrutiny of the most competent judges, before the public can be satisfied on the matter. In the above statement, I have been careful not to express an opinion which is not at the same time an absolute conviction. It is, however, my opinion, gathered from the appearance

of the papers themselves, that all the Bridgewater Shaksperian MSS. which I have seen are forgeries.

The reviewers, in drawing the attention of the public to
an opinion I had formerly expressed in favour of the
authenticity of the documents, somewhat overlook the important distinction between an opinion given merely from
internal evidence, and a conclusion derived from an
inspection of the papers themselves. In admitting, as I
have done, that I confided in their genuineness till the day
on which I saw the originals, I have placed the matter in
as fair a light as possible; and as the MSS. will most probably ere long be submitted to the consideration of competent judges, it is unnecessary to say I should hardly have
incurred the risk of giving an adverse opinion so distinctly,
were I not thoroughly convinced there were forcible reasons
for entertaining it. I can have but one object in such a
discussion—the discovery of the real truth, and the satisfaction of endeavouring to place the materials of Shaksperian
criticism on a sound basis of authenticity. The paucity of
interesting evidences respecting Shakespeare is so great, it
would be a real source of congratulation to all of us could
the Ellesmere MSS. ultimately be acknowledged to be
genuine; but the determination must be obtained from
the closest external scrutiny, as well as from internal
evidence.

The reviewers act injudiciously in insinuating that Mr.
Collier has been in the slightest degree contemptuously or
unfairly treated in my work; and I will give an ample proof
that, so far from this being the case, I have been actuated
throughout by the sincerest feelings of kindness. It is,
I feel sure, sufficient for me, in this respect, to quote the

observations I have made on the following misreading of the Dulwich College MS.

"It may here be observed that a notice which first appeared in Mr. Collier's interesting *Memoirs of Edward Alleyn*, 1841, p. 63, apparently showing that Shakespeare was in London in the month of October, 1603, conveys an inaccurate reading of the original manuscript preserved at Dulwich College, and cannot, therefore, be received as evidence. The following,—

"Aboute a weeke agoe ther . . . . . e a youthe who said he
was Mr. Frauncis Chalo . . . s man . . . . ld have borrow.d
x*s* to have bought things for . . . . s Mr. . . . .
t hym cominge without . . . . . token . . . . d
I would have . . . .
. . I bene sur . . . .
and inquire after the fellow, and said he had lent hym a horse. I feare me he gulled hym, thoughe he gulled not us. The youthe was a prety youthe, and hansom in appayrell: we know not what became of hym. Mr. Bromffeild commendes hym: he was heare yesterdaye. Nicke and Jeames be well, and commend them: so dothe Mr. Cooke and his weife in the kyndest sorte, and so once more in the hartiest manner farwell,"

is all that now remains of a postcript to a letter from Mrs. Alleyn to her husband, the celebrated actor, dated October 20th, 1603. This letter is written on a folio leaf of paper, the commencement of the above postscript being at the end of the first page, the top of the second page, which is perfect, beginning with the words, *and inquire.* The portion of the letter containing the first lines of our extract is in a very decayed state, the bottom of the leaf being rotten, and the writing not very easily to be understood; *but the accompanying facsimile, which was carefully traced from the original by Mr. Fairholt, proves that Mr. Collier's interpretation cannot be correct, inasmuch as it is irreconcileable with the position of words that are clearly to be discovered in the remaining fragment.* The surpassing value of fac-simile copies is here apparent. It is so easy, in a laborious work like the one in which the above error occurs, to misread difficult writing, which even at a second glance, unless most carefully examined in a strong light, may be misinterpreted; the only safe resource,

in all difficult cases, is to substantiate the reading by obtaining the assistance of the artist. It would be bold to affirm, in opposition to Mr. Collier,
that the whole has been misunderstood, and that the name of Shakespeare
has taken the place of some other similar in form ; but even admitting that
it was originally to be found in the decayed fragment, a circumstance
which appears to be extremely uncertain, it is beyond a doubt that the
sentence in which it occurred has been printed erroneously, and that the
true information the letter conveyed respecting the dramatist is now probably not to be recovered. The reader will bear in mind that the original
investigator of a large collection of documents does not possess the advan-
tages that attend those later enquirers, who are concentrating their attention to papers on a particular subject."

Mr. Fairholt's fac-simile of the passage, as it now remains,
is here given ; and the reader will distinctly observe that
Mr. Collier's reading does not correspond with the fac-
simile, and that his transcript must unquestionably be
incorrect. I annex the copy of the MS., as given by Mr.
Collier :—

" Aboute a weeke a goe there came a youthe who said he was M^r
Frauncis Chaloner who would have borrowed x^{li} to have bought things
for * * * and said he was known unto you, and Mr Shakespeare of
the globe, who came * * * said he knewe hym not, onely he herde
of hym that he was a roge * * * so he was glade we did not lend
him the monney * * * Richard Johnes [went] to seeke and inquire
after the fellow, and said he had lent hym a horse. I feare me he gulled
hym, thoughe he gulled not us. The youthe was a prety youthe, and
hansom in appayrell : we knowe not what became of hym. Mr Benfield
commendes hym ; he was heare yesterdaye. Nicke and Jeames be well,
and comend them : so doth Mr Cooke and his wiefe in the kyndest sorte,
and so once more in the hartiest manner farwell."

Now is it not clear from this, compared with Mr. Fairholt's facsimile, that Mr. Collier has misinterpreted the

FACSIMILE OF THE LOWER PART OF THE LETTER, DATED 1603.

TAKEN FROM THE ORIGINAL MS., PRESERVED AT DULWICH COLLEGE, BY F. W. FAIRHOLT, ESQ., F.S.A.

original? *otherwise we should discover in his copy the words that are to be found in the fac-simile.* The fact is, that Mr. Collier probably, in haste, took the words down without sufficient examination. At all events, the fac-simile is an evidence against the exact reception of the discovery.

In this, however, as in other questions, I am contented to appeal to facts, and leave the rest to the determination of the public. The reviewers are perfectly justified in not accepting my *opinion* as to the spuriousness of Lord Ellesmere's MSS.—I adhere to the facts that *prove* one of them not to be genuine, and appeal, as to the whole, to the judgment of those who are best informed in such matters. In the same way, with regard to the Dulwich College MS., instead of entering into an argument on the subject, I give a fac-simile, and scarcely express an opinion. The value of my work depends, and will depend, on the authenticity of its accumulated facts—facts, the importance of which are determinable by any one who studied the subject—and it is with that conviction I may be excused setting too great a value on the censures of the reviewers.

It is, indeed, far from being exclusively on my own account that I publish these few controversial pages. That I am personally nearly indifferent to the mere external acknowledgments of criticism, may be well gathered from the circumstance of my consenting to entomb the results of so many years' labour in so small an impression; a fact which also renders the greatest censure almost innocuous. But I have a far higher motive than any that could result in the hope of accomplishing a successful refutation of an adverse critic. I cannot but think a public service will be rendered

by the exposure of the incompetency and unfairness of a
Journal, which, by its arrogance and subtlety, is calculated
to impose on all but those who have paid peculiar attention
to the subjects on which it ventures to decide. That I shall
incur the well-known undying rancour entertained by its
reviewers towards all who enter into conflict with them, is
certain; but the effect of their animosity will be lessened
by the exposition now given of their animus towards the
writer. An adversary need not be greatly feared, when
his malevolence is generally known.

Brixton Hill, near London,
    July, 1853.

NOTE.

THE Bridgewater MSS. being in private archives, and only used for literary purposes by the liberality of their noble and distinguished possessor, it may be well to observe, lest the strong opinions here expressed as to their want of authenticity be possibly thought to be in any way uncourteous, that the Earl of Ellesmere most generously gave the writer the amplest permission to express any doubts that may be entertained on the subject.

OBSERVATIONS ON SOME OF THE MANUSCRIPT

EMENDATIONS OF THE TEXT OF

SHAKESPEARE,

AND

ARE THEY COPYRIGHT?

BY

J. O. HALLIWELL, ESQ. F.R.S. &c.

LONDON:

JOHN RUSSELL SMITH, 36, SOHO SQUARE.

MDCCCLIII.

OBSERVATIONS, &c.

IN the folio edition of the Works of Shakespeare I am now passing through the press, I have been most careful not to introduce a single harsh observation on the labours of any of the critics, not even on the labours of those who have long been unaffected by praise or censure ; but I have respected in all cases the memory of the dead, and spoken in every way the language of courtesy and kindness towards those who are living. It is, therefore, with the greatest astonishment I discover that I am not only accused of being severe on the errors of others, but also of speaking contemptuously of Mr. Collier's new work—an accusation which is so exceedingly unfair, I am tempted to challenge any reader to produce a single instance in my work in which I have mentioned an error with asperity, or quoted Mr. Collier in any but the fairest and most courteous language. Mr. Collier himself, however, has thrown out one of the most uncourteous implications ever suggested in literary controversy, by plainly intimating that every one who rejects the new readings can only do so from interested motives,—an implication to the consideration of which it may be worth while to devote a few pages. I am the rather induced to take this course, as I have not at present discovered a single *new* reading in Mr. Collier's volume that will bear the test of examination.

In support of the assertion above made, that interested motives are attributed by Mr. Collier to opponents, it appears only requisite to notice the Editor's observations in the threshold of his book, on the well-known passage respecting the " woollen bagpipe" in the *Merchant of Venice*. Mr. Collier, who would read *bollen*, on the authority of his MS. annotator, makes the following singular observation :— *" We may be confident that we shall never again see woollen bagpipe in any edition of the text of Shakespeare, unless it be reproduced by some one, who, having no right to use the emendation of our folio*, 1632, *adheres of necessity to the antiquated blunder, and pertinaciously attempts to justify it."* In other words, no one can sincerely and conscientiously refuse to accept the new reading *bollen*. Let us ascertain more minutely the probabilities of the success of this challenge, by referring to the notes of two of the critics ; merely observing, for my own part, that if any alteration were necessary, I am heretic enough to consider *swollen* a far more natural and likely emendation than *bollen* :—

" *Why he a swollen bagpipe*. We have here one of the too frequent instances of *conjectural* readings ; but it is to be hoped that all future editors will restore the original *woollen*, after weighing not only what has been already urged in its support, but the additional and accurate testimony of Dr. Leyden, who, in his edition of the *Complaynt of Scotland*, p. 149, informs us that the Lowland bagpipe commonly had the bag or sack covered with *woollen* cloth of a green colour, a practice which, he adds, prevailed in the northern counties of England." (Douce.)

"*A woollen bag-pipe*. This is the reading of every ancient copy ; and as we know that at this day the bag is usually covered with woollen, the epithet is perfectly appropriate, without adopting the alteration of Steevens to *swollen*." (COLLIER, 1842.)

Thus the reading that was "perfectly appropriate" in 1842 is not only to be set aside in 1853, in favour of a word of precisely similar meaning to the emendation suggested by Steevens, but it is affirmed that every one who objects to receive the new term can only do so from interested motives. The attribution of motives, as all the world knows, is not only the most easy but the most mischievous and uncertain of all "conjectural criticism ;" and the English public cannot be long blinded by the arrogant assumption that every opponent of these new readings must necessarily be acting with insincerity. Mr. Collier may rest assured that, if he is really and truly restoring the words of Shakespeare, not all the carpings of all the critics may long retard their universal adoption ; while, on the other hand, if they are merely alterations and fancied improvements, the researches of every day will tend to decrease the number of the accepted novelties. Surely, those students who have devoted years to this branch of literature have more regard to their reputations than to join in rejecting what their real feeling would approve—to risk all their claims to the consideration of the public by denouncing that which, if Mr. Collier be correct, a few years must infallibly for ever confirm.

Taking as examples the whole of the annotations in the *Tempest*, mentioned in Mr. Collier's *Notes and Emendations*, I annex, in very brief terms, the reasons for rejecting those readings which are not to be met with in Shakespearian works of common occurrence; without by any means giving entire assent even to the latter :—

6

1. *Have a care.* Given as new by Mr. Collier, but occurring in the alteration of the play by Dryden and Davenant.

2. *Welkin's heat.* New, but characterised by Mr. Collier as "one of those alterations which, though supported by some probability, it might be inexpedient to insert in the text." Mr. Dyce terms it "an alteration equally tasteless and absurd."

3. *Noble creatures.* Theobald's reading, as noticed by Mr. Collier. The old reading is adopted by Mr. Knight, with an ingenious explanation that appears to be unnecessarily refined.

4. *Prevision in mine art.* Given as new by Mr. Collier, but it was suggested by Mr. Hunter, in his *Disquisition on the Scene, &c., of Shakespeare's Tempest,* 8vo, 1839, p. 135, and repeated in the *New Illustrations,* 1845, i. 186.

5. *Thou his only heir.* Given as new by Mr. Collier, but suggested in Kenrick's *Review of Dr. Johnson's New Edition of Shakespeare,* 8vo, 1765, p. 3, and printed in the text of Rann's edition, 8vo, 1786, with another alteration in the next line.

6. *He being thus loaded.* "Perhaps," as Mr. Collier observes, "a questionable change."

7. *To untruth.* This new reading seems to be entirely inconsistent with the context, for this reason, that a person who tells a falsehood makes a sinner of his memory to Truth, not to Untruth.

8. *Fated to the practise.* The old edition reads *purpose,* the new reading removing what Mr. Collier thinks is an

awkward and needless repetition; but see Dyce's *Few Notes*, pp. 128-132. It is rather dangerous to pronounce the original text corrupt, on the mere occurrence of verbal repetitions. Dryden and Davenant read *design*.

9. *Carcass of a boat*. Rowe's alteration, as noticed by Mr. Collier. The same emendation had been previously made by Dryden and Davenant.

10. *Had quit it*. Same as the last.

11. *And all upon the Mediterranean float*. The repetition of *all* greatly militates against the new reading, as Mr. Singer has observed. Mr. Collier adopts it on the incorrect supposition that *flote*, a wave, is not a genuine archaism. It is, however, found in that most common of all dictionaries of the Shaksperian period, that of Minsheu, and it also occurs in Middleton.

12. *Speech assigned to Prospero*. The same alteration was made by Dryden and Davenant, as noticed by Mr. Collier.

13. *A line misprinted*. Adopted by all recent editors, as noticed by Mr. Collier.

14. *As which end o' the beam should bow*. "This interpretation," observes Mr. Smibert, "is decidedly of the cast of Mr. Puff's, harder than the original." The new reading seems to me to be an awkward one, and not felicitous, but it is one of those rather to be decided by judgment than by evidence.

15. *She for whom*. Considered by Mr. Collier as of doubtful character. See his Supplemental Notes.

16. *Measure it back*. This new reading is given by Mr. Collier, with the observation that the old one " seems preferable."

17. *Wherefore thus ghastly looking.* " The change is minute," observes Mr. Collier, " and may be said to be not absolutely necessary."

18. *That's verity.* This reading has long been adopted. Mr. Collier, in his edition of Shakespeare, vol. i, p. 43, says, " Modern editors, *all without necessity*, and some without notice, change *verily* of all the old copies into *verity.*"

19. *The drench of the storm.* The term *drench*, in the sense here used, appears to be *more modern* than Shakespeare's time ; but, independently of this probability, the variation is no improvement of the original text.

20. *Nor scrape trencher, nor wash dish.* Given as new by Mr. Collier, but corrected by Dryden and Davenant in the seventeenth century, and, more recently, by Mr. Dyce.

21. *Most busy,—blest, when I do it.* An emendation characterised by Mr. Dyce as " forced and awkward in the very extreme." The old text is corrupt, but the new reading appears far more improbable than the ordinary one of Theobald, *most busyless.*

22. *A thrid of mine own life.* Theobald's alteration, and most likely the correct reading is *thread.* The passage from Catullus, recently adduced by Mr. Hunter in favour of the old text, does not seem to me to be at all applicable.

23. *Tilled brims.* Given as new by Mr. Collier, but suggested in Holt's tract on the play, 8vo, 1749, p. 69.

24. *Brown groves.* Given as new by Mr. Collier, but long since suggested by Hanmer.

25. *Rain come to you.* Founded on a misinterpretation of the original, the meaning of which unquestionably is,— Let Spring come to you as soon as the harvest is over, so that no Winter shall intervene.

26. *And a wife.* A reading adopted by Malone and others, as observed by Mr. Collier, who, selecting the old word *wise* in his edition of Shakespeare, observes, " It needs no proof that, ' So rare a wonder'd father and a wise,' was the phraseology of Shakespeare's time."

27. *Winding.* This reading is the one recommended by Mr. Dyce (*Remarks, &c.*, 8vo, 1844, p. 7).

28. *Sedge-crowns.* Surely the old reading, *sedg'd crowns*, is more grammatical and appropriate.

29. *The green-sward ringlets.* Given as new by Mr. Collier, but many years ago suggested by Douce. The original compound epithet, *green-sour*, is not only perfectly intelligible, but exactly in Shakespeare's manner. In the previous act, we have, " the *white-cold* virgin snow," an epithet of similar formation; and, in fact, compound adjectives are most common,—salt-green, secret-false, &c.

30. *Noble Gonzalo.* The original epithet *holy* appears to be a most appropriate one as applied to Gonzalo, whose goodness of character is so well exhibited in the play, and has been specially noticed by Dr. Johnson.

31. *To the flow of mine.* The old reading *show* seems to be amply supported by the following passage in *Julius Cæsar*,—

> Passion, I see, is catching; for mine eyes,
> *Seeing those beads of sorrow stand in thine,*
> Began to water.

32. *And a loyal servant.* The original reads, *and a loyal sir,* a phraseology again used by Prospero, who shortly afterwards calls Antonio, "most wicked sir." Compare also *Cymbeline,*—"a lady to the worthiest sir."

33. *Some enchanted devil.* This new reading is perfectly inconsistent with the spirit of Alonso's address to Prospero.

34. *With all her power.* The meaning of the original text, *without her power,* is, independently, or without the aid of her power. The explanation given by Mr. Harness is very neat and to the purpose,—"exercises the command of the moon, without being empowered by her so to do; or, commands the ebbs and flows of the sea with an usurped authority."

It may be well to observe, in reference to the above notes, that the instances of "coincident suggestions," there mentioned, are purposely restricted to the most obvious sources; there being a vast collection of printed conjectural criticism, scattered amongst obscure sources, that will no doubt yield a large number of independent examples of a similar character. It will be sufficient to remark, in reference to this subject, that one volume alone of the miscellaneous collections, published by Messrs. Nichols, contains *at least forty* (I believe many more) of the so-called *new* readings; and such a circumstance is clearly sufficient in itself to show the utter impossibility of any person receiving these as entirely "new lights," inasmuch as the question resolves itself into a simple matter of *fact* resting on proofs alone, and entirely irrespective either of "opinion" or "prejudice." It shows indisputably that Mr. Collier must have been deceived as to the composition of his annotated volume; for no one would otherwise have been rash enough to have presented it to the public as bearing a character so open to contradiction. In the observations given above, it is not to be inferred that Mr. Collier was aware of those which had been previously suggested; but merely that he has not referred to the conjectural readings of his predecessors.

The extent to which the MS. annotator has been publicly anticipated by the suggestions of the critics of the last century, has not at present been fully noticed, and the sources of conjectural Shakespearian criticism are so various, and so widely scattered, it will be long before it can be definitively pronounced that any of the readings in Mr. Collier's volume are unquestionably new. Thus, the writer of a fair article on the subject in *Chambers' Edinburgh Journal*, June 4th, 1853, commences by giving *seven* examples of *real emendations;* but *out of these seven no fewer than four have been many years before the public in other works.* The writer alluded to commences by observing,—

"In the last act of the *Merry Wives of Windsor*, and in the fifth scene, when the fairies approach Falstaff, Anne Page acting the Fairy Queen,

Dame Quickly accompanies them ; and in the common editions we find
that the very authoritative speech addressed to the fairies, and which we
would expect from none but their queen, is put into the mouth of Mrs.
Quickly. The ground for so doing is, that ' Qui.' is prefixed to it. In
Mr. Collier's volume, however, the ' Qui.' is changed to ' Que.,' as a mis-
print ; and thus a speech most inappropriate for poor Dame Quickly, is
given to its rightful owner, the Fairy Queen, Anne Page. *This is one of
the most valuable emendations of its kind.* On the whole, however, the
stage-directions which we find in this volume are not of much importance."

There can be, indeed, little doubt, not only that this
emendation is correct, but that it is one of " the most
valuable of its kind" to be met with in Mr. Collier's
volume ; yet the reader of the latter work may well be
surprised on finding not only that it was proposed by Mr.
Harness, in 1825, with the observation that *Qui* is an
error in the first folio for *Que*, but that it has actually been
adopted both by Mr. Knight and Mr. Collier. Mr. Collier
refers to the very page of his own edition, where he has
adopted the suggestion of Mr. Harness, but so far from
making the slightest remark, that the MS. annotator is
only confirming an established correction, leads the reader
to infer, in the following terms, that it is an original emendation :—

" P. 267. In several preceding scenes we are informed that Anne Page
was to represent the Fairy Queen in the attack upon Falstaff in Windsor
Park. Nevertheless, Malone and others assigned all her speeches to Mrs.
Quickly, the only excuse being that the first of the prefixes is *Qui*. The
manuscript-corrector of the folio, 1632, changed it to *Que*, and made it
Que (for Queen) in all other places ; and after the printed stage-direction,
' Enter Fairies,' he added, *with the Queen, Anne.* It does not, indeed,
appear that Mrs. Quickly took any part at all in the scene, although she
most likely in some way lent her assistance, in order that she might be
on the stage at the conclusion of the performance."

Surely this mode of introducing older suggestions, however useful the emendations are in themselves, is seriously calculated to mislead the reader; and this is by no means a solitary instance where corrections, mentioned by Mr. Collier in his eight volume edition, are introduced into his supplementary work, without the remark that they have been previously noticed. It is readily to be understood that Mr. Collier, compiling his volume of Notes with unusual rapidity, and under circumstances which rendered access to many books exceedingly inconvenient, should have overlooked numerous early parallel conjectures; but the reason he should have ignored coincident suggestions on the very page of his own edition to which he was referring does not appear to be so obvious. The fact, however, is sufficient to increase very greatly the improbability of his being enabled to establish any copyright in the annotations.

It can fairly be stated, without any discourtesy, that Mr. Collier, who so long and in many respects so judiciously adhered to the early editions, has not paid much attention to the vast range of conjectural emendation which appeared during the last century. The very first example in the preface to his 'Notes and Emendations,'—the substitution of *Aristotle's ethics* for *Aristotle's checks* in the 'Taming of the Shrew'—is introduced with the observation that, "many of the most valuable corrections of Shakespeare's text are, in truth, self-evident; and so apparent, when once suggested, that it seems wonderful how the plays could have passed through the hands of men of such learning and critical acumen, during the last century and a half, without the detection of such indisputable blunders;" and, in the work itself, Mr. Collier observes respecting this emendation,—

" Recollecting how many learned hands our great dramatist's works have passed through, it is wonderful that such a blunder as that we are now enabled to point out, should not have been detected and mentioned in print at least a century ago." The oversight here committed as to this reading being a novelty has been necessarily detected,* it being a positive fact that the " new emendation" has not only been mentioned in a great variety of editions, *but has been introduced into the text by no fewer than five editors,* the first, I believe, in point of time, being the Rev. J. Rann, who substituted *Ethics* into the text as early as 1787. I mention this particularly, not in censure, but merely as a decisive proof of the obvious fact that Mr. Collier prepared his book without considering it necessary to consult very closely the emendations suggested and introduced by previous editors. It would also appear from the list already given from the *Tempest*, that even the commonest Shakespearian works have not been duly referred to; and I think it will be found that the list of coincidences will by and by be most materially increased. The early discovery of so many instances of suggestions that have been previously made lead to the inference that any attempt at establishing a copyright in the MS. emendations themselves (Mr. Collier's Notes on them are of course copyright) would signally fail ; and this circumstance will no doubt tend to shield the " disbelievers " from the imputations of interested motives which have been so freely, and, I cannot

* But even so late as June of the present summer, the writer of an article in Mr. Parker's *National Miscellany* mentions it as " one of the quietest and most important of all his notations," and several other reviewers have quoted it in similar terms.

help thinking, so injudiciously attributed to them. There are many of the alterations that are apparently so good, it is not a subject for surprise that they should have been accepted by the general reader, especially when we find so eminent a critic as Mr. Dyce confessing he had at first received several as happy corrections which proved to be questionable on examination : but does not all this lead to the conviction that a hasty assent will probably not be lasting ? In the same way, on the first publication of a portion of the annotations, the suggestion of *bisson multi-tude* appeared to be so peculiarly happy and incontro-vertible, I could not resist the conclusion it was not only truthful, but that it indicated the MS. annotator had derived his alterations from pure sources ; a conviction which was greatly disturbed by an interesting article on the passage by 'A. E. B.' (in the *Notes and Queries*), and further read-ing has furnished reasons that justify the gravest doubts as to the propriety of its reception.

The question of copyright would of course be decided by several other considerations beyond the mere occurrence of the coincident suggestions ; and it may well be doubted whether it could be maintained in any corrections of Shakespeare text derived from early MS. sources. But enough has been said to convince the reader that a critic may reject many of the new readings, without incurring the risk of being fairly included in Mr. Collier's clause of censure. For my own part, not having otherwise written directly or indirectly against the emendations, and having discussed them fairly as far as I have had occasion to do so in my new work, I can only account for the accusation of having treated them with contempt by the circumstance of

my considering most of them worthless, being attributed to
"necessity" and "pertinacity." My reasons for rejecting the
whole of those which occur in the first play in the volume
are before the public ; and I hope the value of all the new
readings will be attempted to be decided in this way by
fair argument, not by mere expressions of opinion.

BRIXTON HILL, NEAR LONDON,
    July, 1853.

For EU product safety concerns, contact us at Calle de José Abascal, 56–1°,
28003 Madrid, Spain or eugpsr@cambridge.org.